The Avebury Cycle

Michael Dames

The Avebury Cycle

with 201 illustrations

THAMES AND HUDSON

To Judy, my wife

*(Pages 2–3) The Avebury
monuments, built more than
4000 years ago, once formed the
metropolis of Neolithic Britain.
In the foreground is Avebury
henge or sacred enclosure, the
world's largest, with Silbury Hill,
top of picture, the tallest prehistoric
structure in Europe.*

© 1977 and 1996 Thames and Hudson Ltd, London

First published in the United States of America in 1977
by Thames and Hudson Inc., 500 Fifth Avenue,
New York, New York 10110
Second edition 1996

Library of Congress Catalog Card Number 95-62448
ISBN 0-500-27886-5

Printed and bound in Spain

Contents

One morning in late July 1995, my wife and I walked from the Avebury henge by the eastern causeway towards the Ridgeway. The day was hot, bright and blue. The only clouds were of butterflies, weaving and hovering among wild flowers that fringed the chalky track. As we climbed, so a panorama of downland came into view. Ample and fecund, limb by limb, a giantess extended herself to the horizon. Here was Britannia-in-miniature, the island landlady, Mother Earth. She was reclining in the last stages of pregnancy as she had done at this season for several millenia. Her maternity gown was of blondest barley interspersed with gussets of red-gold wheat. Clumps of beech trees were stitched to her numerous round-barrow buttons while her loosened girdle was made from water meadows that followed the river Kennet from a spring long-held to be sacred.

At that moment it seemed as if the entire landscape, natural and cultural, including its ancient monuments and modern farms, had merged into an eternally living organism, a divine being whose breath whispered through the ripe grain with the slightest breeze, to be shared by us.

Now that the Avebury district has been designated a World Heritage area, perhaps it is time to suggest that the Earth Goddess, acknowledged on every inhabited continent, and from the remotest stone age to the present, may also be recognized here as having inspired the Avebury chain of monuments, modelled to represent the phases in her life-cycle.

Our July morning advanced, and having walked to the Sanctuary, and across the river at East Kennet, we ascended the long, steepening slope of All Cannings Down, mile after mile, to the escarpment crest at Milk Hill. Overhead, a buzzard mewled like a new-born child. Then a hare shot out from a patch of scrub, and thudded away. A man stacked the first straw bales into towers – an ephemeral golden city awaiting the cart. A red hang-glider bloomed briefly and sank from sight, as two white horses stood in the shade of a blackthorn tree. Everything fitted together.

Then we heard them. Flint nodules, born below the Cretaceous sea, now clinked and clattered beneath our strides, like a congregation of Neolithic figurines about to announce the recovery of a sacred Earth and the mystery of another journey – through and beyond death – which was and is the Avebury cycle.

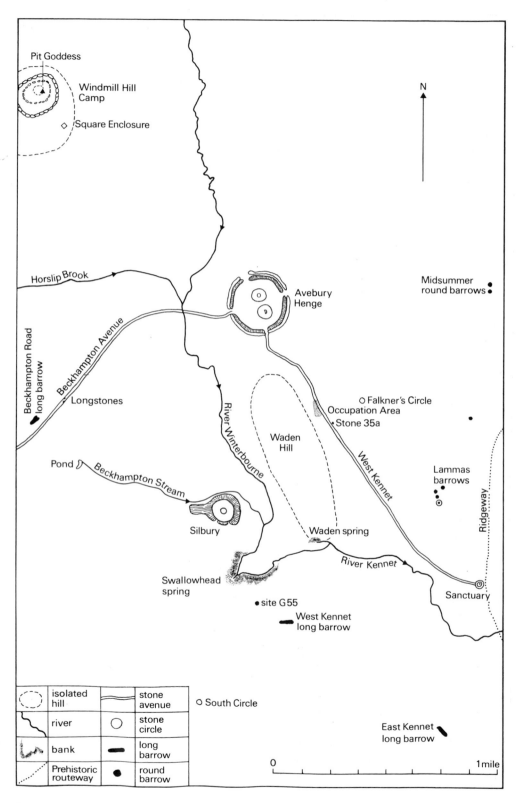

Pit Goddess

Windmill Hill Camp

◇ Square Enclosure

N

Horslip Brook

Beckhampton Road long barrow

Beckhampton Avenue

Longstones

Avebury Henge

Midsummer round barrows

○ Falkner's Circle
Occupation Area
• Stone 35a

River Winterbourne

Waden Hill

Pond

Beckhampton Stream

Silbury

Lammas barrows

West Kennet

Waden spring

Swallowhead spring

River Kennet

Ridgeway

Sanctuary

• site G 55

West Kennet long barrow

isolated hill		stone avenue		○ South Circle
river	○	stone circle		
bank	▬	long barrow		
Prehistoric routeway	●	round barrow		

East Kennet long barrow

0   1 mile

Introduction

The monuments in Avebury parish, Wiltshire, make up the most important Stone Age group in Britain. Included in the complex are remnants of two stone avenues, the biggest known henge enclosure, Europe's tallest artificial hill, and England's largest prehistoric tomb.

These mighty forms lie on the rolling chalk landscape within sight of one another, or even physically linked, and it is generally assumed that they were clustered together on purpose.

What purpose did they serve? What was the unifying idea behind the great metropolis of our first civilization?

In this book it is proposed that the monuments were created as a coherent ensemble to stage a religious drama which took one year to perform, with each edifice offering in turn a special setting for the celebration of a particular event in the farming year, matched to the corresponding event in the human life cycle.

Following the rediscovery that Silbury is an image of the pregnant Mother Goddess in harvest, (described in *The Silbury Treasure*, 1976), it will be argued that the architecture of the entire cycle was designed to be read as a sequence of visual images of the Neolithic deity. These gigantic sculpts of the Great Goddess were regarded as living characters, brought, each in its turn, to a state of maximum vitality by the annual sequence of human rites conducted within.

Such an attitude, though strange to us, was normal in prehistoric times, when 'the whole of creation was thought of as a giant human being, which provided for such an intimate relationship with the whole, that man could expect to find the divine in the depths of his own being'.[1]

The Avebury district was chosen as the centre of attention because there the deity was seen to function through the fortuitous alignment of two river confluences with sunrise and moonset positions at the summer quarter days. This extraordinary chance,

Opposite.
Map of the Avebury monuments.

9

interpreted as a divine exhibition of harmony between underworld, terrestrial plane, and sky, inspired a splendid response.

The Avebury religion sprang from natural physical realities, and crystallized into architectural forms. Studied together, these constructions may give us an insight into the working of the Stone Age spirit.

Ironically, the archaeologists who, through excavation and restoration, have done so much to provide additional data about the West Kennet avenue, the Avebury henge, the Sanctuary, and, most successfully, the West Kennet long barrow, are reluctant to explain how the monuments relate to each other, beyond confirming that they should be regarded as a group built for an unknown religious function. Most workers would agree with Professor Atkinson:

When finally he [the prehistorian] comes to matters of faith and religion, he is usually inclined to take refuge altogether in silence [because] . . . the plain fact of the matter is that on such points there can be no certainty or even any very high degree of probability, as long as written evidence is lacking.[2]

In similar vein, Professor Daniel states categorically, 'The history of ideas begins with writing: there is not and never can be a history of prehistoric thought.'[3]

Perhaps this pessimism reveals a failure to appreciate the operation of images, including big images, in preliterate societies, when every made object was pressed into service to carry coded information additional to fulfilling a narrowly functional role. This code formed a common language valid through vast stretches of time and space, because it was based on people's common experience of the human body.

In a typically preliterate fashion, the body-architecture of the Avebury monuments served practical needs (growing food, burying the dead, etc.) and also enabled these matters to be viewed as aspects of a supernatural metabolism.

The Avebury religion was conceived in terms of physical, measurable matter, and that is why there exists a discernible spiritual dimension to the archaeological remains which can, and should, be deciphered.

Neolithic imagination never lost contact with things. As Lévi-Strauss says, 'In Neolithic science (knowledge), the theory of the sensible order proceeded from the angle of sensible qualities.'[4]

The Avebury monuments deal with order as experienced by a farming community. What did a farming people care about, if not the relationship

Silbury Hill, and the West Kennet long barrow (foreground), landform versions of recognized Neolithic goddess images, flank the tree-lined river Kennet.

A sketch from Stukeley's Abury Described, *published in 1743. Stukeley's devoted fieldwork, carried out at a time when the monuments were under attack, allows us to see much that has been destroyed.*

between earth and sky, worked out in the cyclical progression of the seasons, each different in character, like the Avebury monuments, yet each, like them, linked to its neighbours? The seasons affected their crops and animals, and almost every aspect of human behaviour, as well as that of the surrounding communities of untamed flora and fauna, which were seen to participate in the same great pattern. They found their gods among these mighty, coordinated events. What other theme could have approached the seasonal round in richness and universal fascination? One can understand why most archaeologists prefer silence to an alternative explanation of the Avebury remains.

There has been one previous written attempt to consider the overall meaning of the Avebury monuments – made in 1743 (before the birth of archaeology), by the antiquarian, Dr William Stukeley. His *Abury Described* was based on field work which he had completed twenty years earlier. In July 1723 he wrote to a friend: 'Abury I am perfectly satisfyed about . . . and have little more to do there . . . having by great diligence at last gott a full understanding of that most amazing work, of which before I had but a faint glimpse.'[5]

In Stukeley's case, the material in his field notebooks compiled between 1719 and 1723 was remoulded, following his ordination as a Church of England minister, into Christian bullets for the fight against Deism. His finished work was intended to prove 'that Christianity is as old as creation, though upon a different bottome and principles'.[6]

Through his excellent fieldwork, Stukeley made a unique contribution to Avebury studies, and if, in his conclusions, he fell into the trap whereby prehistorians 'propose to make antiquity intelligible by measuring it according to the popular ideas of the present day (and only see themselves in the creation of the past)',[7] the same could be said of those who now fragment prehistory in the name of scientific analysis.

When a primitive looks at the world there is no gap between himself and what he sees. Therefore, to understand the Avebury builders, 'we need to unthink our seemingly fundamental distinction between self and the world, and with this the distinction between thinking and perceiving begins to vanish too'.[8]

Starting from the belief that 'Man is in nature already',[9] the creators of the Avebury monuments did not so much insinuate the superhuman images *into* the landscape, as draw forth the images already there.

What followed from the conviction that everything, including the land, was alive, was the certainty, based on observation, that everything was subject to change. The monuments were not fixed objects but living events, volatile descriptions of the divine body in different conditions – puberty, sexual maturity, maternity, senescence – reinforced at the right season by appropriate human behaviour, with the last act leading on to the first.

The acts (rituals) of the drama were joined together to make a cyclical play, with the monuments arranged so as to describe and contain the divine narrative in a sequence of architectural stages (symbols) shaped to correspond with the changing condition of the deity's form.

This brings to the fore three interlocking operational modes normal in prehistory, where they were essential to the achievement of coherence amidst continuous motion – namely, symbol, ritual and myth.

In approaching the Avebury monuments, we need these three words in our basic vocabulary, and the ability to use them in combination.

Symbol derives from the Greek 'to throw together, to unite'. Unlike a good visual *sign* (which conveys a narrowly defined message with the utmost clarity) a symbol had a much more complex and important job to do, namely to transmit an entire constellation of meanings through a specially selected (or constructed) physical form. A true symbol was able to tolerate variety and even contradiction in the messages it received and radiated because, before the Age of Logic (which attempted unsuccessfully to drive away contradiction and to separate opposites), contradiction and paradox were accepted, and acknowledged to be embedded in the nature of things.

A natural symbol such as the moon (constantly dying and being born), or an underground spring like the Swallowhead in Avebury parish, could evoke past, present and future in a single form.

The potential for symbol-making was limitless, but in practice attention was collectively concentrated on certain favoured images, often drawn originally from the human body, whence multiple symbolic meanings could be most readily raised to multiple functions.

Where the source material was chosen from animals other than man, or from plants and minerals, 'the symbol (nevertheless) always pointed to a reality or a situation concerning human existence'.[10]

No wonder it is hard to separate symbols from religion. 'For primitives, symbols are always religious',[11] since they contain the world pattern. And what is an alternative name for 'world pattern' so rendered? Why, the Body of God. God is the world pattern, and the symbol is divine because it is an accepted image of God.

Ritual is the active response to symbol, following the patterns visibly suggested in the symbol. It is a human tracing of the symbol, made at prescribed time intervals. The design could be followed and repeated with complete confidence in the relevance of its outline to human fortune, because 'ritual projects man into the era of the gods, makes him contemporary with them and lets him share in their creative work.'[12]

Because of the intimate connection between ritual and symbol, the archaeologist who finds and understands a symbol *should* be able to reconstruct the ritual. Thus Brinton wrote in 1896:

By archaeology we become acquainted with the objective remains of beliefs long since extinguished. We can interpret their symbols, and from rude carvings reconstruct the story of their divine struggles.[13]

When arranged in a grand chain, as they frequently were, symbols activated by rites told the community's master story, the narrative which embraced all others, the Myth Cycle. This explained, regulated and perpetuated the existence of the population in harmony with God.

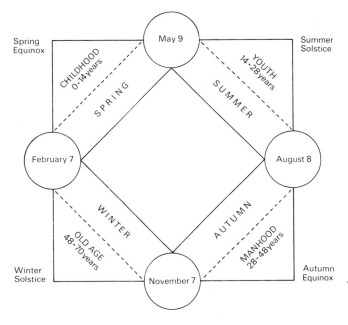

Spring Equinox

May 9

Summer Solstice

CHILDHOOD 0-14 years

SPRING

YOUTH 14-28 years

SUMMER

February 7

August 8

WINTER

OLD AGE 48-70 years

AUTUMN

MANHOOD 28-48 years

Winter Solstice

November 7

Autumn Equinox

The four quarters of the farming year, and the four ages of man, are combined in Byrhtferth's model, AD *1011.*

The Avebury Myth Cycle runs round the entire ensemble of symbol monuments. Together they make up the story, 'for myth, like language, is composed of constituent units',[14] in which 'events or constellations of natural objects are invested with human traits'.[15]

Annual repetition of the story was necessary because 'mythology as a history of the gods could only be produced in life. It had to be experienced and lived.'[16] Every enactment of the Cycle was regarded as definitive *and the first.* The whole universe was 'continually being founded in the primordial mythical events which ceaselessly inaugurated existence'.[17]

Because of this quality of recurrence, the Avebury monuments evade attempts to turn them into history as we know it. Our recent preoccupation with *linear* chronology, summed up by Derek Roe in a book called *Prehistory, the Modern Approach,* constitutes a real obstacle to understanding. He writes:

Pride of place is given to the study of chronology, which is of paramount importance to prehistory, since it is the measurement of time which provides the 'depth' and hence much of the meaning for the narrative picture.[18]

Yet, as we have seen, linear chronology has so far produced no overall picture and no narrative whatsoever for our greatest group of prehistoric monuments. In fact one can only get deep into prehistory either by going round and round, or by following anthropologists into the jungle. There, among living

Neolithic communities, one discovers that 'Myth of its very nature repels historicity', and, in mythic awareness, 'time itself is regarded as a recurring cycle. For such thinking there is no chronology.'[19]

A glance at Christian practice suggests that our culture has not entirely lost touch with primitive timekeeping, for although the year of Christ's birth is used as the starting-point for a linear count (AD I), in many other respects Christian activity moves in an annual circle. We find Christians at Eastertime engaged in something more than a history lesson. The God Christ is crucified and resurrects every year, as a contemporary event in the heart of every believer.

Just as remarkable is the mythical telescoping of the God's mortal life span from a historical 33 years, to fit the solar year. Birth, childhood, ministry, death and resurrection – all these phases are strung unfailingly on each solar orbit, and the scheme is accepted without difficulty, indeed without comment.

Considering this working model, itself firmly based on pagan habit (as scholars unanimously affirm), we should be able to see how the Avebury goddess could run through *her* life in a year, every year, turning from Child to Maiden, then to Lover, then to Mother, and finally to Old Hag.

The habit of equating the seasons with phases in the human life cycle survived into the Middle Ages, even in nature-rejecting monastic circles. In AD 1011 the English scribe Byrhtferth of Ramsey set down what is essentially the Avebury Cycle scheme, employing the ancient quarter days to bisect the solstices and equinoxes.

'We have stirred with our oars the waves of a deep pool', he wrote, tellingly. 'The quarter arises and comes forth like a king from his throne. Spring and boyhood correspond; early manhood and summer are alike; autumn and manhood are allied; winter and old age are periods of decay.'[20]

With this persistent pattern in mind, the recently invented four ages of prehistory – Palaeolithic, Neolithic, Bronze and Iron – seem less fundamental than the four great ages of Spring, Summer, Autumn and Winter.

The Myth of the four quarters was constructed partly out of ephemeral vegetable matter, and is still celebrated in earnest every Old New Year's day (January 6th) at Haxey, Lincolnshire, through the well-known human/corn character called John Barleycorn, male consort of the former goddess:

There was three men came out of the west,
Their fortunes for to try,
And these three men made a solemn vow,
John Barleycorn should die.
They ploughed, they sowed, they harrowed him in,
Throwed clods upon his head,
And these three men made a solemn vow
John Barleycorn was dead.

Then they let him lie for a very long time
Till the rain from heaven did fall,
Then little Sir John sprung up his head
And soon amazed them all.
They let him stand till midsummer
Till he looked both pale and wan,
And little Sir John he growed a long beard
And so became a man.

The song then relates how Sir John is cut off at the knee, rolled, tied by the waist, pricked to the heart with a pitchfork, beaten with sticks, and ground between stones. But after all that he proves in the glass 'to be the stronger man at last'. Here the Haxey drinkers raise their beer mugs and salute the girls, for Sir John, working through the men, desires a female partner.

Contemporary celebration of the annual life/death/life story of John Barleycorn, the mythical character who is also the spirit of the barley – grown, cut, threshed, and turned into beer. On Plough Monday, January 6, the villagers of Haxey, Lincs, continue the ancient tradition.

We should remember that 'folklore is a storehouse of archaic belief',[21] and that the 'astounding uniformity of folklore motives . . . transmitted from the Stone Age until now',[22] arises from a common urge to identify the human life cycle with the seasons.

When the Avebury monuments are reunited with the seasons, a mass of new evidence becomes available to assist in their interpretation: for example, the annual movement of the sun through extreme positions, the rise and fall of vegetation, the annual regime of the chalkland rivers, and the pattern of farm work. The modern Avebury Harvest Supper, and the November necessity to bring the cattle to the barns, are the stuff of the ancient cycle.

What survives of our own folk festival tradition employs the same circular time, through which the monuments could even now come to us from their exile in the land of linear chronology, as an outstanding 'product of a cultural period in which life had not yet broken away from the harmony of Nature'.[23] In the

The midwinter play of the Marshfield Mummers, Glos, commemorates the vegetal cycle of death and renewal. Straw covered the actors before the invention of paper.

Avebury Cycle we shall see how 'everywhere there is a system, everywhere cohesion; in every detail the expression of a great fundamental law whose abundant manifestations demonstrate its inner truth and natural necessity'.[24]

The richness and complexity still visible in the Avebury monuments testify to the majestic quality of all 'primitive' experience. At a time when, in the name of progress, the last primitive communities on earth are being destroyed, the Avebury achievement speaks of the beauty of these decimated groups, and of the others whom they are following into oblivion. The monuments can tell us what we have lost, and also what we are losing.

It is time to get on with the story.

I am a tide: that drags to death.
I am an infant: who but I
Peeps from the unhewn dolmen arch?
I am the womb: of every holt.
I am the blaze: on every hill.
I am the queen: of every hive.
I am the shield: for every head.
I am the tomb: of every hope.

From The Song of Amergin
(*Ancient Celtic calendar poem*),
transl. *Robert Graves.*

The Winter Eve corn dolly

When winter approached, the harvest goddess personified by Silbury was transformed. As surely as winter follows summer, the Tomb Lady took over from the Mother, and invited the Neolithic population to follow her retreat into the underworld.

This meant that the focus of attention switched from Silbury, the August First Fruits temple, designed to operate as the Mother goddess in labour, to a temple devoted to death.

If we stand on the Silbury summit, scanning the horizon for the winter venue, we have not far to look. It lies one thousand strides[1] distant (see map). The Silbury goddess herself points us in that direction. By following the line of her gaze over the narrow east causeway between the Silbury 'moat-nose' and 'moat-hair', we are led to the western tip of the mighty West Kennet long barrow. Yet, close though it seems, between the two sites there is room to put some of the greatest contrasts known to humanity, and a range of thoughts of equivalent comprehensiveness. Sedentary agricultural societies could make journeys of cosmic range within the confines of three fields, in their effort to conserve the epic turning of the universe.

Winter Eve

Three months after the August rites at Silbury had ushered in the harvest, the next quarter day came round. This was called Summer End[2] by later Celts or, alternatively, Winter Eve. Winter Eve was regarded as the most perilous joint in the year, and was marked in prehistoric Britain 'by a solemn and weird festival'[3] which, in decline, had its functions split between Hallowe'en and Martinmas.

Winter Eve lay midway between the autumn equinox and the winter solstice, and is still known as a quarter day in Scotland, though minor calendar adjustments 'have pushed it from November 7th to November 11th'.[4]

(Pages 20–21) The West Kennet long barrow, Neolithic cemetery world of the Death goddess.

Opposite.
A view through the stones of the long barrow forecourt to the Silbury harvest hill. With the start of the winter quarter, in November, the barrow hags came into their own, according to British folklore.

The Neck corn dolly (idol), a traditional form plaited every year from the last of the corn, recalls the shape of the Neolithic long form goddess.

Yet since Thom,[5] Newham,[6] and others have shown that the Neolithic calendar was organized as much around lunar detail as upon a solar framework, it is probably more accurate to think of the Neolithic ceremonies as wandering fourteen nights on either side of the solar midpoint, searching for the most suitable lunar phase.

And what, for Winter Eve, was that? Not the full birth moon of the Silbury Silly season, but the other extreme: a No moon – New moon, to deepen the pitch-black ending, when leaves fall, frost comes, grass dies and, because of the impending shortage of fodder, the great prehistoric cattle slaughter took place.

'Old-fashioned folk still reckon November, December and January as the three winter months,' wrote a Shropshire lady in 1883, adding that in some villages the sexton's wife continued to ring the curfew bell at dusk throughout the winter quarter.[7]

Corn dollies

It was the peasant's disposition to feel and record the autumn-winter transformation in superhuman terms – the Mother who gave birth at Lammas and held sway throughout the autumn quarter was shown turning from Great Provider to Great Devourer.

This dramatic change was until very recently enacted annually among farming communities in the remoter parts of Britain. Every year from the Stone Age till after 1900 the Mother-turning-to-Hag was woven as an idol (dolly), using the vital stuff of the community's life – wheat straws.

The most common form of English corn dolly was known as Mother Earth.[8] Her big-hipped, squatting form stayed close to the more durable Neolithic clay figurines showing the same birth act. As a good symbol, she functioned through her contradictions, her alternative names being Maiden, Wife,[9] and Hag.[10] Thus she was both younger and older than her maternal self. She was the triple Goddess.

'The Corn Spirit appears as both young and old,' reported Frazer.[11] 'There is no difference between the Corn Dolly as Cailleach (wife) and the Corn Dolly as Maiden',[12] and this combined Hag-Mother-Maiden has been recently described as 'the most tremendous figure in Gaelic Myth today'.[13]

Typically, the Hag is represented 'both by the last sheaf, *and the person who cuts it*',[14] he being 'doomed to poverty for want of energy'.[15] The man who brought home the last load of grain was accordingly called Winter. Dirty water was thrown over him, his face was blackened, and he was rolled up in canvas.[16] Even in the nineteenth century it was believed that 'death would fall on the man and his stock who had the Cailleach, Famine of the Farm, put on him'.[17] Yet he accepted his fate with dignity, according to Maclagan's paraphrase of the standard Harvest Supper toast.[18]

Afterwards, in a collective recognition of her triumph, the lads danced with the Cailleach in turn, jogged in procession with her across the countryside, and planted her for a while on the back of a farmer's wife.[19]

Latterly the dance took place in a barn, but because 'in folk belief the spirits of the dead haunted the megalithic monuments, marking the ancient burial grounds, *these* were (once) the main sites of the festival where offerings and sacrifices were made'.[20]

The religion of the barrows, and the making of corn dollies as a communal necessity, have now ceased throughout Britain, but may it not be that the Hag made of straw was carried annually to the West Kennet barrow in Neolithic times, when the goddess image was universally adored?

Our first farmers carved comparable effigies of the goddess from wood and stone, and these indicate the ancient origin of corn dolly designs. In fact there are traditional corn dolly types to match all the primary motifs of Neolithic art in Europe. Mother Earth repeats the squatting goddess figurines, the Devon Cross offers a version of the Eye motif (concentric circles with radial spokes), the Northamptonshire Horns pick up the internationally known Neolithic ox horn theme, while the Somerset Neck and Hereford-shire Fan provide close equivalents to the ubiquitous Neolithic goddess in long form.

Finding these correspondences is much more than a pleasing academic exercise, for the dollies serve to illuminate the connection between the Neolithic figurines and the tombs where they were discovered. The dollies also acclimatize us to accepting very stylized images as representatives of superhuman beings so that, when turning to a Neolithic long figurine like that from Co. Antrim, we can see in its 'trapezoid outline splaying from narrow head to broader foot, with rounded corner, and gently curving sides',[21] the idol from which the dolly derives.

(Top), the Hereford Fan corn dolly repeats the form of a Neolithic idol from Co. Antrim, N. Ireland (below).

Even more important, when the ambiguity of corn dolly naming (Hag-Maiden) is related to her essential work of seasonal transformation *between* the two states, we see that the similar ambiguity which has always surrounded Neolithic long figurines (and long monuments), is integral to their function.

If we stand before the West Kennet long barrow with a long corn dolly in one hand and a long Neolithic figurine in the other, the nature of that dark monument may be revealed, for in a primitive society the smallest visual statements belong to the same image-world as the biggest. As Baldwin Smith says, 'Every man read and depended upon the arts for his conceptual imagery,' and architectural symbolism was 'effective at a popular, instinctive and illiterate level'.[22]

With this in mind, we need to take a close look at the long barrow.

The long barrow goddess

Descriptions of the long barrow

Most people reach the West Kennet long barrow by
following the footpath from the Bath road along the
side of a flat meadow, in the far corner of which the
River Kennet rises at the Swallowhead spring. Then,
having crossed the new-born Kennet by a two-arched
brick bridge, the way lies on to the flint-strewn, bulging
downs. At length the hummocky form of the barrow
mound, stretched east and west, comes into view, with
a dramatic setting of huge sarsen stones standing erect
at the 80-foot-wide eastern end.

We are looking at the most famous of Wessex long
barrows,[1] 'one of the most rewarding in England',[2] and
'one of the most famous megalithic tombs in the British
Isles'.[3] The tomb itself is embedded in the east end of
the barrow mound, and occupies only one-eighth of its
total length.

Estimates of the barrow length have varied so widely
that one might suppose the monument to be unmeasurable in the same way as the Rollright Stones
and other circles were said to be uncountable.

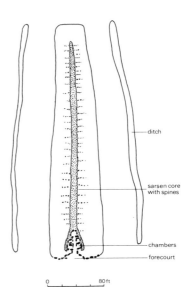

*West Kennet long barrow plan
(after Piggott), showing the five
chambers set in the east end of the
mound, the stone facade, the
mound 'spine' of smaller rocks,
and the flanking ditches.*

*West Kennet long barrow in
1723, as drawn by William
Stukeley.*

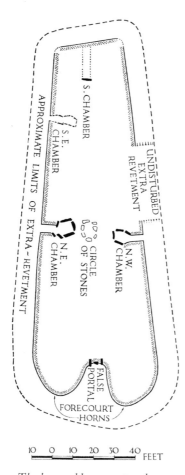

S. CHAMBER

S.E. CHAMBER

APPROXIMATE LIMITS OF EXTRA-REVETMENT

UNDISTURBED EXTRA REVETMENT

N.E. CHAMBER

CIRCLE OF STONES

N.W. CHAMBER

FALSE PORTAL

FORECOURT -HORNS

10 0 10 20 30 40 FEET

The long goddess, great and small. (Above), a plan of the Belas Knap long barrow. (Opposite), a Neolithic bone plaque from Jarlshof, Shetland, 5 inches long. 'Probably the ultimate stylization of a Mother Goddess figure', according to Professor Stanley Thomas.

John Aubrey, (whose drawing, *c.* 1670, shows the entire structure set around the base with stones), gave a mere four perches (65 feet)[4] as the maximum dimension, which casts doubt on whether he was describing the West Kennet barrow at all. Stukeley (1724) reckoned 180 cubits (320 feet) for this 'excessively large mound of earth, ridged up like a house'.[5] Richard Colt Hoare (1814) gave 344 feet,[6] William Long (1858) 'about 300 feet',[7] John Thurnam (1860) 336 feet,[8] and Stuart Piggott (1955) 330 feet,[9] and (1973) 340 feet.[10]

The maximum height of the mound is 14 feet above the Neolithic soil line,[11] but the once smooth profile is now distinctly hummocky, owing to a contemporary of Aubrey's, Dr Toope, alias Took, of Marlborough, who, searching for bones to grind into medicines, 'miserably defaced [the barrow] by digging half the length of it. It *was* most neatly smoothed up to a sharp ridge,' complained Stukeley.[12]

Other attacks on the barrow were described by Thurnam in 1860: 'Later tenants have stripped it of its verdant turf, cut a waggon road through its centre, and dug for flint and chalk rubble in its sides, by which its form and proportions have been much injured . . . [yet] in spite of all this . . . the great old mound, with its grey time-stained stones, has still a charm in its wild solitude, disturbed only by the tinkling of a sheep bell.'[13]

In his classic excavation, 1955–6, Professor Piggott cut through the mound, west of the burial chambers, and found a central core or spine of local sandstone boulders, heaped approximately 6 feet high, from which ran short offshoots at right angles, each composed of 6 boulders of the same material. A thin cover of dark turfy material lay on the core, which divided to pass around the burial chambers, and ended just short of the massive standing stones comprising the east façade.[14]

Overlaying the sarsen spine was a mass of chalk rubble, quarried from two flanking ditches, running its full length at a distance of 40 feet from the north and south mound edges.

The purpose of the long barrow
The biggest question raised by the West Kennet barrow, (and indeed by all English long barrows) is surely: Why is it so long?

Turning to the experts for an answer, we are offered an eerie silence. In most cases, no explanation, however tentative, is forthcoming. Indeed, in most cases, the question is not even asked. Thurnam, in his otherwise diligent report, skirts it altogether, and one may search in vain Piggott's 100-page monograph on the monument to find the issue raised. Perhaps he was discouraged by the experience of the early nineteenth-century antiquarian Sir Richard Colt Hoare, who wrestled publicly but unsuccessfully with the problem.

Colt Hoare asked whether their great length was designed to cover the mass grave of a slaughtered army. No, he decided, because although skeletons were found, and indeed frequently found 'thrown promiscuously together',[15] they were almost invariably confined to the east end of the monument.

The nature of the burials also made it difficult to think of the mounds as emblems of royal prestige: 'At first sight we should suppose them [long barrows] erected in honour of some great chieftain or the head of some British clan, but on opening them these surmises vanish, for they contain no gilded dagger, no stone celt, not any of those articles that might lead to suppositions of riches or grandeur.'[16]

His conclusions perfectly fit what we now know of Neolithic society in England – that it was notably classless and peaceful. But to a titled landowner of 1825 a classless society was unimaginable, and he was 'induced to suppose that long barrows were appropriated to the lower class of people'.[17] Then, 'utterly at a loss to determine the purpose of such gigantic mounds of earth', he eventually 'gave up all researches into them'[18] – an honourable retirement, for what is the use of meaningless research?

In our practical terms the West Kennet long barrow equally makes no sense. But the deeds of every society make sense to its members, whose greatest efforts are usually expended on their highest priorities. The 340-foot length of the West Kennet barrow therefore invites us to contemplate the very spine of the Neolithic rationale, the living body of their Great Goddess.

The long barrow as image

In Avebury parish we are surrounded on all sides by monumental sculpture. Silbury is an image of the squatting Mother; the barrow is the same being, in her Old Hag guise.

Looking again at the many long goddess figurines, frequently found under the barrow mounds of the same period, we may note the close resemblance of their shapes to a typical long barrow plan, while the

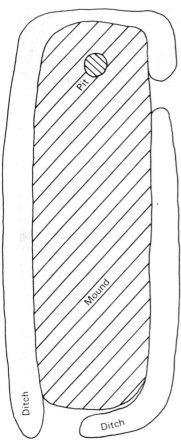

Plan of Giants' Hills long barrow, The goddess with eye pit, landscape scale.

engraved decoration, frequently showing a central spine with horizontal offshoots or bands, again brings West Kennet to mind.

If anything, the barrow scale came closer to describing the community's vision of the deity than the figurines, and in later Celtic tales, we find: 'The gigantic size of the Hag is insisted upon or implied by the strength of her appetite.'[19]

Long barrows are long because they show the Winter goddess as gigantic, and that is probably why in Germany, Denmark and Holland[20] the name Giant is still attached to prehistoric tombs – a pattern confirmed in southern England where 'Neolithic long barrows tend to be called after giants'.[21] Each singular giant was a version of the Great Goddess.[22] In Wiltshire we find Giant's Grave, Downton, Giant's Cave, Luckington, and Giant's Grave, Milton Lilbourne. Further examples in Hampshire and Cornwall also represent the vestiges of a once universal attribution.

A firm statement on the pictorial basis of all Neolithic barrows was made by Cyriax in 1921, in an article which Jackson Knight has called 'important and convincing':[23]

The earth under which men are buried is the mother of the dead. The acceptance of such an explanation would have an important effect on the construction of burial places. The object of the tomb builders would have been to make the tomb as much like the body of a Mother as he was able. The same idea seems to have been carried out in the internal arrangements of the passage grave, with the burial chambers and passage perhaps representing uterus and vagina.[24]

We have here, as Wall says, 'not an architecture of intermediate symbolism, but the reality itself'.[25]

To match the 'eye' perforation characteristic of the bone and stone figurines (and the eye-loop at the head of the long corn dolly), many long barrow heads were given an eye in the form of a circular pit. By 1935, seventeen examples were known. Giants' Hills barrow is typical:

The empty pit (was dug) in the old ground surface on the line of the barrow's central axis. Traces of a hurdle were discovered surrounding the pit, which was 2 feet deep, and filled with clean chalk rubble, capped by a conical mound of loam and soil, rich in the organic remains resulting from human occupation. The loam was found to contain an unusual number of snail shells – 23 species being brought to the spot from lower (and wetter) ground.[26]

These components – fencing, snails from a watery location, layers of loam and chalk, and general cone shape – may be seen as the contracted counterpart to such Neolithic harvest hills as Silbury, which contained precisely these materials in its very core. (At Silbury, the dark hidden eye was expanded, using concentric and radial chalk walling, to turn the entire hill into a fat treatment of the oculi motif, appropriate for harvest.)

In Stone Age imagery and belief, the long goddess grew from and returned to the squatting goddess. We are dealing with two aspects of a three-in-one trinity. For that reason the two modes frequently combine in a single figurine. Consider for example the pillar-headed goddess from Cernavoda, Romania, *c.* 5000 BC, with its deliberately extended neck-head.

We might also see this principle rendered monumentally in the elongated neck and head of the Silbury squatting figure, which offers more than a hint of the West Kennet barrow shape, and the season to come.

Is it no more than a coincidence that farmers in many parts of Britain called the last handful of standing wheat the Neck, and then ritually plaited it into a similar long shape? They were helping the Harvest Mother to decapitate herself, so concluding the necessary annual sacrifice, involving her transformation into complete Long Hag.

Archaeological evidence reinforces this possibility at Silbury. In the south east perimeter of the Silbury mound, facing the long barrow, a perforated stone of a hard grey schist was found, two inches long and half an inch thick, shaped like the long goddess of a thousand schist idols, *and used as a sickle sharpener.*[27] This object makes the point that Neolithic art was intended to present agricultural processes and technology in terms of the superhuman body.

By scraping and cutting, the thin winter witch is extracted from her summer apron, or rather she undresses herself, as described in the Welsh Hallowe'en rhyme:

> *A white Lady on the top of the tree*
> *Whittling an umbrella stick.*[28]

This is Death, carving herself to the bone. Her other name was Cyhiraeth. She 'displayed her shrivelled arms before those she called' to join her as a skeleton.[29]

To see a monumental Welsh lady engaged in the same work, we can inspect the Neolithic barrow at Bryn yr Hen Bobl, Anglesey, where the mound-neck stretches three times the length of the squatting body.[30] Neolithic monuments were built to live, and living

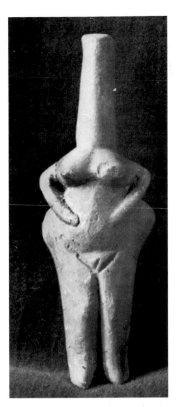

Columnar neck and full body of a goddess figurine from Romania, c. 5000 BC, combines the two modes of the deity.

implies continuity and transition between Maternal and Hag shapes. It may also imply periodic ritual scrubbing of the West Kennet chalk mound, as Grahame Clark suggests[31] – the body, like the Uffington White Horse, had to be cared for.

The west chamber

Reading from Silbury, William Stukeley called the West Kennet barrow 'South Barrow', and noted 'a very operose congeries of huge stones upon the east end'.[32] 'Here', wrote Colt Hoare, 'if uncovered, we should probably find the interment.'[33] In 1849 Dean Merewether counted 'at least 30 sarsen stones in which might clearly be traced *the chamber* and the covered passage leading to it from the semi-circle of stones [forecourt] at the east end'.[34]

Ten years later John Thurnam arrived to dig. He made straight for the chamber roof close to the east end, marked by 'three large flat stones, lying in a row', with glimpses of upright slabs, 'jutting up below them'.[35] By use of 'screw jacks and rollers of timber', a capstone was removed, and the chamber entered. Two days later, another party of men bored in via the prehistoric passage which followed the barrow mound's central axis for eight yards.

Exploration of the forecourt end of the passage was blocked by fallen slabs and the owner's refusal to allow them to be moved, but enough was revealed to show that the passage was more than a yard wide, with walls 'formed of rude [undressed] upright blocks, four or five feet in height'.[36] Above this level, two or three horizontal courses of sandstone drew the tunnel roof progressively inwards and upwards to a ceiling height of 8 feet along the central axis.

Like the passage, the west chamber was stuffed almost to the ceiling with compacted chalk rubble, heavily studded with fragments of prehistoric pottery representing parts of at least fifty vessels, which originally ranged in size from 'salt cellars to two-gallon containers'.[37] Flint tools were also found, and (unexpectedly), horizontal layers, '3 to 9 inches thick . . . of a blackish, sooty and greasy looking matter', judged to be decomposed plants, but containing in addition 'bones of sheep, goat, ox of a large size, roebuck (including part of a horn) and swine . . . including boars with large tusks'.[38]

When cleared, the west chamber proved to be exceptionally large by English standards – nine feet

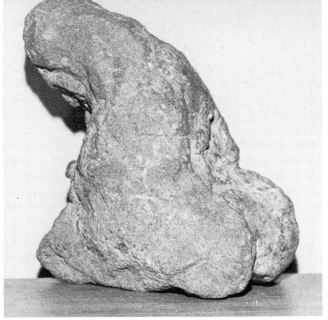

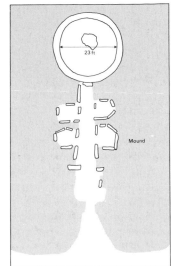

Plan of the Neolithic chambered long barrow of Notgrove. (Left), a limestone figure of the Hag goddess was found on the roof of the circular head of the chamber complex.

wide and eight feet long, with walls created by six huge sarsens, set on end to penetrate the ground by a foot or so, and supported by chunks of stone rammed into the gravelly subsoil. These megaliths were linked by 'panels of dry stone walling built from tile-like stones'[39] – limestone flags quarried 20 miles west, near Bath.

On the chamber floor Thurnam found the dishevelled skeletal remains of five adults and a child, buried without personal possessions or 'grave goods'.[40] Their long skulls suggested a Stone Age date, as did the total absence of metal. Thurnam filled up his excavation, replaced the capstones, and published his report.

The side chambers

Piggott's investigation, 1955–6, confirmed the existence of the straight east façade, the 'shallow semicircular forecourt, and the passage leading from it to the west chamber'. Then he made 'the wholly unexpected and entirely gratifying discovery'[41] of four additional chambers, opening off the sides of the passage as matching pairs.

Somewhat smaller than the west chamber, they were constructed in precisely the same manner, at the same time (*c.* 3250 BC),[42] and for the same purpose – tombs containing untidy multiple human burials, interred over a long period. Like the west chamber they had then been filled to the roof 'with chalk rubble and occupational debris . . . containing large quantities of pottery, bone and stone tools, beads and other objects'.[43]

(Above) the squatting harvest goddess emerges from a plan of the West Kennet long barrow chambers. (Below), a possible flint image of the hooded winter Hag was found in the west chamber of the long barrow.

Viewed together the passage and five chambers comprise 'a plan for which many parallels exist'.[44] Thanks to Piggott, they can be seen to fit an orthodox Neolithic pattern or figure, illustrated nearby in the Gloucestershire chambered tombs of Hetty Pegler's Tump, Notgrove, Nympsfield, and at Parc le Breos and Tinkinswood in South Wales. Piggott writes: 'The architectural similarities between the tombs ... [means] we are dealing with the formal architectural setting for prescribed liturgical and ceremonial performances.'[45]

Liturgies, whether ancient or modern, usually offer a description of the deity and an invitation to the congregation to enter the body of the godhead. In prehistoric times those twin objectives were literally repeated in the shape of the temple, just as a Christian church repeats the body of Christ. The building and the prayer were in harmony. Using different media, they both said: 'Here is the God. Let us enter.'

The chambers as squatting image

On that account, many writers have interpreted the east end chambers of long barrows like West Kennet as the womb of the goddess in long form, representing death,[46] and Grinsell points to the tendency for the corpses to be buried in the foetal position as consistent with this intention.[47]

But acceptance of the West Kennet chambers in this uterine role does not explain why they were laid out in five lobes. What is this five-lobed image? The problem loses its intractability when we recall that old hags were once mothers, and that the great giver of life and the great destroyer were essentially one and the same wherever the Great Goddess held sway.

Consequently the goddess in long form was frequently *merged with* her maternal squatting representation. Thus the chambers offer a version of the squatting goddess known from a thousand figurines.

In winter, the Harvest Mother (Silbury) does not vanish from but *into* the earth, into the bone mound, there to receive the dead. For this purpose her body, though preserving the squatting pregnant posture, was made suitably hollow.

With varying degrees of 'realism' the chamber plans of southern England and Wales tell the same story. The pregnant Harvest goddess goes into hibernation, just as the Mother Earth corn dolly was shut up in a barn every winter, to be returned to the fields the following spring.

The stone rivers

The vanishing river

The siting of the barrow, high above the Kennet valley on the lowest layers of the Upper Chalk, ensures a perennial dryness. The ditches on either side, 23 feet wide, and 12 feet deep, are now full of soil, but they were never full of water, being well above the maximum level of the underground water table, and in this respect they differ fundamentally from the intentionally wet Silbury ditch. Indeed, running throughout the long barrow is the theme of desiccation, reflecting the nature of the skeleton under the flesh, and the late autumn condition of the surrounding landscape. The barrow is at one with the bare November trees, drained of sap.

An English proverb also talks of the scarcity of surface water in late autumn: 'Between Martinmas and Yule, water's worth wine in any pule,' a conviction vividly supported by the behaviour of the Kennet headwaters, where miles of river simply disappear every November.

Following heavy surface evaporation all over the downs during the summer months, the saturation of the underlying chalk strata is so reduced that the Swallowhead spring generally dries up and the river and its tributary, the Winterbourne, cease to flow. No matter how much rain falls in November, it usually takes two months for the underground reservoir to be replenished sufficiently for the flow to start again.[1]

Irrespective of fluctuations in climate, says Professor H. L. Hawkins, the Kennet autumn sinking effect would have applied throughout the prehistoric period. This rhythm has consequences almost as startling as the appearance of mud flats around a tidal estuary. In early winter the Kennet is sour and shocking in its emptiness. Where, a few months previously, vital running water had supported fish, insects and mixed communities of water plants, now all appears in a state of collapse. To stand on the empty bed is to be sunk half underground, among dead and dying populations.

What did the Neolithic population make of this spectacular change? To answer, we should first recall

Main source of the sacred river Kennet, the Swallowhead spring ceases to flow in the winter months of November and December – a hydrological fact which applied equally in Neolithic times.

that, in prehistory, the land was not regarded as an 'It' but as a 'She'. The land was the extended body of the deity, and the rivers were the superhuman 'bloodstream'. In *The Silbury Treasure* we have shown how this attitude inspired the erection of the Silbury Mother image to fit the summer behaviour of the nearby Swallowhead and Waden springs.

But the summer mood passed and the water level dropped, preparing the scene, perhaps, for the appearance of the traditional British figure known as the Divine Cleanser or, in Scotland, as the Washer at the Ford, 'a sinister hag who may be encountered on the river bank, washing the bloodstained garments of those who are about to die'.[2]

By Winter Eve, the Kennet goddess had swallowed her own river head (still called Swallowhead), and turned her river bloodstream into stone. At the same season, the Swallowhead is left dry as a bone. The familiar trickling sound is not heard. Nothing comes from the dark orifice in the curving rock wall. The natural semi-circle has been transformed from life-giving spring to barren womb, or skull; a memorable sight, and one which must be accepted, because it is natural. There is room for half a dozen people to sit here on the flat dry ground. Then the embracing chalk cliffs, only four feet high, cut off the view of Silbury. Old Stone Age hunters, with their well-known sensitivity towards the religious meanings of cave mouths, probably visited this place. Certainly the common people in Stukeley's day regarded it as holy – the chief natural symbol in the area. Only in modern times have we and our archaeologists chosen to ignore it.

Yet even today, though divorced from the land, architectural historians reiterate the old message: 'An early symbol was the cave which extends into the motherly earth from which all life arises. The cave represents the first spatial element. Artificial caves were created as dolmens.'[3]

Dolmen is another word for burial chamber, and Swallowhead is only 500 yards from the most notable burial chamber in England, the natural counterpart and likely model.

Because the prehistoric mind 'does not separate *what* a thing is experienced as being, from the place *where* it was experienced as being',[4] we may suggest that the west chamber represents the winter Swallowhead, transferred into architecture. Horseshoe-shaped, it has four standing sarsens (massive sandstone blocks) linked together with thin, horizontally laid slabs of limestone, imitating the plan, elevation and bedded texture of Swallowhead, but using materials with a higher load-bearing strength than chalk.

Set in the 340-feet-long barrow, the west chamber may also have registered pictorially as the contracted winter womb of the long barrow goddess, and simultaneously provided the skull or head to the squatting deity whose body was outlined by the four adjoining chambers.

The stone rivers

Running between the sarsens which make up the walls of all five chambers are sections of the peculiar dry-stone walling previously noted. Composed of layers of little flags half an inch thick, this material is a creamy coloured limestone, pitted like fish row, or decaying bone.[5] At the same time, its curving arrangement carries the idea of the continuous stream from the northern end of the façade, into the forecourt, through the left thigh and arm, and on to the head of the sitting goddess. From there it flows outwards via her right side, and eventually emerges as the wall of the south forecourt.

No local material could have carried the eye horizontally around the chambers so effectively. But what was the builders' intention in creating this effect? Similar wall coursing exists in other barrows, including the inexplicably 'wavy' undulation around the Parc le Breos tomb, which is built directly over a subterranean stretch of a little stream. The barrow goddess would naturally epitomize the streams of the underworld, since she was queen of that realm. A leading water diviner has declared that 'every long barrow had an underground stream running its full length',[6] and this conviction is shared by the former Keeper of British Antiquities at the British Museum, R. A. Smith.[7]

It seems possible, then, that the ragstone walling at West Kennet long barrow may have reference to the local river – the Winterbourne, which becomes the Kennet at the sharp bend marked by the Swallowhead spring (K1).

The Winterbourne-Kennet abandons its surface course in November to disappear underground. Might not the Neolithic architects have followed its downward movement and represented it in the West Kennet long barrow walls which, as at Parc le Breos, were designed to incorporate the qualities of the underworld goddess? Support for this view may be found in British folklore, where it is said that, in November, the divine hag exercises her power to convert water into stone, and sea into solid land, with a touch of her wand.

Opposite.
The west chamber of the long barrow, representing the head of the hollow chamber-figure within the mound. Limestone courses convey the line of a stone river between sarsen uprights, while massive corbelling rounds off the skull. (Below), similar undulating stone courses in the Parc le Breos long barrow, built over an underground stream, may have been intended to indicate the sacred current.

Verbeia, the Romano-British goddess of the river Wharfe. River serpents flow from her body and coalesce in her gut.

Since British folklore, not to mention Romano-British inscriptions, also equates rivers with superhuman or divine females (the river Wharfe, for example, is the goddess Verbeia), we can understand the iconographic necessity of making the walls describe the rivers *and* the squatting goddess plan. The stone rivers were the actual body of the divinity.

But if her chamber head is identified with Swallowhead, we should expect some architectural reference to the other important spring in the vicinity, that flowing from Waden Hill and joining the Kennet half a mile further downstream. For the Waden tributary undoubtedly played a vital role in determining the proportions and siting of Silbury Hill. To be consistent with the barrow plan, it should be represented 'downstream' of 'Swallowhead', in the south forecourt. Sure enough, running to meet the main wall of the south forecourt, Piggott found an inexplicable ragstone 'tributary', four feet long, emanating from Stone 4, an eccentrically placed sarsen.

It is significant that, when in later Neolithic times five more stones were erected in the forecourt, they were *not* joined together with limestone coursing, and therefore did not confuse the river image.

The relationship of the two springs, recorded in the barrow design, was important because the 70°–250° axis joining their confluences marked moonrise and sunset position at the two winter quarter days, Martinmas (7 November) and Candlemas (2 February). This extraordinary coincidence complements the phenomenon observable at the May and Lammas quarter days, where sunrise and moonset (70°–250°) may be observed along the selfsame water axis.

West Kennet long barrow may therefore be regarded, like Silbury, as architecture incorporating 'rhythms, acting in time', which Zevi asserts was a normal feature of ancient buildings.[8]

Units of measurement

Pacing the dry tributary beds leading from the two sacred springs to the Kennet, a Neolithic designer would have observed the following lengths:
Swallowhead spring – Kennet (K1) = 65.25 feet, or 24 megalithic yards.
Waden spring – Kennet (K2)   = 400 feet, or 147 megalithic yards.

Whether expressed as megalithic yards, (i.e. the likely average pace length of a population whose average height is known to have been 5 feet 6 inches), or in modern units, the evidence from Silbury and other Neolithic monuments clustered around the Kennet headwaters suggests that the two tributaries were employed as linear modules in the building programme. This seems to apply to the barrow, of which Piggott writes: 'It is clear that some kind of regular plan was envisaged, presumably to define units of measurement, and with a knowledge of ratios.'[9]

The purpose of all the Neolithic monuments in the area was to celebrate the Great Goddess *as locally revealed*. 'For the mind of the primitive, the location-form-deity relationship was not arbitrary . . . but representational'.[10]

Our search for units of measurement might start at the most striking features of the deity's local revelation, her sacred springs, the source of two *real*, rather than abstract, measuring rods.

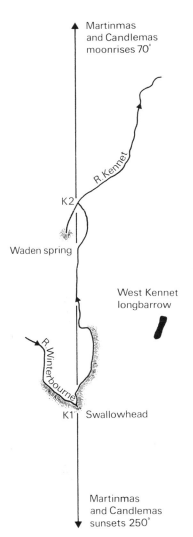

Winter quarter days and sacred springs. Moonrise and sunset lines connect, at Martinmas and Candlemas, the confluences of the Swallowhead and Waden springs.

SH-K1 represents length of Swallowhead tributary (65.25 ft)

SH-K2 represents length of Waden tributary (400 ft)

Feature	feet	meg. yds	river unit
Long axis of mound, west end to forecourt	326	120	SH-K1 × 5
Long axis of chambers, west chamber to forecourt	43.5	16	SH-K1 × $\frac{2}{3}$
Mound, greatest width, (east end)	80	29.4	WS-K2 × $\frac{1}{5}$
Mound, least width (west end)	32.6	12	SH-K1 × $\frac{1}{2}$
Sarsen façade, overall length	65.25	24	SH-K1
Forecourt, greatest width	32.6	12	SH-K1 × $\frac{1}{2}$
Internal chambers, periphery (i.e. from stone 8 to stone 35)	130.5	48	SH-K1 × 2

INTER-SITE DISTANCES FROM THE WEST KENNET LONG
BARROW, MEASURED FROM THE BARROW FORECOURT

To	feet	meg. yds	river unit
Silbury top	3132	1152	Sh-K1 × 48 or SH-K1^2 × 2*
Sanctuary entrance	4398	1617	WS-K2 × 11
The 'Obelisk', Avebury henge	7196	2646	WS-K2 × 18
Waden spring	1999	735	WS-K2 × 5

*N.B. Exactly twice the Silbury-Swallowhead distance

Bones and pots

Necessary confusion

The nature of the Winter goddess at West Kennet is revealed as much by her furnishings (now housed in Devizes Museum) as by her overall form. Her tomb-body was built to contain that primary chaos of natural and man-made things – the undifferentiated rubbish from which new life annually arises.

Within the tomb there was a blurring of distinction between corpse and corpse (their bones were muddled up), between the living and the dead (the tomb was designed to be visited),[1] and between pot and skull (both were rounded, containers, and of practical use in ritual).

Forty-six bodies are represented by the surviving bones. The remains were treated with scant respect for individual origin. As in other Neolithic barrows,[2] there

A Neolithic confusion of skulls and bones, discovered by Piggott in the long barrow's southwest chamber, attests to the culture's collective attitude to burial.

is no trace of hierarchy, precedence, or segregation on the basis of age or sex. Lynch found the same at Bryn Celli Ddu:

> Men, women and children were buried together. There is no sign of any distinction between rich and poor. Neolithic chambered tombs would seem to represent vaults in which all members of the tribe or community were entitled to burial.[3]

The bones

But this muddle should not be misconstrued as indifference. At West Kennet certain limbs – the upper arm bones, for instance – were the subject of particular attention to the people of the Neolithic, for 'the humerus was detached from other arm bones in many instances'.[4] In his report, L. H. Wells formed the 'ghoulish picture of a Neolithic visitor to the barrow picking up a partly decomposed arm, detaching the humerus, and flinging the other bones into a dark corner'.[5]

Perhaps there is more to it than that. We should note, for instance, that the humerus bears a strong resemblance to the shape of the entire long barrow mound, and may very well have been regarded as a reference to, or version of, the long goddess. The ambivalence of arm bone messages has persisted in primitive ritual usage. In 1962 the forearm of an ancestor was used, in New Guinea, to promote fertility, while pointing an arm bone at someone was thought to be a sure way of inducing his or her death.[6]

A similar double notion may be implied by the arm bone which was found through the north forecourt wall at West Kennet long barrow. It pointed straight to Silbury Hill, the harvest womb.

It may seem strange and even offensive to our Western sensibilities that the tomb was frequented by the living as well as by the dead. But here again the belief that the living can find meaning and reality within putrefying chaos was once widespread, and is still held in modern India, where Tantric belief has incorporated practices from Neolithic times. The seeker even today 'makes use of the graveyard in several ways. The Sadhaka (worshipper) is supposed to make it his home, at first literally, later metaphorically. He must confront and assimilate in its most concrete form the meaning of death . . . His goddess, his loving Mother in time, who gives him birth and loves him in the flesh, also destroys him in the flesh. His image of her is incomplete if he does not know her as his tearer and devourer.'[7]

The bone goddess. A human legbone, carved to represent the goddess in long form with eye motif, was found at a Neolithic site in Portugal.

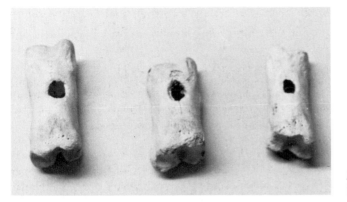

Perforated ox bones from the West Kennet long barrow.

At West Kennet, the encompassing 'Mother tomb' design undoubtedly sustained and gave meaning to the hard task of handling the decomposing wreckage. To call the behaviour 'ghoulish' is to miss the connection perceived so clearly by Piggott when, in the Zhob valley of north Baluchistan, he confronted Neolithic figurines of the death-dealing goddess. They were, he wrote, 'a grim embodiment of the mother goddess who is also the guardian of the dead – an underworld deity concerned alike with the corpse of the seed-corn buried beneath the earth.'[8] That is the Great Goddess, East and West.

On balance, as always in the world of myth, the life-giving force enjoys no absolute triumph, but always survives. This is shown in the traditional game, 'The Farmer's in his Den' where the child selected to be Bone is destined to be chewed by Dog, and to receive a shower of blows from the others, who shout: 'We all pat the bone.'

The bone disintegrates, but the end of one game is the start of another, because that very bone is changed into a new being. Bone becomes Farmer in the next round.

The widespread identification of bone with death goddess is further supported at the West Kennet barrow by the discovery in the south side chambers of six ox phalanges or foot bones, each perforated with a single hole at one end. They resemble other perforated animal bones from Neolithic graves, which are generally recognized as idols – for example, the group from Stone Age Jericho in the Ashmolean Museum, Oxford. From the long barrow at Belas Knap, Gloucestershire, comes a similar bone figurine,[9] and another was found in Nympsfield long barrow.[10] At West Kennet, as elsewhere, the perforated bones of

45

oxen recall the close association of the goddess with that animal – the drawer of the plough and chief provider of milk and meat. Indeed, the creature was universally regarded as a form of the goddess, and both horns and feet were given a place of honour in many tombs of the period.[11] Ox vertebrae were embedded in the primary mound of Silbury Hill, and Thurnam found 'ox bones of a large size' in his excavation at West Kennet west chamber.[12]

The roebuck antler

Thurnam's dig also unearthed the antler of a roebuck. Another, found carefully placed on the floor at the entrance of the northeast chamber, should remind us again that 'the primary goddess of the Old European pantheon . . . was a composite image',[13] inclined to put on antlers.

Unlike other deer, the roebuck casts its antlers in late October and a new set begins to grow immediately, being fully developed by March.[14] Therefore, the antler is seasonally connected with the deathly Winter goddess, the Bone Lady, and for that reason well represented in the tomb.

In late October, the doe is pursued in a tight circle by the buck around a tree, or some other pivotal point, flattening the grass in the process. (Doe and buck invariably run anti-clockwise, or widdershins. In many fairy stories, the entrance to the fairy hill is gained by running three times around it, widdershins.) Sometimes a double ring is made, in a figure of eight,[15] resembling the two circles within the Avebury henge, and perhaps referred to in the long barrow by two rounded sarsen nodules, with a rib placed between, which were found lying within four inches of the antler.[16]

Using the skulls

There is a shortage of skulls and thigh bones at the West Kennet barrow, and this is generally assumed to mean that these were used in Neolithic rituals, perhaps at the nearby causewayed camp on Windmill Hill, where Keiller found fragments of human craniums in the ditches 'related to rites which involved the use of skulls and other bones, taken from the tombs'.[17] The widespread use of skull and femur in fertility rites was maintained down to classical times,[18] when the rotting flesh fell off to reveal the clean tools of a new sexuality, with skull acting as female container, encompassing the thigh bone-phallus. Our own civilization has seen this ancient statement of harmony converted into a pirates' flag.

Some skulls, however, were left in the barrow, and perhaps none was more significantly placed than that of a one-year-old infant (no skeleton) found by Thurnam on the central axis, against the back wall of the west chamber. One year is the time which the agricultural myth cycle takes to be completed. The cranium, shell-like in its delicacy, therefore perfectly fits the nature of the goddess's massive tomb head. With this little skull were three artifically struck flint flakes, and 'one of these', Thurnam observed 'is actually transparent'.[19]

In the southwest chamber three skulls were placed in a row. They were of an old woman, a young woman and a child,[20] and may have served to record the three states, sharing a common fate. Their deliberate grouping reminds us that the habit of divination, using three bowls, was a persistent Winter Eve activity in Britain down to modern times.[21] And drinking from a skull 'to ensure health, or to possess the owner's qualities, or to cure illness, continued at one Pembroke-shire well, into the present century'.[22]

Of all the bones in the human body, the skull is the most evocative container. When set up in the normal way, it is the womb of thought; inverted, it becomes a bowl or cup. In Neolithic culture there is no firm boundary between the skull and modelled forms,[23] and the skull is the most likely model for the first pottery ever made in Britain – the round-based, dark-grey, largely undecorated ware of the Neolithic Windmill Hill culture, found in the West Kennet tomb.

The pots

There are 'practical' disadvantages in creating pots with round rather than flat bases – they have to be either suspended in the air or sunk into the ground – but the symbolic importance of the shape remained paramount for over 1,000 years, 'showing how far away [the potters] were from a merely profane activity; every housewife, potting, exercises a part of the creative activity of the gods.'[24]

Many writers go further and affirm that the pots, like the skulls which they resembled, were the Goddess: 'The Mother Pot is really a fundamental conception in all religions and is almost worldwide in its distribution. The pot's identity with the Great Mother is deeply rooted in ancient belief through the greater part of the

A Neolithic pot (above), found at the barrow, imitates a skull with its round base. Used for religious purposes, the Great Goddess (top) was the pot.

world.'[25] Erich Neumann writes, 'We arrive at a universal symbolic formula for the early part of mankind: WOMAN = BODY = VESSEL = WORLD. This is the basic formula for the matriarchal stage.'[26]

But a Neolithic formula does not produce uniformity, because the basic idea is always worked out in accordance with local conditions. The pot known as P.12, for example, large fragments of which were found in the forecourt and east chambers, represents a Neolithic pot of a type peculiar to southeast Britain, manufactured in the middle of the third millennium BC, and known as Fengate ware. The vessel has the characteristically truncated conical form which, inverted, offers a schematic version of many a harvest hill-womb. Yet something prompted the P.12 potter to go further, adding features which, in Piggott's words, are 'remarkable in many respects . . . [and] without counterparts in the British Neolithic series'.[27] The vessel's hollow neck shows a series of widely spaced circular impressions. Are these mere decorative dents, or are they eye images? The latter possibility is reinforced by the rows of deep paired 'eye holes' which march from the neck, across the broad collar, to the vessel's open mouth. These designs bring to mind the Avebury stone avenues (West Kennet and Beckhampton), crossing the ploughed fields on their way to the world's biggest henge, especially since the collar is also incised with 'boldly channelled ornament of filled triangles [fields?], difficult to parallel'.[28]

Because these furrows are arranged in triangles, they also suggest the classic, internationally known, female pubis symbol.

In any Neolithic community, potter and architect collaborated in rendering to society a coherent account whereby the Mother might bear fruit. Accordingly, the P.12 pot's version of the Silbury wheat may be the finger and thumb impressions which turn the entire cone into a waving corn stook.

The local interplay between goddess-pot and goddess-monument clung on tenaciously in the folk-lore fragment, reported by Aubrey in 1660, that Silbury 'was raysed while a posset of milk was seething'.[29] Is P.12 that very posset, forerunner of the Iron Age magic cauldron, and the medieval Holy Grail?' Probably not, for though one has a clear view of Silbury from the barrow forecourt, where most of the fragments were found, the barrow season pivots on Midwinter rather than Lammas.

The pot known as P.12, found in the barrow forecourt, carries a unique configuration which may refer to local features: the Silbury lower hemisphere, with indented eyes beneath the collar, and two 'avenues' of smaller indentations (see Ch. 9).

A nineteenth-century Welsh wassail bowl retains Neolithic references in the squatting goddess figurine (pellet-encrusted, on the right of the lid), as well as in the snake handles, the eye motif, and the harvest hill slope.

Yet precisely this paradox attends those splendid conical mounds festooned with signs of plenty, the lids of nineteenth-century Welsh wassail bowls. In their own way, they too offered a clear view of harvest in the depths of winter. Designed for midwinter house-to-house group drinking, as part of the Mari-Lwyd hobby horse fertility rite, these vessels often retain eye patterns around the neck, and the traditional serpents, whose ancient ancestors were probably the megalithic stone rows. Here they weave among a zoological garden of birds and beasts.

And who should we see, sitting on the St Fagans Castle lid, (right side), but the descendant of the Great Goddess – a squatting female figure, moulded in clay, and covered from shoulders to knees with the pellet-symbols of fertility.

Associated with the wassail bowl is the puzzle jug, used in traditional midwinter revels to mark the season of chaos, and the collapse of sound form. Perforations around the lip of the vessel cause the would-be drinker to get drenched rather than quenched.

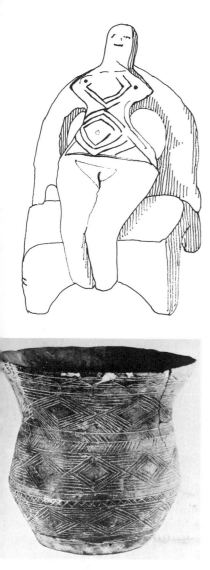

The same result would have been obtained from the pot, 'perforated with a series of holes . . . so as to form a kind of strainer',[30] which Thurnam found under a sarsen slab in the west chamber, next to a man's skull. It may well belong to the same tradition.

In the northwest chamber, a splendid Late Neolithic bell beaker, lacking a base, was found in an inverted position, suggesting perhaps that the pot deity of winter was to pour her juices back into the ground.

Hipped and waisted, this version of the deity is patterned with lozenge shapes. Comparable lozenges are incised or painted around the womb and breasts of many Neolithic figurines, such as the little enthroned goddess from Kolekovats, Bulgaria,[31] and testify to the working human reality underlying an apparently abstract pattern.

As a superhuman summary the lozenge still conveys a bisexual message in many parts of the Orient, being composed of a downward-pointing female triangle and an upward pointing male element, the totality achieving the comprehensiveness of the Chinese Yin-Yang symbol.

To judge whether or not the bell beaker diamonds were drawn with comparable urgency, one has only to look around the contemporary Avebury monuments. There one is faced by stone diamonds, weighing up to 50 tons, which have been deliberately balanced on one tip in order to exhibit the right shape. Prehistoric art was a weighty business.

Pots and myths

Although some of the West Kennet pots display special features, it would be wrong to imply a firm division between ritual vessels and domestic vessels. If the Elizabethan clergy could, without incongruity, conduct holy communion from secular flagons and wine cups, we may be sure there was domestic-ritual exchange in the days before Original Sin. Drinking, (like eating, and food preparation) has always been recognized as an inherently sacramental act, requiring only the intensification brought by ritual.

Among modern workers, Lévi-Strauss is one who *has* fully appreciated the extent to which prehistoric religion emanates from and returns to the domestic hearth. A religion which did not eat, did not work. In these circumstances, cooking was a vital medium for myth. The story was told in the carefully managed stew, with the pot goddess as the vehicle of ordered change.

The lozenge or diamond motif, associated with the goddess in Neolithic art, appears (above) on a beaker from the barrow forecourt; (top), on the belly of a goddess figurine from Bulgaria, c. 4000 BC; and, in monumental form (opposite), as the Diamond Stone of Avebury henge.

The soft fabric of British Neolithic pottery allowed boiling through the insertion of hot stones, rather than direct placement on a fire, and 'traces of carbonized food frequently found on the inner surfaces',[32] show that both Windmill Hill and the later type of vessels were so used.

Lévi-Strauss believes that 'in the universal principles underlying food preparation'[33] among primitive peoples, boiling always carries democratic, plebeian, non-hierarchical associations, which are entirely in keeping with the arrangement of human bones within the barrow, and the tenor of Neolithic life.

The Avebury Cycle was a cooking cycle, which naturally extended into the grave, where 'natural corruption was paralleled by cultural cooking'.[34]

As the Avebury Cycle unfolds, we should keep an eye on the pots found among the monuments, especially when approaching the Avebury henge itself, because often 'the myths about the origin of cooking refer to physiology of marriage alliance, whose harmonious functioning is symbolized by the culinary art'.[35]

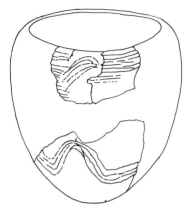

The pot known as P.11 appears to show water spurting from a spring while, below, the course of the river is outlined: references, perhaps, to Swallowhead and the river Kennet.

Because the mythic narrative in Avebury parish is intimately involved with the local springs and rivers, cross-references between watercourses and pots were inevitable, and are possibly displayed in permanent form on the vessel known as P.11, found in the southeast chamber among a scatter of children's bones. This was 'a small cup of fine, almost gritless smooth pink ware, with a slight sandy texture. The ornament of loops, arcs and lines is made probably with a fingernail, to imitate fine, twisted cord impressions.'[36]

To us, 'ornament' usually means pattern for pattern's sake, but this was not so in prehistory. Preliterate people used pattern as a repeated reference to an observed working reality which they wished to extend. For them, pattern clarified the ideas contained in the natural model, and drew messages from the very body of the thing seen. In view of the consistency with which the spring-river theme runs through the barrow imagery, from the monumental to the minute, there is some justification for seeing the P.11 design as a rendering of the Swallowhead spring, with the Winterbourne-Kennet meandering below. Near the rim, a version of the Swallowhead spurts from a series of carefully incised horizontal lines, which might be descriptive of the bedded character of the chalk around the spring, and the layered deposition of chalk rubble, interspersed with stripes of organic material, that were subsequently spread across the tomb chambers to the ceiling. (The sherd was located in the ninth layer down, and nine layers are incised to the right of the spring, as drawn on P.11.) Perhaps, before it was broken, the vessel contained water from the spring, which was poured from the lip at that point on the circumference where the image was described.

P.11 was located among the bones of children, including those of a foetus, close to the emergence in the south forecourt of the ragstone 'river'. In Scottish folklore the stone hag, Gyre Carlin, was said to visit every house, spinning the future, at the end of the winter quarter (early February). She was 'always accompanied by a child, and as she made it a regular point to bathe the latter before retiring, it was necessary to have some clear spring water in the house for that purpose'.[37] The water design on P.11 possibly symbolized the same necessity.

Martinmas

During the middle of the third millennium BC, when the barrow itself was at least five hundred years old, five massive sarsens were set up in its forecourt. Described as 'blocking stones',[1] the megaliths are arranged in a way which resembles the monumental body of a stone ox, with its legs (stones 44 and 46) thrust towards the barrow passage, and its carcass the 11-feet-high stone 45, aligns with head and tail stones. Thus, though the setting has been interpreted as 'blocking stones', what seems to debar progress may in fact lead to it, for it was axiomatic throughout the Late Neolithic world – and long afterwards – that 'the Great Goddess emerges miraculously out of death *via* the sacred bull'.[2]

To demonstrate the credentials of the forecourt ox, we should begin at the start of the winter quarter, at Martinmas – or Martmas, as it was called in many parts of Britain. In Christian terms Martinmas is the feast of St Martin of Tours, who died on 11 November 397, but this saintly feast does not wholly conceal the pagan Winter Eve ox lying just below the surface.

In Gaelic, Irish and English, the word Mart *means* ox, particularly a cow or ox fattened for slaughter. Marts, the *Oxford English Dictionary* says, 'were usually killed at about Martinmas',[3] and in eighteenth-century Cumberland 'it was a rare circumstance to slaughter a fat beeve at any other season but in November.'[4] Impending fodder shortage and ritual habit combined to support the tradition: 'The marts or mairts to be salted must be killed when the moon is on the increase, else the meat would not keep well.'[5]

The animals were still touched, it seems, by the ancient moon goddess, reflecting the fact that in the Age of Myth there was a 'morphological relationship between the bull, on account of its fast-growing horns, and the waxing aspect of the moon'.[6] Both were seen as displays by, and of, the Great Goddess. She was moon and ox, and her bisexuality has passed into the English term free-martin: 'A heifer, the twin of a bull calf . . . not a true heifer but an undeveloped male, with many of

The forecourt ox (top) of the West Kennet long barrow. Comparison with an ox cult vase c. 4000 BC, from northeast Greece, provides an indication of the builder's intentions.

the characteristics of an ox, and generally fattened and killed about Martinmas.'[7]

If the goddess is the ox, it should follow that corn dolly and ox should also be related, and indeed this old fusion was once widely known. At Chambéry in France, for instance, the corn Mother and the ox were conjoined in the ritual words of the threshers, who cried out, '"The ox is killed," and thereupon a real ox is killed and eaten by the threshers'.[8] In Scotland, the end-of-harvest Christian newcomer, St Martin, was said to have been 'cut up and eaten in the form of an ox'.[9]

The monumental ox

The Stone Age horned graves of Western Britain bring the ox goddess into the architectural ground plan, and the markedly horned forecourt of the Beckhampton Road long barrow plants the same image firmly in Avebury parish. By way of confirmation, the neighbouring Firs long barrow has three ox skulls, with horns, placed under the mound's central axis.

Ox architecture springs from ox bones, and the pierced phalanges of the West Kennet barrow are seen again at stone 44, a long form image of the goddess with eye cavity. That megalith also represented the front legs of the ox figure. Ox and goddess were synonymous, which explains why in France the Neolithic goddess is frequently found in the form of a carved menhir-statue in churchyards dedicated to St Martin,[10] and why, in the classical Greek distortion of the myth, Europa is bound to the bull's back.

Standing as it does between the symbolic stone 'rivers', the West Kennet forecourt ox prefigures the annual English compulsion to drive an ox to death in a river, best recorded at the Stamford Bull Run ceremony:

> *Come take him by the tail, boys,*
> *Bridge him, bridge him, if you can.*[11]

This meant driving the selected animal onto the bridge and tipping his (by then) mortally wounded body over the parapet. Afterwards, bull dirt was ritually smeared on every face, for 'he who gets no Bull dirt gets no Christmas'.[12] Then, 'the Great Gut or Pudding, commonly known by the name of Tom Hodge, was given to the most worthy [bravest] adventurer'.[13]

From the recent to the remote past, there is overwhelming evidence to support a November slaughter of oxen, with a persistent sacrificial quality. Thus the beast upon whose broad back the Neolithic Queen of Death rode in annual triumph may perhaps have been killed, at the start of every winter, at her West Kennet forecourt, and this event was ultimately expressed in the monumental forecourt stones, presiding over 'ox bones of large size' (Thurnam), and the perforated phalanges incorporated into the tomb filling.

Monumental art 'always depends upon a tension between the ephemeral and the lasting'.[14] The myth revolved. The animated stones marked its regular passage. Only when the real ox *ceased* to die, did the force depart from the sacred sculpture. Then, destitute of meaning, the stones lost first their power, and eventually, in the eyes of a new generation, their former resemblance to the animal. For want of a splash of bovine blood they froze into perpetual Blocking Stones.

Yet Piggott himself unwittingly demolishes the label when he turns his attention to the Avebury henge North Circle (see p. 158). There, set up in the middle, he found three massive stones which he does not hesitate to compare with those in the barrow forecourt, calling them 'a concept represented by one symbolic element

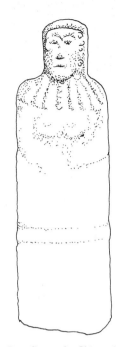

La Grand'mere du Chimquière, St Martin's Church, Guernsey. The menhir-statue was referred to locally as both a female and St Martin – a vestigial memory of the Neolithic ox-woman.

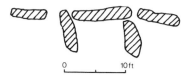

0   10ft

The forecourt ox, in plan, recalls the stone 'oxen' found at other Neolithic sites (see illustration on p. 158).

abstracted from tomb architecture'.[15] The symbolic concept is the ox, which dies and yet survives death.

By pointing to the connection, he has put his finger on an essential quality of the Avebury Cycle (and all myth) – namely the desire to engineer cross-references between the parts. Every aspect of the Late Neolithic modifications to the barrow can be satisfactorily explained with the help of this principle.

Sealing the tomb

The age of the long barrow is now generally given as 3250 BC,[16] with the stone ox being added *c.* 2600 BC, when the huge mass of chalk rubble, speckled with broken pottery, and bits of bone, and striped with organic material, was packed into the chambers and forecourt. The barrow remained in this condition from the mid-third millennium until modern times.

The chalk rubble and organic matter, carefully arranged in layers through the chambers, resembled the chalk, soil and vegetable layering found around the core of Silbury Hill. Both deposits were laid down *c.* 2600 BC.[17]

Thurnam's 'blackish, sooty, greasy-looking [west chamber stripes] . . . arising from the decomposition of vegetable matter',[18] and 'the black peaty substance' noted at Silbury by Merewether,[19] affirm that we are dealing with the world of vegetation rites. The cyclical nature of those rites was eloquently expressed in the number of layers – at least nine in the barrow, alternating with chalk, giving light and dark, rock and leaf, hard and soft.

The decision to forego access to the barrow chambers must have been painful, but perhaps was justified on the grounds that only the old barrow could successfully nurse the new harvest hill into full efficacy. Silbury, in chronological terms, was the newcomer, and her sacredness could best be established if her primary mound could somehow find an echo at the barrow. This the barrow filling provided.

Authority to make such a change at the barrow may be seen in the many mid-Neolithic long mounds (e.g. Horslip barrow) which were designed as solid versions of the goddess from the outset, and the West Kennet filling, one may suggest, no more marked the end of the barrow's life than the contemporary primary mound of Silbury marked the end of Silbury. Here, as so often in the world of myth, the end turns out to be a new beginning.

The slow fermentation of Spring was begun by the barrow goddess *from* the filling material. 'After the destruction of the Universe, at the end of the Great Cycle, the Divine Mother garners the seeds for the next creation.'[20] At the Wiltshire barrow she then performed the standard miracle, known in Neolithic realms wherever cattle were kept, and described by Professor Gimbutas: 'The Great Goddess emerged miraculously out of death, out of the sacrifical bull, and in her body the new life begins.'[21]

A design executed on a conical flat-topped pot from Linwood, Hampshire, illustrates this. Hawkes calls it 'a puzzle pattern of the old, not yet forgotten sort . . . a female body with squatting leg curves and her vulva indicated by a shallow S-smear'.[22] She emanates from an unmistakably horned ox.

Goddess and sacrificial ox, separate and conjoined, are seen (top) in a Sassanian figurine, (left) in the Romano-British Linwood pot, horns surmounted by a squatting figure, and (above) in an Iron Age form of the myth, depicted on the Gundestrup bowl, where the goddess kills the sacred bull on the Candlemas quarter day.

The pot was made in the third or fourth century AD, which goes to show that firmly engraved patterns of mythic behaviour disregard linear chronology. The ox was sacred to British farmers long before the long barrow was built, and remained so, far into the historical period; Piggott correctly sees in the Roman coins found near the West Kennet stone ox 'something more than casual losses by Roman visitors, but rather an association between Roman cults and pre-existing native traditions'.[23]

He detected the same 'continuity of ritual concern for the tomb by more than one community alien to that responsible for the initial building' in the two hundred and fifty pots incorporated in the tomb rubble. 'Half a dozen pottery styles were included in the assemblage.'[24]

With freshly broken edges the pot fragments were thoroughly mixed up, dispersed laterally and vertically throughout the tomb goddess's chambers. Her potent stuffing reached across the forecourt, and by pressing up against the stone ox, enabled her to enter the bovine torso during the Martinmas quarter, and eventually rise through this sacrificial victim (her animal self), and return to the surface world.

Stone 44

If further evidence is needed to show that in erecting the forecourt ox the community continued to venerate the long goddess of the original barrow design, it can be found at stone 44. In addition to operating as the ox front leg, stone 44 carried on its south face a very substantial rendering of the long goddess. The traditional trapezoid is here five feet tall, with a deep eye pit at the narrow upper end, a swelling torso, and a suggestion of feet at ground level.

Whether this stone was specially worked or specially chosen is debatable, though Keiller and Piggott, writing of Avebury parish megaliths, convincingly manage to combine both possibilities: 'There can be no question that the stones were dressed to conform to certain required shapes, and to this end were selected as near to the required form as possible.'[25]

The long goddess was the form required in the barrow forecourt. Unrecognized in modern times, stone 44 ought to be seen as one of a large company of Neolithic megaliths set in tombs, and acknowledged to be statues of the goddess. Professor Daniel identifies 'one of the Mother Goddesses' in a megalith with much less strongly carved features at the Rodmarton long barrow, Gloucestershire,[26] while Anglesey provides good examples at the Bryn Celli Ddu and Bryn Yr Hen Bobl passage graves.[27]

Summing up his work at the West Kennet barrow, Piggott wrote: 'The evidence demands that we assume continued veneration of the tomb during phases of Late Neolithic culture.'[28]

This means that the barrow is part of the Avebury Cycle. In the midst of change, the figure of the long goddess remained as much a part of people's experience as winter itself.

Stone 44, in the barrow forecourt, belongs to the class of menhirs identified as images of the goddess. The eyehole and the trapezoid outline are two typically Neolithic features.

Approach to the Sanctuary

Sanctuary sightline

Through at least 4,000 years (as Stukeley's drawing of 1723 makes clear),[1] the 'eye' of stone 44 projected above the level of the forecourt filling. Standing there, one could (and can) peer through the narrow gap separating ox head from body (stones 43 and 45).

What can be seen? Part of the river Kennet in its tree-lined valley, downstream from the Waden spring confluence, and beyond the trees a slice of Overton Hill, where the fence surrounding a famous Neolithic site, called the Sanctuary, can be discerned. The barrow goddess looks at the Sanctuary, just as the Silbury goddess looks at the barrow.

The barrow-Sanctuary passage is much more than a clear sightline; the architectural links in the Avebury myth interlock to form a physical chain, as Piggott *almost* said when contemplating the 'cardinal problem in interpretation'[2] created by the barrow filling pottery:

'We have to assume a separate covered structure, an offering house, where successive ceremonies of ritual deposition took place as at Tustrup, Jutland, where there was a "temple" adjacent to and contemporary with a group of passage graves.'[3]

He therefore hinted at the Sanctuary as 'the temporary storage place for offerings, including or contained in pots, until the contents of the building could be swept in basketfuls and ritually mingled with the chalk rubble filling which has been inserted into the tomb chambers'.[4]

If Piggott is right, the barrow goddess carried Sanctuary pots and bowls[5] inside her body for over 4,000 years – a fact which might seem to go against the annual sequence of ceremonies, running in a chain from Silbury, through West Kennet long barrow, to the Sanctuary. But every strongly flowing mythical tide tends to create a sort of backwash, which may be represented by the Sanctuary pots found in the barrow, just as the long grey figurine buried in Silbury is evidence of a minor reciprocity operating from barrow

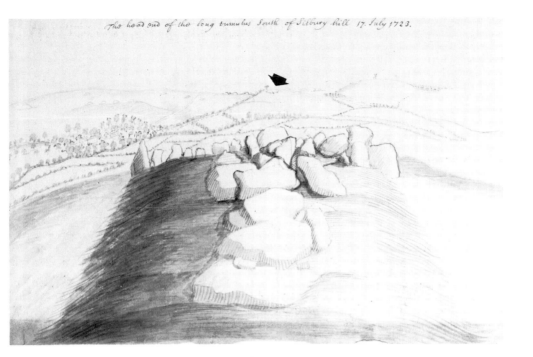

The head end of the long tumulus South of Silbury hill 17. July 1723.

to harvest hill. Similarly, a backwash from Silbury will be met at the Avebury henge, and all these counter-movements testify to the strength of the main seasonal flow in the opposite direction.

The earliest period of building at the Sanctuary is now believed to date from *c.* 2600 BC, so that the barrow stones in question can be legitimately regarded, among other things, as a siting device, set up to focus attention on the distant Sanctuary structure, thus preserving and enhancing the inter-monumental traffic. The architecture helped to roll the seasons round, with the path to Spring beginning in the barrow forecourt.

Stukeley's drawing of the long barrow chamber capstones and the façade, 1723, points the barrow straight at the Sanctuary, indicated by the arrow to the right of the skyline tree, whereas it actually runs almost due east-west.

The river crossing
One of the names of the pre-Celtic British goddess, which has survived into modern times, is Bride (christianized into St Brigid). According to Scottish belief, Bride is on the move at Candlemas, the February quarter day, and her desire to restore liquid circulation brings her down to the river:

> *Bride put her finger in the river*
> *On the feast day of Bride* [February 2nd, Candlemas]
> *And away went the hatching mother of the cold.*[6]

This river-reviving act may also be recorded in the Avebury Cycle, for the direct line from forecourt to

The Eyestone, four feet long and set in the riverbed exactly on the barrow-Sanctuary line.

Sanctuary crosses the river precisely where a 'bride-stone' (an alternative local name for sarsen) sits in midstream. Here called the Eyestone, it is four feet long and two feet six inches wide, with a long axis following the river.

In summer it lies beneath the water, and only the weeds rooted onto the rock are visible. With the arrival of winter and the disappearance of the water, the stone emerges in the shape of a gigantic fossilized head, having a huge roll of stone hair to replace the summer locks which hang and shrivel. Beneath the brow, set close together, are two concave eye sockets interconnected beneath a nose bridge.

The case for regarding the Eyestone as an intentional placement is helped by recognizing that, in every region of Britain, the Neolithic community set evocative stones on significant sightlines, which the barrow-Sanctuary line certainly is. Intervisible, linked by sighting devices, exchanges of contents, and other factors yet to be described, the two monuments shared the river goddess.

Washed by the sanctity and birth association of that famous intermittent stream, the Eyestone bring to mind the water connection attaching to other sarsens in the locality, reported by Stukeley in 1721. He mentioned particularly 'the great stone where is the remarkable fountain, [which] lies in the plowed ground in the Valley E. of Kennet Avenue near Abury. It is a sort of pentagonal figure . . . flat on the ground hollowed a little, like a bowl that has a round hole in it, very deep, and brim full of water. [Here] the shepherds lead their dogs ordinarily to drink . . . I thrust the staff down a yard into it. The shepherd told me he had thrust a rake staff down to the end and the water does not go out. This is not the lowest part of the valley, for it runs down to Kennet. There is probably a spring here. 'Tis mightily talked of, and may be for ought I know.'[7]

An unresolved statement of John Aubrey's might also relate to the subject: 'On the brow of the Hill above Kynet, on the right hand of the highway which goes from Bristow to Marlborough, is such a monument as called the Sanctuary . . . I do well remember there is a circular trench about the monument or temple, by the same token that Sir Robert Moray told me that one might be convinced and satisfied by it that the earth did grow.'[8]

When Mrs Cunnington excavated the Sanctuary in 1930, she discovered many surprising features, but not

the expected trench, although the investigation was extremely thorough and carried well beyond the limits of the circular building.

Perhaps Sir Robert was referring to the natural semicircular trench created by the meandering Kennet – a vulva shape which defines the spur of Overton Hill. By February the Overton Hill meander would be dry no longer. Water animated its parched bed – the first waters of the new year. Fertility and river regime were linked together, so that even in the seventeenth century AD a man 'might be convinced and satisfied that the earth did grow'. Bride had 'put her finger in the river'.

To follow her progress up the spur of Overton Hill to the Candlemas Sanctuary ('also known locally as Kennet Hill'),[9] it might be appropriate to carry a torch, since 'pagan processions' marked the beginning of the Canting quarter, as it was known in Shropshire.[10] And Professor James writes that on 'February 1st, per-ambulations with lighted torches connected with the return of the Goddess from the Underworld, and the rebirth of Nature in the spring, had long been observed in the pre-Christian Feast of Lights.'[11] Other authorities confirm the connection between the date of Candlemas and the Celtic quarter day.[12]

The dry Kennet is flowing strongly again by the time of Candlemas, the February quarter day, an important event in the annual cycle caused, then as now, by the rising level of the underground water table.

Rundway   10. road   Rc Camp   Silbury

R.

Come in, come in, thou bonny wild worm!
For thou hast ta'en many a lucky turn.

Revesby Plough Play,
Lincolnshire, *c.* 1790

Windmill boll

Abu

Sanctuary circles

On 15 June 1668, Samuel Pepys passed the Sanctuary in a coach and saw 'great high stones pitched round, which I believe was once some particular building, in some measure like that of Stonehenge'.[1]

His contemporary, John Aubrey, described two concentric sarsen rings: 'The stones are fower and five feet high (but) most of them now are fallen downe,'[2] though, as Stukeley discovered in 1719, 'the country people have a high notion of it [the site]. . . . They still call it the Sanctuary. The veneration for it had been handed down thro' all successions of times and people.'[3]

On his next visit, 13 May 1724, he reported, 'This day I saw with grief several of the few stones left on Overton Hill carryed downwards towards West Kennet (village), and two thirds of the temple plow'd up this winter, and the sods thrown into the cavitys, so that next year it will be impossible ever more to take any measure of it.'[4]

Two farmers, Green and Griffiths, were responsible for the damage: 'The loss of this work, I did not lament alone; but all the neighbours (except the person that

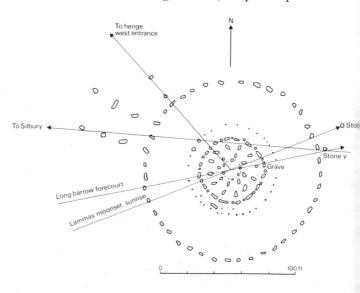

gained the little dirty profit) were heartily grieved for it'.[5]

With the passage of time the location of the former structure was lost. Its rediscovery in 1930, and the excavation which followed, enable us to see that the site once formed an integral part of the grand cycle, relating through symbolic architecture to the Great Goddess in her early spring state. In fact, Cunnington found the cavities of the two concentric stone rings and, in addition, six concentric rings[6] of post holes dug c. 2600 BC (according to the latest estimates)[7] to receive timber uprights. At the very centre was a single slender post hole.

The posts, she decided, had 'faded away in situ'. The central part of each filling, being softer and darker, represented the decomposed timber: 'As the post gradually decayed, fine rubble and silt trickled in from the top, yet remained distinct from the packing of hard chalk, originally rammed around the butts.'[8]

By reading from the Sanctuary's centre to the other major Neolithic structures, it becomes clear that, within the general area of the river bend, it was so placed as to satisfy simultaneously several outward-looking re-lationships summarized in the Table on p. 69. The only major site (Avebury henge) which is not visible from the centre is physically linked to it by the West Kennet avenue.

What is more, these inter-site distances conform to multiples of the two river lengths SH-K1, and WS-K2, which also permeate the internal dimensions of the monument.

The Sanctuary today, looking northwest across Waden spring towards Silbury. Concrete markers indicate positions of the stones and posts, and the mown area corresponds to the 65-foot diameter of the temple-hut.

(following the designations used by M. E. Cunnington, 1931)

Ring		Number of holes	Diameter feet	River unit	Equivalent to
A	Outer stone	42	130.5	SH-K1 × 2	Silbury Hill, height. W. Kennet chambers, inner periphery.
B	Fence ring	34	65.25	SH-K1	Silbury inner fence, diam. W. Kennet façade, width.
C	Stone and post	32	44.16	SH-K1 × $\frac{2}{3}$	W. Kennet chambers, long axis.
D	Bank Holiday	23	32.63[10]	$\frac{SH-K1}{2}$	W. Kennet forecourt, max. width.
E	Ten foot	8	22	$\frac{SH-K1}{3}$	W. Kennet north façade, length.
F	Seven foot	8	14*		
G	Six foot	6	13	$\frac{SH-K1}{5}$	

(*acting as supports to G ring, acc. I. F. Smith)

It will be seen that the diameter of the larger stone circle (A ring) is the height of Silbury Hill (130 feet or SH-K1 × 2), while the largest of the Sanctuary's six timber rings (B ring) has a diameter identical to that of the circular wattle fence found inside the Hill. This diameter also exactly matches the distance from Swallowhead to Kennet at K1 (entry of the spring's tributary into the river proper), which is 65.25 feet, or 24 megalithic yards. All the inner rings are simple fractions of this unit (SH-K1), which confirms both the fundamental importance of SH-K1, as revealed at Silbury and the long barrow, and the integration of the Sanctuary into a broader scheme.

Reminders of the long barrow can also be seen in the 42 stones set up to make the Sanctuary A ring; the same number of sarsens was used in creating the façade and chambers at the long barrow,[11] where 30 of the stones were set in permanent darkness, while 12 (forecourt and façade) enjoyed the light. Newham suggests that the 30 uprights of the sarsen circle at Stonehenge represented the 29.5 days of the lunar month (with the small stone 11 as the half-day),[12] and perhaps the 12 barrow forecourt stones represent solar months, and the 30 chamber stones a lunar month count, with months and days brought into a single circle at the Sanctuary A ring.

The Sanctuary-barrow axis

From the barrow forecourt, the Sanctuary centre lies 79° east of north. Following this line through the Sanctuary, one encounters five features which lend the axis special emphasis.

In hole 11 of the D ring there was a lump of haematite iron ore. Heavy, shiny, liver-coloured, and formed like a cluster of soap bubbles, haematite is completely foreign to the district. Wessex has no iron-stone; nor, prior to the Iron Age, beginning *c.* 800 BC, did she need to import any for smelting. Neither swords nor plough-shares were made of iron when this piece was dropped into hole 11 before the erection of a pair of massive timber posts, which were part of the Stone Age Sanctuary. Traces of decayed timber from these posts

Powerful cult indications at the Sanctuary include the 'bloodstone' or haematite nugget found on the barrow-Sanctuary sightline, which yields a powder the colour of dried blood.

DISTANCES BETWEEN THE SANCTUARY AND OTHER SITES

From	*To*	*Feet*	*River unit*
Sanctuary	Silbury (centre)	6264	SH-K1 × 96 or SH-K1² × 4
Sanctuary	Silbury (moat 'breast')	6398	WS-K2 × 16
Sanctuary	W. Kennet (forecourt)	4398	WS-K2 × 11
Centre Sanctuary	E. Kennet (forecourt end)	4000	WS-K2 × 10
Centre Sanctuary	Obelisk (Avebury S. Circle)	7997	WS-K2 × 20
Centre Sanctuary	Waden Spring	4000	WS-K2 × 10

were sufficient to prove that the hole had not been disturbed in Roman or later times.[13]

After bisecting the Sanctuary centrepost, the barrow sightline crosses hole 2 of the innermost, or G ring. This hole was found to contain a red deer antler. The next hole to be crossed is no. 5 – on the opposite side of the D ring to no. 11. All the holes of the D ring except no. 5 are oval in shape and contained 2 posts, set side by side. Only hole 5 is circular and meant for one upright, although 'upright' is a misleading term, because this particular hole was dug at a noticeable angle to the vertical, and the top of the post leant east-north-east, following the sightline from the barrow.

This singular shaft pointed straight at a feature dating from the last phase of Sanctuary construction – the body of an adolescent male, aged 14, interred only 6 feet away, in front of Stone 12 of C ring. The death line from the barrow forecourt is thus given its due, in the form of a human sacrifice.

The body of a sacrificed youth, buried in a foetal position within the Sanctuary precincts.

His body lay 'much crouched' in the foetal or pre-birth position: 'The arms were crossed in front of the face, the two hands seeming to enfold the face.'[14] Lying on his right side, facing east, 'he almost touched the face of stone 12', so that 'the probability seems to be that he was interred at the time of the stone's erection'.[15] Between his knees was a pot or beaker, but his skull was long, matching those laid in the long barrow before 3200 BC. All the youth's bones were broken, and placed on the body were bones of a young ox, including a phalange reminiscent of the bored ox phalanges which featured as goddess figurines at the long barrow.

'Oh Goddess, we offer to thee this sacrifice: give to us good seasons, crops and health,' sang the Khonds, in nineteenth-century Orissa, as they slew the consecrated being, the *meriah*. This was done 'at the feast before sowing'.[16] His body was cut to shreds, and pieces of flesh were carried to distant villages and planted in the empty fields. 'Human sacrifice' says Campbell, 'is everywhere characteristic of the worship of the Goddess in the Neolithic sphere.'[17]

If the 79°–259° axis is projected across the grave and through the A ring, it touches a solitary stone hole placed 3 feet beyond. The location of the hole puzzled the 1930 team. Now it can be proposed as the terminal point of a track through the monument of quite exceptional richness (haematite, deer antler, leaning post, and grave), and the connecting route between winter and spring.

River snails

A curious feature of the Sanctuary site as a whole was the extraordinary number of snail shells found in the stone and post sockets, mostly belonging to creatures known to inhabit very damp or watery surroundings, rather than a high and dry chalk hillside.[18]

Since peat accumulation rates and pollen analysis show that the British climate between 3000 BC and 850 BC was considerably warmer and drier than at present,[19] the snails found at the Sanctuary were not in their natural habitat (any more than were the riverine flora and fauna, including snails, found in the heart of Silbury Hill). Snails were brought to, and incorporated in, both sites, probably because they came from the holy river, and their shape presented a natural three-dimensional version of the spiral motif to be found in Neolithic stone carving and ceramics.

Woolley and Hawkes have found that the snail/spiral was a Neolithic symbol expressing 'eternal continuance through fecundity'.[20] And Eliade, in his survey of primitive and archaic religion, has written that 'snails . . . figure constantly in aquatic cosmology, as well as in sexual symbolism, and participate in the sacred powers which are concentrated in the Waters, in the Moon, and in Woman'.[21]

Amulets called 'snail stones', which displayed aspects of this ancient theme, continued to be popular in Britain till at least the seventeenth century AD: 'The snail stone is a small hollow cylinder of blue glass, composed of 5 or 6 rings. Among other mysterious virtues, the snail stone cured sore eyes, and was beneficial in parturition.'[22]

Circles, spirals and mazes

When the snail stone is enlarged, it becomes the Sanctuary ground plan, of which G. R. Levy has written:

'Such circles designate, like the spirals, the paths of entry between worlds, and the pacing or dancing of such designs in imitation of the journeys of the Gods, offers a perfect explanation of these structures.'[23]

The Sanctuary posts lent themselves equally well to ring and spiral dances, and the architectural pattern belongs to the very widespread maze or labyrinth class. Many examples from antiquity are known, including the Bronze Age Baltic stone labyrinths, and the aptly named Stone Dances from Norway.'[24]

The turf maze of Wing, Rutland (top), is a survivor of many such mazes, built on the archaic pattern, and used in springtime 'turning dances' till the middle of the last century. A Scandinavian stone labyrinth (above), suggests the outline of a snake's coiled form, recalling (right) the labyrinthine rock engraving of the third millennium BC from Italy.

In England the 'turning', or 'troy', as it is variously called, survives as a turf labyrinth to this day, and behaviour which underlies the names persisted in some places into the nineteenth century. People alive in 1908 were able to recall treading the ancient maze on Ripon Common.[25]

Matthews lists over 20 British examples of turf mazes (excluding decorative mazes in gentlemen's parks) having, like the Sanctuary, a hilltop location, a circular shape 40–80 feet in diameter, enclosing concentric walls, with a round space or 'home' in the centre. At some sites, (Gillian's Bore, Yorks., and St Martha's Hill, Surrey), springtime gatherings of young people are known to have occurred.[26]

'There is no doubt', concludes Matthews, 'that the custom of cutting these devices in the turf was formerly very widespread throughout the land.'[27] It was widespread because what eventually degenerated into the setting for a 'game' had previously contained a rite of the utmost importance, which we have a chance to reconstruct at the Sanctuary.

8

The Candlemas womb-eye

The cone

By common consent the Sanctuary is part of the Avebury complex. It therefore speaks the same architectural language as the other buildings, while (like each of them), having something special to say about one passage in the divine seasonal narrative, with the message contained in and described by the architectural form. But whereas the other sites are plainly visible, though damaged, all that remains of the Sanctuary are rings of modern concrete markers set over empty holes. We are dealing with the ghost of a building, so how can we proceed?

Ever since the 1930 excavation, there has been a surprising degree of unanimity among archaeologists attempting to reconstruct the Sanctuary. The timber rings have normally been interpreted as the foundations of a circular temple, with a conical roof rising from a low wattle wall, 65 feet diameter, to a central vent, 14 feet across – the overall shape being a truncated cone. The wattle wall hypothesis is well sustained by the relatively shallow and closely spaced holes in the 65 feet ring, with a single entrance denoted by the pair of larger doorpost holes, 34 and 35.

Most of the roof weight is thought to have been carried by the C, D, E and G ring timbers, with the slender centrepost interpreted (by Cunnington) as a free-standing pole, coming up through the central aperture.

Cross section of the Sanctuary hut, reconstructed, showing the post hole rings and centrepost.

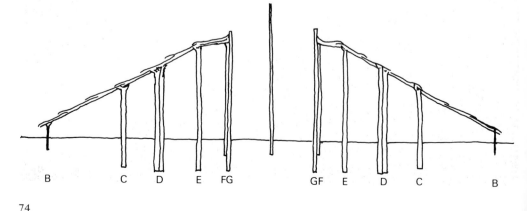

B   C   D   E   FG   GF   E   D   C   B

An airview of the Sanctuary (left) shows its resemblance to the partly excavated Durrington Walls (below) a circular temple-hut which probably served the same function.

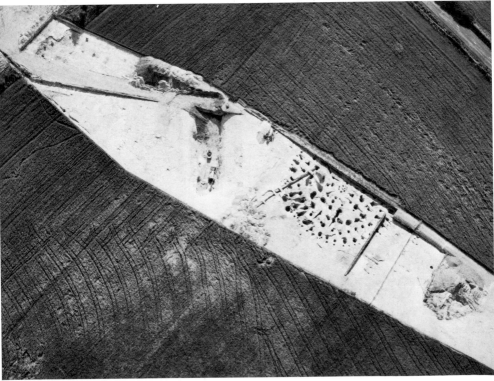

Puzzled by the number of timbers, Piggott sought to modify the scheme by explaining some of the rings as the footings of smaller, earlier buildings, eventually superseded by the 65-foot temple. But C. R. Musson has pointed out that the innermost Sanctuary post holes, though slender, are far too deep to fit this theory comfortably.[1] Nor does the pottery from the different rings show the necessary chronological sequence which his theory implies. On the other hand, 'sarsen fragments, many of them showing scorching or fracture by fire', were 'present in practically all the holes'[2] of *all* the post rings, indicating a single plan.

No explanation of the scorching has been advanced to date. Wood fibre from post bases was found uncharred, so the stones were not burned in a general conflagration. Instead, they were submitted to intense heat *before* the timbers were erected. This treatment, and the ritual deposition, may amount to a recognition that springtime preparation was literally founded upon the earth-cleansing fires of winter.

The discovery of other massive circular huts at Woodhenge (6 rings) and Durrington Walls (6 rings), shows that complex timber structures were definitely part of Neolithic life in Wiltshire. The Sanctuary 'maze' should therefore be allowed to stand as a conscious roofed design, especially since, in the ancient world, labyrinths were often roofed, as Pliny makes clear.[3] Viewed together, the post rings transcend the modest functionalism discerned by the twentieth century. Both in plan and in three dimensions they describe what Renfrew calls 'the cognitive basis ... the symbolic means which the culture has at its disposal for comprehending and using the world.'[4]

The six-ringed roofed temple of Durrington Walls, Wilts, is contemporary with both Sanctuary and Silbury, and probably very similar in structure.

Sanctuary and Silbury

In Neolithic terms that meant Great Goddess. The world was comprehended as her ever-changing body, and how can we forget it, standing at the Sanctuary, when to the west the pregnant womb of the Mother goddess rises before our eyes in the magnificent truncated cone of Silbury Hill?

The Sanctuary *is* Silbury, at a different season. The Sanctuary is Silbury's Candlemas beginning. That is why the two versions of the goddess were sited in such a way that the vital Lammas harvest moon rose over the Sanctuary. That is why there is, concealed beneath the centre of Silbury, a circular wattle fence, supported at

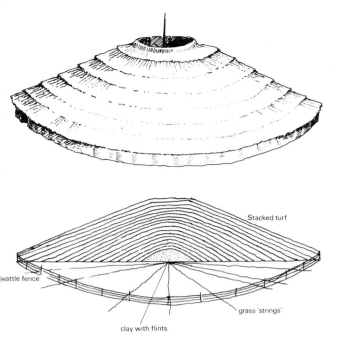

The identity of the Sanctuary with the primary mound hidden inside Silbury Hill is demonstrated in this drawing of the two structures, same scale. (Above), the Sanctuary hut, with central vent and thatched roof leading down to the 65-foot diameter of the wattle wall. (Below), the core of Silbury Hill, with wattle fence and turf layers, stacked over a central clay mound.

Stacked turf

wattle fence

grass 'strings'

clay with flints

intervals by vertical stakes, which in circumference, materials, and mode of erection, exactly duplicates the outer wall of the Sanctuary hut.

Sanctuary	Silbury core
Wattle wall	Wattle wall
Diameter: 65.25 ft (SH-K1 × 1)	Diameter: 65.25 ft (SH-K1 × 1)
Material: wattle	Material: wattle
Secured by: stakes	Secured by: stakes

At the centre of this fence enclosure inside Silbury Hill, a low circular mound of clay with flints was laid down, matching the area of the Sanctuary vent. Above this clay core, turf and soil (dug from the area later to become the chalk quarry) were stacked in a conical manner extending outwards to the fence, recreating in solid form the hollow, dark interior of the Sanctuary.

Besides being necessary to support the overlapping mass of chalk, this 'solid' version extended the farming narrative, for while the actual Sanctuary hut was a place where, it will be argued, the secrets of agriculture may have been disseminated, the Silbury inner mound contained their realization in the upturned sod and the seed bed – the basis in every sense of the Mother goddess's August achievement.

Silbury Hill multiplies the Sanctuary kernel by 8, to make a chalk cone diameter of 522 feet or SH-K1 × 8. Why eight? Conceivably because there are eight moons between the shortest day, December 21st, and the August quarter day, the start of harvest, when the Hill was completed.

Atkinson's discovery in 1968 of the hidden Silbury fence was unknown to the archaeologists who had earlier recreated the Sanctuary hut in Silbury's image. Yet the size of the Sanctuary vent, as proposed by them, is precisely one-eighth of the diameter of the Silbury summit. Even the terrace running around the Silbury top could find its equivalent in a 2-foot-wide ledge held up by the closely grouped E and F rings.

Professor Atkinson has proved that the Silbury flat top *was* accurately centred over its primary mound (the hidden Sanctuary): 'It is evident that the central point was projected upwards as the work proceeded. . . . Careful survey has shown that the original centre, the centre of the flat top and the centre of the cone which is best fit to the present surface of the mound all lie within a circle less than 1 metre diameter.'[5]

The tip of his cone takes us into the sky, and we have shown in *The Silbury Treasure* how the tiered chalk hill as solid eye was complementary to the solar and lunar eyes, and integrated with them through reflection in the surrounding moat-body.

At the dry Sanctuary, the need to involve the heavenly eyes was no less great, and this was achieved by a different means – by the deliberate decision to leave the flat summit open. The sun's and moon's rays could therefore penetrate through this architectural pupil to the Sanctuary floor.

The contemporary Durrington Walls temple presents the same working image, and there the eye goddess theme is also closely stated in the accompanying pottery. On four vessels, the oculi motif, of concentric circles, widely accepted as an orthodox representation of the Neolithic deity, was 'a major component of the decorative scheme, immediately below the rim'.[6] Pot and building offered two views of the one reality.

Silbury and Sanctuary called to each other across the Waden spring, and since Silbury's particular concern was the 250° harvest moonset, we might expect this event to be recorded as Sanctuary prophecy. From the

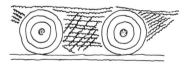

The Neolithic womb-eye synthesis is corroborated by ceramic eye goddess motifs found at the Durrington Walls conical temple.

centrepost, the 250° axis bisects only one of the post holes – no. 27 in C ring, and this hole *was* found to contain a unique deposit: '20 pieces of lava (nephrite) from the eastern side of Eifel, Rhineland ... with a hard cavernous nature and rough surface, unknown in Britain prior to introduction during the Roman Occupation.'[7]

Yet Cunnington 'proved that the hole had not been disturbed for 4,000 years'; the deposit was Neolithic. The Romans later employed this mineral, called Neidermendig lava, throughout the Western Empire as a corn-grinding stone – an extraordinary coincidence, since hole 27 is aligned on the Lammas moonset, which signalled start of harvest, and the grinding of new flour.

The Sanctuary's stone circles maintained the Silbury connection. The smaller circle preserved the dimensions of the hut, while the larger A ring, diameter 130 feet (SH-K1 × 2), reflected the full height of Silbury Hill. The A ring plots on the ground what Silbury lifts into the sky. Viewed together, the two rings also reaffirm the eye motif.

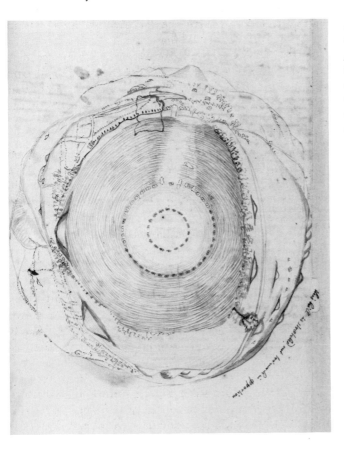

A drawing from Stukeley's notebook vividly describes the powerful Silbury-Sanctuary link, while also stressing how the smaller Sanctuary could be experienced as the centre of the drama at the appropriate moment in the Cycle.

Approximate date	Sanctuary	Silbury	West Kennet long barrow
c. 2700 BC	Wooden temple, 65 feet diam.	Primary mound built, 65 feet diam.	Chambers still open.
c. 2600 BC	Wooden temple replaced by stone ring, outer diam. 130 feet.	Silbury completed, height 130 feet.	Silbury-type primary mound layers introduced, incorporating pots from the Sanctuary. Forecourt ox stones erected.

Whether the two Sanctuary stone rings were erected during or after the wooden temple's lifetime is a matter for conjecture. In the C ring, post and stone holes share a common diameter, and this proclaims either contemporaneity, or at least continuity. Though the sherds of pottery found were 'similar' in both types of hole, Mrs Cunnington eventually interpreted them as 'not contemporary but nearly so'.[9]

Assuming she was right, we might speculate on how the evolving characteristics of the three monuments, Silbury, long barrow and Sanctuary, were kept in harmony.

The puberty temple

In almost every primitive society, the passage from childhood to sexual maturity is marked by a long period of instruction, accompanied by physical tests.

'The candidates prepare by a period of separation from their families. They are herded together in an isolated place where they are instructed in the traditions of the tribe, in the laws that regulate communal life, and in matters affecting procreation. Frequent recourse is made to ancestral communion. . . . The blessing of the dead is invoked to strengthen the ties uniting the individual candidates with the tribal forefathers.' The girls' instruction covers, among other matters, 'sex, the upbringing of children, and domestic management'.[10]

Numerous ethnographic studies show that the sexes are separated during these puberty events, when girls are much more likely to be shut in a building than boys. Tanganyikan practice, for example, was for the boys to be kept in a camp in the bush, whereas the girls were placed in a womb-hut.[11] Similarly, Thompson Indian girls (British Columbia) were taught to mime the birth process, using stones and baby porcupines, within a conical hut.[12]

To this worldwide pattern we can add Byrhtferth's summary of pagan synchronization in Britain, whereby puberty is made to coincide with the Candlemas-May Eve quarter, and the corresponding agricultural preparations.

The Sanctuary, frequently called by Stukeley the Temple of Ertha[13] (Ertha = Nerthus, the North European goddess of spring), and facing as it does the maternal Silbury model, provides a very suitable setting for female puberty rites.

The serpentine maze aspect of the Sanctuary ground plan also points to the female sex. Neolithic art frequently stresses the connection, and Jackson Knight finds that, in prehistory generally, the maze symbol is associated with maidenhood.[14]

The Sanctuary probably occupied a position in the annual cycle where generations of children died to be reborn as adults, following the pattern set by the hibernating snake goddess herself.

Campbell reminds us that the puberty threshold passage was 'comparable to a birth, and has been ritually represented practically everywhere through an imagery of re-entry into the womb'.[15] We can now see why it was necessary to shape the Sanctuary hut and stone circles to match the greatest womb in the world, Silbury Hill.

We may therefore reasonably give the Sanctuary to the girls, and offer the adolescent men a site at the start of the Beckhampton avenue (though not necessarily a monumental structure), balancing the Sanctuary's position.

By their sojourn in the Sanctuary, the girls died to an outworn childhood, and were born to the prospect of fruitfulness. But that prospect lay over the horizon, and could only be realized through action, because the Avebury Cycle was a sequence of deeds.

The path to maternity was indicated by the only three stones in the outer ring which had their long axes at right angles to the circumference. Viewed from the centre of the monument, these stones point at Silbury Hill, and initiated what Aubrey called 'a solemne walke . . . of stones pitched on end, about 7 foot high . . . very probable this walke was made for processions'.[16]

But this West Kennet avenue does not lead directly to the Silbury harvest. Instead, it veers off to the right, towards the Avebury henge monument and perhaps a May Wedding. At any event, the long incarceration is over, and a great procession is about to begin.

A prehistoric maiden-goddess, five feet high, from Scotland. Found at the centre of a circular wattle shrine-hut comparable to the Sanctuary, it suggests that the Sanctuary 'centrepost' may have been a similar carved image.

The avenue snakes

The Stukeley snake

The West Kennet avenue is nearly one and a half miles long, 50 feet wide, and was originally defined by 100 pairs of stones, set at longitudinal intervals of 80 feet. It links the Sanctuary to the Avebury henge, but not by the shortest route.

'We may observe the two great curves it makes,' wrote Stukeley.[1] At the time of his first visit to the area its course was clearly visible. Modern excavation has confirmed the line, and writers continue to use words like 'serpentine' and sinuous'[2] in their accounts, while rejecting the explanation offered by Stukeley of the peculiar meanders. For him, the curves 'imitated the figure of a snake as drawn in the ancient hieroglyphics'[3] in a planned design, with the Sanctuary as the head and the two avenues (Beckhampton and West Kennet) making a single body three miles long, on which was threaded the Avebury henge, at a point midway between head and tail.

For two hundred years antiquarians and archaeologists rained furious blows on this theory, until today it is considered absolutely harmless because quite dead. Most experts now feel no need even to mention the

As an earth and water reptile, the avenue incorporates zig-zag straight lengths – chevrons of the archaic water symbol – into the landscape's undulations.

The avenues are seen to meet at Avebury henge, in Stukeley's engraving, with the Beckhampton avenue on the left, and the West Kennet avenue extending from the Sanctuary.

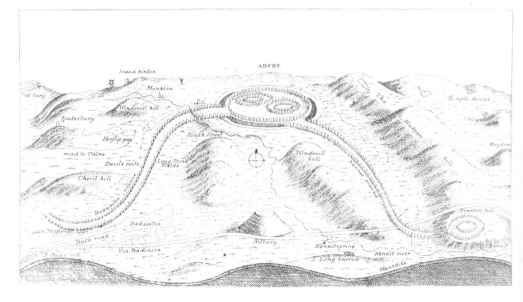

Oldbury   Abury

Windmill ball

corpse. Those that do usually dismiss it with a phrase such as 'cannot be taken seriously',[4] and return to the world of facts.

Yet, it will be argued in this account that one more chop, delivered midway between the serpent's head and tail, will bring not one but *two* snakes back to a life which they enjoyed for thousands of years. They meet at Avebury henge. One is called the Beckhampton, and the other the West Kennet avenue.

The West Kennet avenue remained intact from the time of its construction in the late Stone Age until the reign of Charles II. 'Mr Smith, living here, informed me that when he was a schoolboy, the Kennet Avenue was entire from end to end,' wrote Stukeley.[5] And Aubrey's statement concerning the northernmost part suggests no deliberate destruction: 'The great stones at Avebury's townes end where this Walke beings, fell down in Autumn 1684 and broke in two or three pieces.'[6]

The human attack on the stones in the early eighteenth century was related to the enclosure of the common land by the wealthier and therefore more powerful farmers, turning from ancient communal values to private profit. Stukeley is explicit:

Where the cornfields or pasturage have infringed upon the sacred ground, our work generally goes to wreck. Where the heath remains it is still perfect enough. Near a hedge belonging to the enclosures of West Kennet, in the year 1720, I saw several stones just taken up there and broken for building; fragments are still remaining, and their places fresh turf'd over, for the sake of the pasturage.[7]

Sometimes, as between Sanctuary and West Kennet, the stones were toppled and incorporated into the line

'Enclosure', the annexing of common land by wealthy farmers, brought about the destruction of the stone avenue serpent, as Stukeley's contemporary sketch shows.

The West Kennet avenue as it appears today: the stones represent broad-hipped and long forms of the megalithic goddess.

of the new hedge, where they may still be seen. The concept of the land as the source of communal good, and therefore the object of collective responsibility, which survived to some degree until 1700, was finally overturned by a new emphasis on individual progress. The removal and breakup of the firmly rooted stones occurred at the same time, and was part of the same process as that which created the landless proletariat.

Of the original 200 (100 pairs), there were 72 left in 1722,[8] while in 1934, in the best preserved half of the avenue there remained only four standing, and nine fallen.[9]

But not all those which had disappeared since 1684 had been smashed to rubble: 'Many of the farmers made deep holes and buried them in the ground and they knew where they lay,' wrote Stukeley.[10]

By measuring the intervals, both transverse and longitudinal, between the few surviving stones, those working in the 1930s were able to re-erect 27 sarsens in the northern third of the avenue, and to locate another 37 prehistoric stone holes, which were subsequently marked with concrete plinths. The tallest stone recovered, 13N, was 14 feet high, but most were between 7 and 12 feet. (In this account, the stone pairs are designated 'N' for north and 'S' for south, and numbered from head to tail with low numbers at the Avebury end.)

The hibernating archetype

There is general agreement among archaeologists that the avenue was intended as a processional way between two monuments whose functions cannot be explained – a wavy line joining two mysteries.

Here it will be proposed that the avenue represents a snake on its way from hibernation in the Sanctuary to copulation at the henge. The avenue presents us with an archetype, one of a small repertoire of working images, through which the human race came close to declaring its unity. The energy generated in the Sanctuary coils is seen unleashed in the avenue, which is the great serpent searching for fulfilment, with the advance of spring.

Versions of this event have been witnessed and celebrated all over the world. To take one example: in spring, after the rains, the adolescent girls of the Bavenda tribe, Transvaal, still perform a processional dance to imitate the python awakening from hibernation.[11] 'In most parts of the world, the snake is used as a symbol of the beneficent forces of life and growth,'[12] states Lommel.

The swelling life force of human libido and vegetable spring found classic embodiment in the serpent form. Anthropologists, art historians, folklorists, psychologists, and students of comparative religion know this to be true, while millions of the earth's inhabitants continue to know, feel and act to the West Kennet avenue pattern.

'The meaning of these serpents', writes Campbell, 'is . . . the naked goddess in her serpent form,'[13] and in describing the 'several representations of snakes' from Neolithic Malta, Professor Evans recalls their association 'with chthonic and fertility deities in many cults'.[14] Where the supreme deity took female shape, an accompanying snake is very frequently portrayed, as in the well known faience statue from Knossos. The serpents she holds are 'the survival of Neolithic Mother Goddess iconography'.[15]

The snake coiled in the Sanctuary, and emanating as the avenue, was designed to carry the seasonal drama from Candlemas to the Spring quarter day, and from bud to flower. The actors were the adolescents, entering, at puberty, from the Sanctuary into the vital length of a snake's body composed of bridestones.

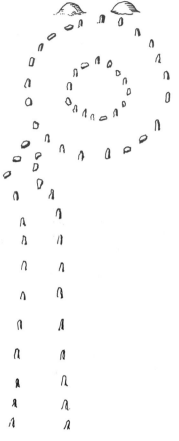

The Sanctuary and the tail end of the West Kennet avenue, from a drawing by John Aubrey, c. 1685.

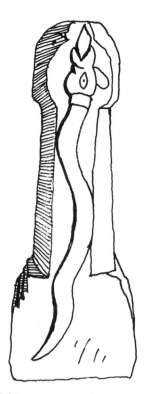

Celtic serpent stone from Maryport, Cumberland. Forty-five inches long, the snake was 'apparently connected with phallic rites' (A. Ross).

British form of the integration of maiden with serpent ('The Virgin naked on a dragon sits') drawn by Henry Peacham, 1612.

Bride, the pre-Celtic goddess, is thus referred to in a later Gaelic poem:

> *'The Day of Bride, the birth of Spring,*
> *The serpent emerges from his knoll. . . .*
> *The serpent will come from his hole*
> *On the Brown day of Bride'.*[16]

Another verse describes the serpent as a 'noble queen'.[17]

Elsewhere in the Scottish Isles the snake was called the Damsel (An Ribhinn), and the Milkmaid of Bride.[18] The serpent belonged to Bride, and the serpent *was* Bride.

In fact Bride as Serpent permeated the whole life cycle, which is why, when a Hebridean child was about to be born, 'A stocking with a knob of peat inside is jiggled on the doorstep, while this verse is said:

> *Bride! Bride! come in*
> *Thy welcome is truly made*
> *Give thou relief to the woman.'*[19]

This stocking-serpent corresponds to the snakes of plaited grass which were found inside the Silbury Mother. At that season the eye (hill) is big and the snakes small, whereas in the avenue, designed for late spring, the snake is gigantic and the eyes, found engraved on the face of stone 25 S, are tiny. Recognized by Piggott as being contemporary with the stone's erection, and executed in the standard 'pocked technique', he calls them 'two well-preserved examples of "cup and ring" type ornament, showing irregular double concentric circles, surrounding a pair of depressions, one natural, the other worked'.[20]

The continuity between Celtic goddesses and Neolithic prototypes is well established. Scholars recognize in the Celtic forms 'restatements of an age-old theme . . . that of a Mother Goddess, which had evolved in much earlier times and which persisted through and beyond the Celtic period'.[21]

Dead Neolithic monuments are truly resurrected in Gaelic song, and Bride in her threefold original form emerges once more:

The Celtic Brigid or Bride was frequently regarded as a triple goddess . . . she was a goddess of Plenty, and had additional functions as tutelary deity of learning, culture and skills.[22]

As an aspect of the triple goddess, the avenue snake leaves the immature Sanctuary womb, in order eventually to find itself multiplied beneath the mature

Silbury womb, in the form of the twisted grass ropes noted by Merewether.

The goddess could never shake off the snake, because it was part of her. It went with her when she flew from the West Kennet barrow to the Sanctuary, where it hibernated. The spring warmth, and the return of water to the Kennet, aroused her again; and the year was on the move.

Thus the life force swung without a break into the avenue track, which was waiting to receive it. The great locomotion to Avebury had begun.

The fully extended avenue snake was intended to run from Sanctuary to Avebury and not, as Stukeley supposed, in the opposite direction. That is why an expanding tail section can be found at the Sanctuary end, where the width between the stones is gradually increased as the extended body is traced down the hill from the Sanctuary.

At the point of junction with the Sanctuary A ring, the tail tip is only 20 feet wide. This increases to 28 feet at the penultimate stone pair, and as it runs down Overton Hill, gradually expands to the full body width, 50 feet. This was proved during pipe laying operations, carried out in 1942.[23] The serpent plainly heads for Avebury, and there is no constriction at the neck end.

The Neolithic snake goddess in a Sumerian version of the fourth millennium BC. The maiden, plainly human, is also a snake.

The goddess's eye motif, found in all the Avebury monuments, reappears in the West Kennet avenue on the south face of stone 25S, where it was engraved when the stone was set up.

The Rainbow Serpent, a traditional sand drawing by Australian Aborigines, reveals many features in common with the Sanctuary-avenue snake.

The serpent in modern times

For Stukeley, who was both Anglican minister and classical scholar, the mental conflict surrounding the snake was acute. His Bible equated serpent with Satan and the birth of sin, while his classical education told him the opposite:

The ancients concluded this to be the most divine of all animals . . . the poets are luxuriant in their descriptions [of serpents], comparing them to the most glorious appearance in the universe – the rainbow.[24]

In the end, loyal to his experience at Avebury, he wrote of 'this great and wonderful work, and the magnificent plan upon which it is built . . . the whole figure representing a snake transmitted through a circle'.[25]

But what did it mean? Here he stuck to what he knew and liked best – history, patriarchy and Christianity, and saw the entire complex as the memorial to a dead warrior who was buried under Silbury – a patriarch who was a Christian in all but name, because 'the patriarchal religion and the Christian is but one and the same'.[26]

But if they shared an abhorrence of snakes, it followed that the great and wonderful work was based on the epitome of evil. Stukeley saw the contradiction, and countered: 'It was one of the arts of inventors of symbols and emblems to picture out the highest things by what we may esteem the lowest subjects: to picture out the greatest good by its contrary.'[27]

The real importance of Stukeley's interpretation is that, while erroneously tying the monuments into Christian knots, he rightly recognized that he was dealing with architectural *imagery*, whereas professors of prehistory now declare that buildings are, and *therefore always were*, necessarily inanimate and non-pictorial.

Yet despite this imposition, the old avenue snake shows some signs of revival, because our needs are about to change (though these vibrations do not at first penetrate heavily upholstered chairs). In the world at large the brief experiment with scientific linear progress, based on analysis, is beginning to appear as an irresponsible interlude. Uneasy about a rationale which can glibly justify poisoning the planet for the sake of a brief spasm of 'peaceful' nuclear energy, we start to hanker after stability and wholeness not least because we want to survive. Therefore, walking the avenue, we may come across the ancient circular reality again.

The Avebury monuments show architecture as a language made from 'the joining of a few ideographs of immense ramification . . .' which 'draws upon the origin of all sense of wholeness; builds upon the deepest foundations.'[28] Is it possible? How can we allow *them* to have enjoyed a richness which our own buildings do not register? 'A kind of cultural censor intervenes, one which will militate against such speculations themselves, even apart from the matter of their proof.'[28]

Yet even with nihilism at its recent zenith, the prehistoric serpent has occasionally been glimpsed as a major architectural form in temples and monuments of primitive agricultural communities. For example, its body has been admitted in the Great Serpent Mound at Ross County, Ohio, a relic of Hopewellian culture, which flourished 2,000 years ago and knew both cereal cultivation and squatting goddess figurines. The serpent is a 1350-foot-long bank, curled up at the tail and meandering to a head, whose open jaws surround a large egg-shaped feature, which is not a tomb.[29] Other 'imitative mounds' in Wisconsin 'consist of the figures of animals raised on the surface of the open country, and covered with grass, [and] . . . many of them include considerable areas'.[30]

Coiled beginning, extended body, jaws opening on an enclosure, the Great Serpent Mound of Ross County, Ohio, shares many of the Avebury Cycle characteristics.

Stone rows and cursuses

British architectural serpents may be represented in the stone rows of southwest England.

On Dartmoor, half buried under accumulating peat, these wind across the land, sometimes for miles, as single or double placements of boulders. Like the West Kennet avenue, R. N. Worth found 'the rows of Dartmoor are invariably connected or associated with stone circles', and he goes on to say that 'in its complete form this class of rude stone monument connects a circle to a menhir [tall upright or orthostat], . . . indicating a possible association with the widespread worship of the productive powers of nature which, in forms more or less disguised, finds place in symbol if not in doctrine, in all the elder religions.'[31]

Worth drew a direct comparison between Dartmoor and other English sites: 'So at Avebury, Stanton Drew and Shap, the rows are connected with circles.'

The comparison holds with regard to orientation. Researchers have hunted in vain to find an overall preferred direction, for the serpent in each particular

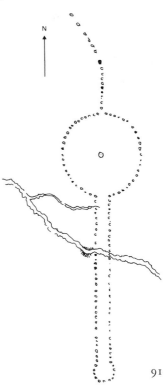

The Dorset cursus, a well-known
type of Neolithic earth serpent.

The Shap circle and avenues,
drawn in 1859, follow the
Avebury pattern: a small circle
linked to a larger by one avenue,
with a second avenue coming in
from the other side.

location concentrates on the special features of the
topography and follows where they lead. Only then can
it be the true genius of the place.

A variant on the stone row is the cursus, described by
Piggott as 'certain extremely long and narrow bank and
ditch enclosures. The largest known examples have a
width of 250–350 feet between the parallel ditches with
internal banks.'[32] The Dorset cursus is over 6 miles
long, and the one lying close to Stonehenge exceeds
9,000 feet. All these structures 'are certainly to be placed
somewhere in the Neolithic'. The Stonehenge cursus is
'contemporary with the first phase of that monument',[33] and therefore as old as Silbury Hill.

As with the Kennet avenue and the Dartmoor stone
rows, the great snake is associated with the springtime
journey between death and renewal. On the one hand,
long barrows are both set across the line, and even
incorporated *into* the line of the bank, while 'the
proximity of many cursus enclosures to henge monuments implies that some connection exists between the
two groups of structures'.[34]

91

Snakes form the arms of a Cretan maiden goddess, c. *1400* BC. *Three streams flow from the right-hand serpent.*

With the approach of the late Neolithic period in Wessex, the proximity of snake to henge becomes increasingly evident. Thus the chalk banks of the Stonehenge avenue meander nearly two miles from the river Avon to Stonehenge, and are copied 'in part from the nearby cursus and in part from the avenues of standing stones which form the approaches to Avebury'.[35] The same writer says:'It would not be too rash to suggest some kinship of intention and function between avenue and cursus'.[36]

The living model

Stone rows, cursuses and avenues were probably all designed as monumental snakes. The snake became 'the constant archetypal symbol for the inner energy of libido, both sexual and cosmic'[37] because prehistory consorted with natural history. Understanding the avenues depends upon familiarity with the qualities of the living reptilian model.

The snake evokes bisexual power. The rounded head and muscular body suggest the male phallus, particularly when rising nearly perpendicular to the ground, as in the territorial 'dance of the adders'. Yet this thrusting member can open its jaws so wide as to become the epitome of the human vulva, the great female swallower. The final limit to a snake's swallowing capacity is not skeletally controlled, but is set by the elasticity of the skin. The two halves of the lower jaw are united only by ligaments. Thus the snake was felt to be as suitable for the female West Kennet avenue, as for the male Beckhampton.

Then, as Campbell writes, 'the wonderful ability of the serpent to slough its skin, and so renew its youth, has earned for it throughout the world the character of the master of the mystery of rebirth.'[38]

In addition, both British snakes – adder and grass snake – have a period of courtship in April/May, in phase with the Avebury Cycle.[39] Both the grass snake's white eggs and the adder's young appear in July, corresponding with the start of harvest. Both have a high reproductive rate.

Snakes have no eyelids, and, like the eye goddess, always look. Hence hypnotic qualities are traditionally attributed to snake's eyes (even a sloughed skin has transparent eye coverings).

Once the serpent had been accepted as a vehicle for symbolic truth, the primitive integrating impulse sought more and more correspondences, real or imagined. So we find the belief, widely held in antiquity, that the male snake puts its head into the female's mouth during coitus:

'I know not', wrote Charas in 1670, 'on what ground the ancient writers on this animal had to say – that in the copulation, the male did insert his head into the throat of the female, and there emitted his seed into her matrix.'[40]

The related conviction that the mother adder was capable of swallowing and regurgitating her young survived until AD 1900 – among writers in zoological journals.

Finally, as a matter of fact, snakes, like the Great Goddess and her river Kennet, run into the ground in late autumn, and re-emerge in the spring, when they make excellent swimmers.

This consideration leads back to the holes from which poured the inspiration for the entire complex of monuments, the Swallowhead and Waden Hill springs. These contained and gave forth, according to the season, the serpentine spirit of the place.

The Waden spring lies a significant 4000 feet (WS-K2 × 10) from the Sanctuary, where the West Kennet avenue begins, and aligns exactly with the centres of the twin wombs – maternal Silbury and daughter Sanctuary. The genius of the West Kennet avenue might therefore come from the Waden spring, especially since the avenue describes the length of Waden Hill in its progress to the henge.

Stukeley placed the start of the second avenue closer to Swallowhead than the Waden spring, and recent resistivity surveys have proved him right. The Beckhampton avenue might be tentatively ascribed to Swallowhead.

But another possibility exists in the form of the inconspicuous stream which rises in a pond at Beckhampton near the Waggon and Horses public house, and runs eastwards past Silbury to the Winterbourne above Swallowhead. The pond is 4000 feet from the Fox Covert where the Beckhampton avenue began.[41] Since the same distance lies between Waden spring and *its* avenue tail, one can say that a pair of tributary streams and their respective avenues balanced nicely around the primary spring of Swallowhead.

Both avenues were built to be 8000 feet long from their tail ends to the point of impact in the henge: 8000 feet = 4000 ft × 2 = WS-K2 × 20.

The serpent phallus displayed: an oak representation of the Broddenbjerb god, male partner to the goddess Nerthus.

In the summers of 1934 and 1935, the northern third of the West Kennet avenue was excavated by Alexander Keiller. Many buried stones were found and re-erected, and 'great care taken to ensure that each stone was returned exactly to its original position'.[1]

As a result of Keiller's work, several interesting features came to light, which further indicate how the avenue was attached to the Avebury Cycle as a whole.

Stone 35N

The designers were apparently at pains to connect their work to Silbury (which lay out of sight behind Waden Hill), as stone 35N demonstrates. Of those surviving, it alone is set at right angles to the long axis of the processional way, standing today in its Neolithic stone hole precisely at odds with the general policy regarding avenue stone setting, which was described by Stukeley and confirmed by modern workers: 'If of a flattish make, the broadest dimension was set in the line of the avenue.'[2]

The unusually flat face of 35N is over 7 feet broad and is emphatically not so directed. It agrees neither with the avenue's long axis, nor with its partner on the other side of the processional way.

These targets are ignored in favour of the biggest artificial eye in Europe, Silbury Hill. The centre of Silbury Hill is 3,200 feet (WS-K2 × 8), from the stone.

We should not pass this stone without recalling the traditional belief, still explicit from Cumberland to Cornwall in such names as Long Meg and the Merry Maidens, that all megaliths were superhuman beings. To us this may sound like casual whimsy, but it embodies a once sacred truth. Megaliths, whether carved or natural, were set up as effigies. If, then, *we* can see an eye and mouth on one side of 35N, and the hunched body of the Grandmother on the reverse, it is likely that 'savages who converse in figures'[3] saw them more, rather than less, clearly.

An observer standing at 35N on Midsummer Eve (the midpoint between the May and August quarter

days), would see the full moon sink at the Silbury end of the axis, and, in the opposite direction, would witness the midsummer sun rising at *c*. 51°E. between two closely set round barrows silhouetted on the shoulder of Avebury Down.

These first rays simultaneously bisect a little-known stone circle, called Falkner's Circle,[4] which lies in the valley bottom only 800 feet (or WS-K2 × 2) from the viewing position.

Of Falkner's Circle only one stone now remains. 'It was one of a circle that had existed at some former period. There were (in 1840) two other stones lying on the ground, and nine hollow places from which a stone had been removed, making twelve altogether.' The ground was 'quite flat within the circle, which was 120 feet in diameter'.[5] Today, the remaining sarsen is 6 feet wide at the base and 4 feet high. From this spot stone 35 N is clearly visible, but Silbury is not.

From the twin barrows (one wooded) on the horizon, along the line of the hedge, through the stone circle (the remaining stone is at the hedgerow corner), through stone 35N, and over Waden Hill to Silbury summit: a unique series of monuments mark the midsummer sunrise alignment.

How, then, was the line set out to incorporate Silbury so accurately? Perhaps by posting an observer on the crest of Waden Hill on Midsummer Eve. But even without this simple form of help the line could have been achieved, if Professor Thom's view is accepted: 'There is evidence that Megalithic surveyors could range in a straight line between mutually invisible points.'[6]

The overall length of the axis from Silbury centre, through 35N, to Falkner's Circle, is 4000 feet, or WS-K2 × 10 – a reiteration of the distance separating both avenue tails from their respective springs.

But Falkner's Circle is not the end of the line; rather it was built precisely halfway between the Silbury summit and the midsummer sunrise barrows,[7] which extend the axis by a further 4000 feet to the northeast horizon. Ultimately, the end point is the rising sun itself.

'Earth, Divine Goddess, Mother Nature, who generates all things, and brings forth anew the sun, which you have given to the peoples', runs an ancient prayer which even found its way into English monastic manuscripts, *c.* AD 1100.[8] The people who built the midsummer barrows may well have expressed the same attitudes, and almost certainly appreciated the complementary midwinter event – the lunar moonrise marked by the same axis.

Neolithic observers were forever following the solar and lunar eyeballs in their critical plunges to and from the underworld. Sympathetically, they placed beneath stone 35N (the most skyward orientated of all the avenue stones) a lump of Neidermendig lava, the corn-grinding rock. Deposited prior to the stone's erection, this specimen from Germany marks 35N in a unique manner, reciprocating its celestial importance.[9]

Midsummer bonfires, the successors of the Baal fires, were formerly lit all over Britain to celebrate the summer solstice.

The pipes

Four hundred feet (WS-K2 × 1) further along the avenue, the procession entered an area demanding and receiving full subterranean attention. Stones 30S and 29S were sited near the centre of a patch of coombe rock,[10] where deep, cone-shaped natural funnels led into vertical pipes. Five of these had been filled throughout with dark soil and charcoal. The remaining five had soft black central cores surrounded by rings of clay. In some cases, flint nodules and pieces of sarsen were packed round as well.

The charcoal was of hazel, blackthorn and hawthorn twigs,[11] yet the surrounding lining of clay was not burnt or hardened by heat, and, Smith says, 'It must be presumed that the charcoal had been gathered up from nearby hearths.'[12]

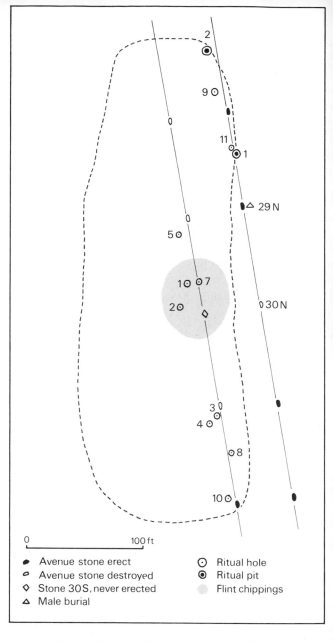

Within the plan, the following labels appear:

2

9 ⊙

11 ⊙ ⊙ 1

△ 29 N

5 ⊙

1 ⊙ ⊙ 7

2 ⊙ ◇

⊙ 30 N

3 ⊙
4 ⊙

⊙ 8

10 ⊙

0   100 ft

●	Avenue stone erect	⊙	Ritual hole
⌐	Avenue stone destroyed	◉	Ritual pit
◇	Stone 30 S, never erected		Flint chippings
△	Male burial		

Plan of the avenue's Occupation Area, the 'place of ancient worship'.

Smith is certain that 'the holes, especially those with cores of charcoal, cannot be interpreted as adjuncts of normal occupation'.[13] On the basis of the earliest pottery styles represented, she concludes that interest in the site began before the avenue was built and lasted into the Bronze Age.[14]

In addition to 600 potsherds,[15] 70 pieces of the same shelly oolite used in the construction of the West Kennet long barrow were discovered. Bits of a ferruginous greensand, brought from afar, and over 1000 worked flint artefacts were also found.

All this material was concentrated in a blunted rectangular area, known as the Occupation Area, approximately 400 feet long and 130 feet wide[16] – the long axis being parallel to that of Waden Hill.

The Occupation Area and Waden Hill

The Avebury Cycle monuments are grouped around Waden Hill. Detached on all sides from the rest of the downland mass, the hill forms a major feature of the horizon, from whichever monument one looks. One end dominates the view from the south entrance to the henge; the other, with the Waden spring and tributary lying directly on the Silbury-Sanctuary line, is involved in the most sacred moment of the Neolithic year, the Lammas Birth. From the West Kennet barrow forecourt the hill's long profile seems reflected by the long goddess image on stone 44, rearing up in the foreground, and by the barrow in its entirety, reminding us that prehistoric man made 'the outside world to be like himself . . . according as he saw resemblance'.[17]

The name Waden derives from Anglo-Saxon Weadhun, meaning 'the place of pagan worship',[18] and it is possible that in the eyes of the Neolithic pagans Waden Hill was seen as an explicit topographic version of the long goddess, prompting a vivid architectural response in kind.

Does the mysterious Occupation Area make sense in these terms? Was it designed to concentrate the long goddess/Waden Hill shape around the natural orifices, the pipe holes?

Grounds for believing so include the close proximity of the Waden Hill model, the close resemblance between the outlines of the two forms, the orthodox archaeological view that the Occupation Area was a 'ritual cult centre',[19] and the fact that the Area was found to be the same length as the Waden Hill tributary, 400 feet (WS-K2).

Even after 4000 years the Area was clearly defined by flint scatter, and there was a marked peak in flint tool concentration (over 100 per 500 square feet, compared with 25 per 500 square feet in the rest of the figure) around holes 1 and 2, a position corresponding to the womb of the goddess figure. The material was 'identical with the flint from the Upper Chalk on Waden Hill . . . a dark flint with occasional brownish streaks',[20] which occurs only towards the south end of the hill torso, in a corresponding womb position.

Hollow, funnel-headed figurine of a female form from the sanctuary of Petsofa, Crete, c. 1600 BC. In ancient Greece it was customary to offer pigs to the goddess down subterranean cavities in the earth.

The nodules had been reworked within the Occupation Area, as several hundredweight of chippings testified. Patination showed that they were collected from the surface of Waden Hill, and were difficult to work on that account. Unlikely to have been chosen for narrowly functional purposes, they might have been employed in a ritual act of embryo-making by, or on behalf of, the avenue virgins, hoping through sympathetic magic to enhance their own fecundity.

An interpretation of this kind would be consistent with the use of coiled clay linings around the holes, which display the conventional snake-maze-snailshell imagery, and produce an inverted form of the tiered Silbury structure.

Antiquity affords many examples of sculpture where access to the goddess's interior is gained through a ribbed and inverted cone, often taking the form of a head-dress. The implied underground hemisphere beneath Silbury Hill is an inverted duplicate of the Hill itself. This lower half had to be reactivated before the harvest hill could be expected to make a proper annual show – hence the need for ritual holes, which provided both access to the underworld and a natural mould for the Silbury shape.

The moon stone
The Occupation Area goddess had her flint-knapping womb within a few feet of avenue stone 30S. But there *is* no stone 30S. Nor was there ever one. An intensive search for the stone hole, marking the former site of a destroyed upright, has revealed the extraordinary fact that the builders did not erect a sarsen to match 30N.

Reading from Avebury, their design ran for 29 full pairs, followed by an eccentric half pair, 30N, before full pairs resumed to the Sanctuary. What was the significance of this break? We may find the answer in the moon. There are $29\frac{1}{2}$ days in a lunar month.

Snake, Woman and Moon – these three components are essential to Neolithic imagery and belief.

According to Professor Eliade, 'The whole pattern is Moon – Rain – Fertility – Woman – Serpent – Death – Periodic – Regeneration.' As the moon waxes and wanes, so the snake hibernates and emerges, and 'dies' repeatedly into new life by shedding its skin.

'What emerges fairly clearly from all this varied symbolism of snakes is their lunar character – that is their powers of fertility, of regeneration and immortality – through metamorphosis'.[21]

The moon controlled the womb, including the menstrual flow. The avenue architects accordingly chose to join their snake to the Occupation Area 'Woman' at a point 29.5 stone pairs (days) from their common destination – the Avebury henge,[22] thereby reaffirming the Snake-Woman identity. The avenue, which originated in the goddess's Sanctuary eye, did more than cut *through* the Occupation goddess – it united her torso with its mighty stone body, so that she rode the snake, *was* the snake, and had the snake emanating from her vulva.

Where was her vulva? One would expect it at the south end of the Occupation Area, close to stone 32S, and corresponding to the Hill's Waden spring position. Meeting these requirements is the specially treated hole 10, uncovered in 1935. Typically filled with a thick clay lining and charcoal core, the hole was special on account of the large sarsen stone, closely resembling the tall goddess shape, set vertically in, and emerging from, the charcoal core.

For her eyes, the Occupation Area goddess was given two artificially scooped pits, 4–5 feet in diameter, bowl-shaped, and 1–2 feet deep. Each had a top dressing of clean natural silt from a river bank. Beneath this 'seed bed' layer were fragments of Rinyo-Clacton pottery, arrow-heads, sarsen lumps and, in pit 1, an ox skull. This skull was so arranged in relation to a red deer's antler as to suggest the birth process enacted in bone with the antler as offspring emerging from the U-shaped ox horn womb. The eye pit prophetically 'sees' the birth.

Analysis of the charcoal in the pits showed that hawthorn predominated. Hawthorn, the white flower otherwise called May, which blooms in time for the May quarter day (May 8th), is considered lucky in folk tradition, and is preeminently the plant associated with the May festival and with weddings. (Flaming hawthorn brands were carried before wedding processions in ancient Rome.)

Smaller amounts of hazel charcoal (autumn), and the deadly blackthorn (winter), draw attention to the other aspects of the trinity – and raise an awkward question, namely: How can the Occupation Area represent the long goddess of spring, when the shape was claimed in Chapter 3 as the barrow mound winter goddess?

A reply can be based partly on Neolithic figurines. Compare for example the long goddess-as-bone from the Almizaraque tomb with a slim maiden goddess from

Metamorphosis of winter bone goddess into spring maiden is apparent in a Seleucian bone figurine 'connected with the great Oriental Goddess of fecundity and love'.

Susa, or from Maiden Castle, Dorset. The similarity and the difference underlies the standard fairytale miracle whereby the boney hag becomes the willowy princess. In the world of myth, the baton is passed from season to season, and its skin is transformed in the process.

The Occupation Area may relate to the barrow mound as Sanctuary does to Silbury – the first in each pairing being the adolescent version of the adult image.

Within the body of the Occupation Area goddess the pits and the natural pipes may have become the focus of worship because they provided a direct way to contact the subterranean long goddess – she who had swallowed the midwinter Kennet, and who had devoured the previous summer. The desire to call down to her is a world-wide impulse.

Farm art

'No Ashanti would till the ground without first asking permission of the Earth Mother,' writes Parinder. 'When the season for cultivation comes round . . . the farmer kills a fowl, and pours its blood into the ground, then the corpse is cut up and mixed with cooked plantain or yam. Meanwhile, he prays to his grandparent who had cultivated the land and to Asase Yaa (Earth Mother) to give help in cultivation.'[23]

This brings to mind the squatting maternal form, found in the long barrow chambers. Was it to her that the avenue worshippers offered their plump hazelnuts?

The pregnant goddess, part of the trinity, is never far away from the long image, and she may again have been portrayed in the pattern of shallow pits around the stone hole 27S (Keiller's hole 21), which lies immediately beyond the Avebury end of the Occupation Area. Here the three unexplained Neolithic excavations may be intended as head and breasts of the Mother figure, with the torso created by the shallow stone hole.

By contrast, the sculpture of our urban civilization, though often made of materials extracted from the ground, is typically arranged on a plinth. In fact the plinth eloquently describes the difference between us and Neolithic people. They made *farm* art, wherein the earth plane was the fundamental horizontal axis around which the whole notion of sculpture was balanced. For them, above-ground images were true to life only if concave counterparts could be established, either by inference, or physical exploration.

The agricultural imperative may also be seen in the treatment of Neolithic figurines. In addition to the frequent burial of maiden-goddess figurines, (at least some of whom were probably playing out the role of a Stone Age Persephone), the carver often chose to cut a deep groove across the belly of his female subject. A good example of this impulse comes from a Windmill Hill chalk idol. Iron Age goddesses, like the maiden-goddess Nerthus from Denmark, display similar cuts. Because the surface plane of the torso was simultaneously read as the surface of the land, it had to be farmed.

Traces of the rationale survive in most European languages. Thus the Latin word *sulcare* means to plough *and* to cut the skin.[24] The English word sulcus means a trench in the land, *and* a groove in human tissue.[25] This identification is further supported by the vast folk inheritance, where maidens are 'ploughed', or referred to as fields.[26]

In springtime the maiden-land was wounded by hoes and ploughs. Her skin was lacerated, so it is no surprise to hear of naked youths at the Roman festival of Lupercalia whipping all the young women they came across. They were engaged in a form of fertility magic.[27] 'Whipping', states Money-Kyrle, was a 'commonly used practice in vegetation rites',[28] and may well have been a feature of Sanctuary-West Kennet avenue behaviour.

Having scored the land, the seed corn was planted, and complementing the suggested scourging of the avenue maidens is the known sacrifice and burial of several men, whose remains were found in the underlying 'mother-ground' along the northern section of the West Kennet avenue. They 'were' the seed corn in a more than metaphorical sense.

Today, Mother Earth may be no more than a figure of speech for Europeans, but to Neolithic Europeans figures of speech were figures of fact, and their subterranean lady may be found again in the assemblage constructed around stone 22S. A flat area was carved into the chalk, measuring approximately 120 square yards with an edge describing broad curving arcs. In this they set a deeper pit where a youth in foetal position was buried on his right side. A bowl, found almost complete, was placed behind his shoulders.[29] The excavation was also slightly deepened at the narrow south end, to receive stone 22S, since removed.

Looking at Piggott's plan and photograph of this refilled area, the typical maternal image, dare we say, stares us in the face. Eyes are carved into the rock wall

'Ploughing furrows' mark the stomach of the spring goddess, Nerthus, represented in stylized form with two eyes bored into the head, and a natural cleft. The image was carried from the sacred grove annually into the surrounding fields.

A possible squatting goddess image, hollowed out of the chalk below and around stone 22S, was found to carry in its 'womb' a youth lying in a foetal position, together with a lozenge-marked, Silbury-shaped bowl (below).

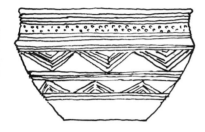

above the stone socket, the pit is her womb, the youth her seed-child, and the bowl the lower springtime hemisphere of the harvest hill to come. The sculptor described the fruitful mother in the rock where she was hiding.

Human sacrifice

'Human sacrifice', writes E. O. James, 'was most prevalent among the relatively higher grades of agricultural peoples and associated with calendrical sequence.'[30]

So far as can be judged from the fragmented human remains found at or near other stone holes, (29N, 25S, 18S, and 5S) all the interments were of young men. At 25S, under the eyes carved on the face of the standing stone, parts of three individuals were discovered, one being not more than 16 years old. 'These were unmistakably foundation burials, made when the stone was set up'.[31]

Such burials were normally of victims specially killed for the purpose, rather than of people who had died of natural causes, and the marks of ritual violence were plainly discernible in this instance. Cross-reference to the long barrow possibly emerges in the fact that 'part of a humerus had been forced through the jaws, and well into the skull of the adult'.[32]

Was this a bone version of the sexual act, played in the head and therefore complementary to the ox-skull birth process suggested for pit 1? Smith is surely right when she speaks of 'the concept of a close relation between death and fertility'[33] pervading the monuments, and the attitude of the population towards the avenue victims is likely to have been one of veneration. Apart from the vast ethnographic testimony, common sense suggests that a great and holy work would not have used despised bodies (if such a category existed).

For the victims, the opportunity to end their lives in physical incorporation with the Great Serpent *may* have been regarded as an awesome privilege,[34] an ultimate union with the godhead – son and parent united in divinity.

Whatever the religion, 'when someone embraces freely the symbols of death, or death itself, then it is consistent with everything that we have seen so far, that a great release of power for good should be expected to follow'.[35] 'The community can live on as a rational order, because of the unafraid self-sacrifice of its priest.'[36]

The snake's neck

When in June 1935 Keiller and his team reached the north end of the avenue, they found that the characteristically long waves of the snake's body were replaced over the last 500 feet by a much more agitated rhythm, amounting almost to a zig-zag.

The erratic course of the stone pairs 5 to 1 is no longer misconstrued as 'looking like an afterthought on the part of the builders',[37] as was once suggested. Instead, the dynamic form signals the fact that the avenue serpent which glided out of the Sanctuary is about to reach the climax of its one-and-a-half mile journey. The puzzling knots in the avenue's neck can be unravelled by the realization that the avenue reptile, in common with the young people in procession along its length, was probably about to mate.

The changing shape and condition of the snake would naturally have influenced the mood of the procession, for in primitive society resemblance is taken past simile to a state of real union. The more pronounced the convolutions of the snake, the greater probably became the excitement among the dancers contained within its body, accentuating the normal African pattern whereby an 'unceasing wavelike ripple runs down the muscles of the back and along the arms to the fingertips of every dancer who joins the chanting serpentine columns at the time of planting.'[38]

'Stop!' commanded the Christian Fathers, for whom snake worship was the epitome of pagan depravity. 'Stop!' says the bishop on the twelfth-century font in Avebury church, raising a spiked crozier and clutched Bible over the heads of the advancing dragons carved beneath his feet.[39] By 1750 the command had been

Excavation of stones (white patches) at the henge end of the avenue, reveals a sharper undulation of the avenue serpent as it nears the sacred enclosure.

The serpents are anathematized by a bishop, armed with crozier and Bible, in a carving on Avebury font. Thus did Christianity challenge the recurring life of the snake avenues.

The serpents or genii are venerated, in a Pompeiian house shrine, c. AD 60, as they approach the marriage altar, watched by the enthroned goddess of the home, Vesta.

obeyed; both avenues were destroyed, and by dint of an ingenious Christian inversion, 'Avebury was regarded in the neighbourhood as so holy that no reptiles could live there. If any were taken into the sacred precincts they immediately died.'

Tis remarkable that all this holy country has no snakes, tho' all the country round abounds with them, nay at Lockeridge many, yet they never reach up the Kennet to Overton. Ruben Horsal has known this country forty or fifty years, and neither he, nor the oldest man alive, ever heard of a snake being seen here.[40]

The serpents in congress, carved on a slab in Strathmartin, Forfarshire.

And yet we know that in the Middle Ages the reviled reptile had symbolized beneficial power in Wessex. The dragon standard which flew beside Harold at Hastings – 'a twisting snake with two legs and small wings' – had appeared for Cuthred of Wessex at Burford in 752, and was regarded as 'formidable, wise, protective, and a good friend'.[41]

Therefore one cannot but admire the perverse courage of the font cleric in his attack on the avenues, for at that time they represented the most splendid expression of earthly energy to be seen anywhere in Wessex, epitomizing, through adoption, the very life force of the new English nation.

English, Celtic, Bronze Age, and Neolithic peoples followed the yearly myth through its ever-new ancient course, and had good reason to walk the length of Bride's body to the great Avebury Wedding Ring. There the divine serpents, which had died in the long narrow ditches, and had hibernated in the Sanctuary (and its lost male counterpart at Beckhampton), at last unleashed magnificently into full life.

Every peasant community knows in its bones that death is the prelude to life, and while the peasantry survived, something of the truth and relevance of the Avebury monuments (designed to honour the natural world), survived with them.

Here we have tried to trace the old monumental goddess through half her annual round, and have come to the very door of the summer quarter and the henge wedding. But we may not be admitted, since for us, the Age of Myth is over.

Yet as the sun works its way through the quarters and the Kennet vanishes and returns, the raw material of myth is evidently still available, dynamic as ever, implicitly offering us a harmonious and enduring place on earth – a marriage which could last for a thousand years, if only we would accept.

PART THREE
Henge Wedding

My mind is bent to tell of bodies changed
into new forms. Ye gods, for you
yourselves have wrought these changes,
breathe on these my undertakings, and
bring down my song in unbroken strains
from the world's very beginning, even unto
the present time.

Ovid, *Metamorphoses*,
Book I, 1–4

The royal topographer

When King Charles II lay in Salisbury in 1662, he heard rumours of an ancient monument so large that it would dwarf Stonehenge, and traced these claims to a Wiltshire man called John Aubrey, who later wrote:

His Majesty admired that none of our chorographers had taken notice of it, and commanded Dr Charlton to bring me to him the next morning. I brought with me a draught of [the monument] donne by memorie only . . . with which his Majestie was pleased; gave me his hand to kisse. . . .

About a fortnight after . . . I shewed him that stupendious Antiquity . . . and His Majestie commanded me to write a description of it.[1]

Accordingly, in the September following, Aubrey returned to the site, but found it hard to obey, because 'within the circumference or Borough of this Monument is now the village of Aubury [Avebury]' and 'it was no easy task for me to trace out the vestigia . . . by reason of the cross streets, houses, gardens, orchards and several small closes . . . altogether foreign to this Antiquity [which] clowded and darkned the reall Designe.'[2]

The prehistoric components were 'huge stones pitched on end, as big, or rather bigger than those of Stoneheng, but rude and unhewen as they are drawn out of the earth'.[3] (Actually, they are sarsens of Eocene sandstone, brought from the surrounding chalk downs, where they lie on the surface.)

With the appetite of a young parasite, the growing village was consuming the Avebury megaliths:

(Pages 108–109) Avebury henge which, in Aubrey's words, 'did as much excell of Stonehenge as a Cathedral does a Parish Church'. A view of the southwest sector of the Great Circle shows the design to be U-shaped rather than circular, with the corner also registered by the bank and ditch.

The houses are built of the fustrums [fragments] of those huge stones which they [the villagers] invade with sledges. . . . These mighty stones (as hard as marble) may be broken in what part of them you please without any great trouble, *sc.* make a fire on that line of the stone where you would have it crack; and after the stone is well heated, draw over a line with cold water and immediately give a knock with a smith's sledge, and it will break like the collets at the Glasshouse.[4]

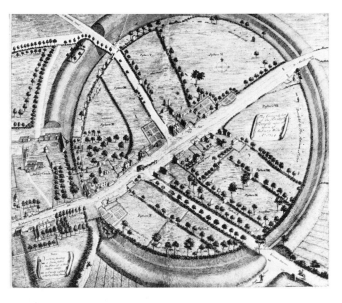

(Left), William Stukeley's 'ground plot of the British Temple, now the town of Aubury, Wilts' (1724). An airview of the henge, taken in the 1940s, shows the extent of the monument, with much of the village – but not the church, bottom right – contained inside the ancient precinct.

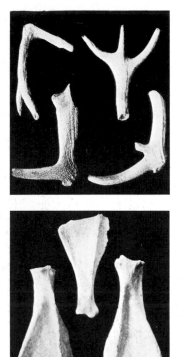

Antler picks and oxbone shovels, the tools used to construct Avebury's massive ditch and bank, were found during H. St George Gray's excavations, 1908–22.

Opposite.
The full magnitude of the Avebury ditch achievement can be seen with the removal of the silt, southeast sector, 1922.

Yet enough remained standing in 'curvilineous segments' for him to 'boldly conclude that heretofore they stood quite round about like a crowne'. This 'crown' originally consisted of 98 stones, up to 18 feet high, enclosing $28\frac{1}{2}$ acres. Within this area he saw remnants of two smaller circles – 'so within Christian churches are severall chapelles'.[5] Despite the damage he could say:

Avbury is peradventure the most eminent and entire monument of this kind in the Isle of Great Britaigne. It is environed with an extraordinary great vallum [bank] . . . within which is a Graffe of a depth and breadth proportionable to it.[6]

Today, it is customary to refer to the Avebury monument as a henge, a henge being defined as 'a monument or temple used for religious rites . . . a roughly circular area of ground, bounded by a ditch with a bank outside it, often enclosing a stone or wooden circle or circles. It was usually built on low ground, often near water. The earthwork was broken by entrance gaps.'[7]

Judged by any of these criteria, the monument at Avebury is a henge, and takes its place with 77 other British examples surviving from the Late Neolithic and Early Bronze Age. Twelve of these, like Avebury, have an internal stone circle.[8] Yet Avebury's unparalleled scale calls forth superlatives from even the soberest of observers:

'In its original condition, surely the most outstanding monument of prehistoric antiquity in Europe' (G. Clark, 1936).
'The grandest relic of an ancient heathen temple in Europe' (A. C. Smith, 1885).
'The greatest and most remarkable circle in Britain, if not in the world' (A. Thom, 1967).

Using red deer antler picks and ox shoulder blade shovels, they raised the bank no less than 50 feet above the ditch bottom in a circuit nearly a mile in circumference. This Dyke of the Britons (Waledich), as it was called in an Assize Roll of 1289, had four entrances through the bank leading to causeways of undisturbed chalk across the ditch.

In Aubrey's time, a northwest section of the bank was levelled by Lord Stowell[9] in order to build the manor barn which still stands in its place, but we know now that many of the missing stones reported by Aubrey were in fact toppled and buried much earlier – in the fourteenth century.

Medieval destruction

This phase of destruction was conducted by the Christian authorities trying to stamp out what, in 1939, Emerson Chapman called 'the many superstitions and questionable practices still connected with stones at that period'.[10]

Involved in the work of destruction was a barber-surgeon, who was killed and incarcerated by the premature fall of stone 9 in the Great Circle. He carried a metal probe and a pair of scissors, and coins in his purse enabled his death to be placed between 1320 and 1325.[11]

Around that time, most of the stones in the southwest sector of the Great Circle were felled, in addition to a number of smaller megaliths which formed a central setting within the South Circle.

Whether accidental or contrived, it is possible that the surgeon's death brought an end to one round in the medieval battle for the henge fought between the peasantry, (committed to a form of nature worship stemming from the Stone Age), and the bishops of Christ. As we have seen, the battle is portrayed on the twelfth-century Avebury font, where a prelate, with raised crozier, defies the forces of nature in the shape of two serpentine dragons – a representation of the conflict which began, in Dr Smith's opinion, in AD 634, when the first Christian church was built 'outside, but

Skeleton of the barber-surgeon identified by the tools found on him, crushed beneath stone 9 of the Great Circle during the Medieval onslaught on the stones.

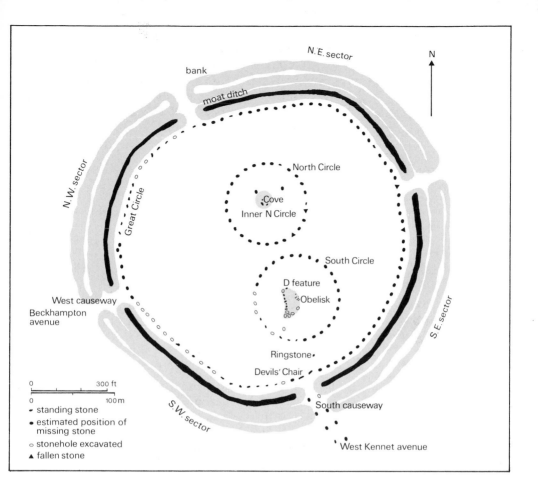

Inside the plan, the following labels appear:

N.E. sector

N

bank

moat ditch

North Circle

N.W. sector

Great Circle

Cove

Inner N Circle

South Circle

D feature

Obelisk

S.E. sector

West causeway

Beckhampton avenue

Ringstone

Devils' Chair

S.W. sector

South causeway

West Kennet avenue

0   300 ft
0   100 m
- standing stone
• estimated position of missing stone
○ stonehole excavated
▲ fallen stone

Plan of Avebury (after I. F. Smith)

right up against the henge bank, implying a challenge from the new faith to an old one, whose followers were still numerous'.[12]

The clash between world-rejecting, sin-laden Christianity and the entrenched matriarchal folk heritage was bound to be violent, and in 1249 we find the Prior of Abury, together with his brothers Robert and Ralph, jailed in Marlborough on a charge of murder.[13]

The Puritan revolution

In the end, the Church defeated the monument, but the victory was not achieved till long after the Reformation, and then not by the power of the bishops, but by the single-minded exertions of a Nonconformist preacher called John Baker.

Based at nearby Chisledon, this Puritan was dispossessed of his Anglican living by Charles II in 1660. Thereafter, Baker stalked the Winterbourne valley, forming his own congregations. By 1670 his first Avebury flock had formally come together. In 1676

The partitioning of the monument with property boundaries, and the division of common land into plots of individual ownership, have never concealed the massive scale of the original conception.

they numbered 25, compared with 181 Anglicans in the village.[14] By 1715 there were no less than 130 attendants[15] at the Meeting House, built, *c.* 1670, from demolished megaliths between the North and South Circles.

The erection of the Avebury chapel from fragments of shattered Stone Age megaliths neatly epitomizes a turning-point in human affairs on this planet. As Max Weber says: 'That great historical process . . . the elimination of magic from the world . . . came here to its logical conclusion.'[16]

What he describes as 'the entirely negative attitude of Puritanism to all the sensuous and emotional elements in culture and religion' was enough to break the weakened ring of communal conviction which had imbued the henge with positive meaning through the ages.

Moreover, because the new morality raised the private profit motive to the status of a cardinal duty, the inhabitants of Avebury became iconoclasts in the name of the god of business acumen.

The process was recorded with much regret between 1719 and 1724 by William Stukeley during a series of visits to the area.

Of the stones in the Outer Circle, he learnt that 'ten of the remainder all contiguous, were at once destroyed by Tom Robinson *anno* 1700, and other places perfectly levelled for the sake of the pasture'.[17] Concerning the North Circle, he wrote:

People yet alive, remember several [stones] standing in the middle of the street; they were burnt for building *anno* 1711. . . .

Most of the houses, walls and outhouses in the town are raised from these materials. (The stone) at the corner of the lane going to the North gate of the town, not many years since, lying on the ground, was used as a stall to lay fish on, when they had a kind of market here.[18]

'In 1700 both inner circles were standing almost entire.' He attributed the first act of destruction directed at the inner circles to 'Walter Stretch, father of one of the present inhabitants', who demolished 'one of the stones standing in the street before the inn'.[19] Subsequently, 'John Fowler owned to us that he had burnt 5 of the South Circle'. Farmer Green and Tom Robinson were also named.

And so, 'within the space of twenty years, a few miserable farmers destroyed this, the noblest monument which is probably on the face of the earth; which has stood so many ages, and was made to stand so many more.'[20]

THE AVEBURY HENGE STONES

	Diam.	No. of stones Orig.	Now	Av. dist. apart	Height
GREAT OUTER CIRCLE containing	1305 ft	98?	30	36 ft	9–18 ft
1) *North Circle* with	320 ft	27?	4	36 ft	9–13.5 ft
a) Inner North Circle	65 ft	12		30 ft	9–13.5 ft
b) The Cove	22 ft	3	2	6 ft	15.5 ft
2) *South Circle*	340 ft	29?	5	36 ft	9–13.5 ft
D feature	80 ft	13	6	12 ft	4 ft
Obelisk		1			21 ft (Obelisk)

The Great Circle restored. In 1937 the Scottish industrialist, A. Keiller, had re-erected a number of stones in the northwest sector.

The henge, 1719-1976

In Stukeley's day, the main road from London to Bath ran into the world's largest henge by the east causeway and out via the south causeway, where the West Kennet stone avenue joined the monument. Midway between these two entrances, stage coaches drew up outside the Catherine Wheel inn[21] between what remained of the North and South Circles. The North Circle, 320 feet in diameter, once contained 27 stones, while the South Circle was composed of 29 stones, on a 340 feet diameter.

Both north and south rings held central stone settings. Near the middle of the latter once stood the tallest megalith of all, the Obelisk. Subsequently broken up, it was 'of a circular form at base, of vast bulk, 21 feet long when standing'.[22] By 1723, when Stukeley drew the stone, it had been felled and lay close to a group of relatively small buried members which, now restored, are referred to as the D feature.

In the centre of the north ring, there was a massive three-sided sarsen box, called the Cove.[23] One side collapsed in 1713, leaving two stones erect, the bulkier being 16 feet broad. Around the Cove, concentric with the North Circle, ran an inner ring of 12 stones, 65 feet

in diameter, whose former presence was confirmed by
I. F. Smith's excavation on 1964.[24]

What Stukeley saw, he plotted in words, drawings
and maps, eventually publishing his *Abury Described* in
1743. But the interest aroused by his book did not stop
further destruction.

In 1821 we find Colt Hoare 'with awe and diffidence
entering this once hallowed sanctuary . . . the wonder
of Britain',[25] to discover some of the remaining
megaliths being broken up by the Commissioners for
Roads.

When the Scottish industrialist, Alexander Keiller,
reviewed the state of the monument in 1937, he saw 'a
condition of indescribable squalor and neglect' – a
tangle of rusty pig wire, accumulations to a depth of
nearly three feet of old tins and broken bottles, and
refuse heaps which filled part of the ditch almost flush
with its edges. The once majestic site of Avebury had
become the outstanding archaeological disgrace of
Britain.[26]

Having already restored part of the West Kennet
processional avenue, adjoining the henge, Keiller
began buying up land within the monument in order to
effect a restoration, involving the demolition of houses,

*The Great Circle unrestored: a
view of the northeast sector. On
Keiller's retirement the work of
restoration ceased.*

the re-erection of the buried stones, and the marking of the sites of those which had been destroyed.

He had the writings of the Rev. A. C. Smith to encourage him; that Victorian clergyman, 'with a gang of five labourers had probed the Avebury ground (using a crowbar) . . . and found 18 large sarsen stones . . . sunk deep in the ground'.[27]

First in the northwest and southwest sectors of the Great Circle, and then in the South Circle, Keiller and his team re-erected a large number of buried megaliths – 43 stand today – and accurately marked the site of 31 others. Then the war brought the work, 'scheduled to last for at least a decade', to a premature close, and afterwards, due to declining financial fortune and health, Keiller never resumed his colossal self-imposed task.

The Department of the Environment, which now looks after the monument and Keiller's museum, has not re-erected any more stones, but has set up a bookstall, a large car park, and public lavatories within the sacred precinct for the convenience of us visitors.

The pamphlets on the bookstall say that it would be misguided to hope for an explanation of the monument's purpose, and we are warned of certain heresies that linger on:

You may have heard all kinds of stories about sun worship, serpent worship and so on, but there is absolutely no foundation for any of these tales which have been put about by people with more imagination than knowledge.[28]

Professor Stuart Piggott is not one of those. Writing of the Avebury parish monuments, he positively asserts: 'The nature of the beliefs which prompted the activity of which the monuments are the tangible memorial must remain unknown.'[29]

A similar attitude suffuses G. J. Wainwright's recent survey of British henge monuments, where interpretation has hardly begun before it is snuffed out by professional evasion:

The accepted function of henge monuments is that they were intended for non-utilitarian purposes connected with ritual practices, our concept of which lies beyond the limitations of archaeological inference.[30]

What then are the grounds for the unanimous belief among archaeologists that Avebury was the scene of indescribable ritual practices, when a ring bank and ditch normally suggest practical defence?

Aubrey was the first to emphasize that the Avebury bank 'could not be designed for a fortification, for then the Graffe would have been on the outside of the rampart'.[31] His perception has rightly been accepted ever since, and further supported by the fact that circles of standing stones 'are found in many parts of the world, and whenever we know anything about their purpose we always find that they are connected with religion or ritual'.[32]

At this point the train of orthodox archaeological thought comes to a halt, though whispers of 'fertility worship' can be heard from some compartments, amidst the persistent clatter of typewriters repeating the facts of Keiller's fieldwork.[33]

Archaeologists are quite right to say that, from the confines of their isolated discipline, the question 'What was Avebury for?' can never be properly answered. Archaeology's important contribution must first be returned to the ancient world from which it sprang – a world which knew nothing of our '-ologies' and '-isms', a world whose shattered fragments now lie incongruously in the hands of art historians, anthropologists, astronomers, folklorists and students of comparative religion.

If we want to restore meaning to the damaged Avebury ring we must try to reintegrate their separated findings. Only then may the wholeness of prehistoric sense emerge.

Stone 98 of the Great Circle, as it has looked since its erection, c. 2600 BC. One of the stones which has never fallen or been toppled.

The henge as image

The Maiden, a traditional corn dolly which was carried back to the fields in spring to ensure the continuing fertility of the land. A reference to the Neolithic eye motif may be seen in the pattern of her dress.

Henge and annual cycle

The Avebury henge was built in the late New Stone Age, *c.* 2600 BC.[1] That much is clear from a few fragments of pottery found under the banks. It is therefore part of the great complex of Neolithic monuments in Avebury parish which includes Silbury Hill, West Kennet long barrow, the Sanctuary, and the West Kennet and Beckhampton stone avenues.

In looking at the henge we should remember that, before the invention of writing, people concentrated their most important thoughts and beliefs (arising from their experience of the natural world) into objects, including buildings. As Forge says:

'Primitive architecture is an art often very highly charged with value and meaning for the society concerned . . . and is an effective form of communication.'[2]

Writing of British henges, Professor Clark states: 'Some light is thrown upon what went on in these sacred places by the plan of the monuments themselves.'[3]

Though damaged, the Avebury henge still describes *through its form* an important episode in the seasonal Neolithic myth-narrative. Indeed, partly because such prodigious efforts were expended there to make the general henge message particularly explicit, and also because the monument is plainly related to the surrounding contemporary monuments, which collectively tell the rest of the annual story, the Avebury henge offers us an exceptionally good opportunity to find the lost meaning.

As we have seen, the overall purpose of the entire ensemble was to celebrate the annual life cycle of the Great Goddess, at temples which were her seasonal portraits.

The worshippers moved around this extended gallery of symbolic architecture in time with the changing seasons and the farming year, synchronized with the comparable events in the lives of the human community, namely birth, puberty, marriage and death.

The solar year, now as then, is naturally divided by equinoxes and solstices, but because there has always been a climatic and vegetational time-lag in response to solar behaviour (June is not the hottest month, nor is harvest ready then), the quarter days, midway between solstices and equinoxes, were used as the cardinal points in the ritual calendar. These fall in early August, November, February and May. In this chain of events, each of the four climaxes was almost certainly attached to the appropriate lunar phase (waxing or waning, full or new) nearest the solar quarter day.

Thus the First Fruits festival was conducted at Silbury at the full moon nearest August 8th, when the moon rose over the moat (which was shaped to describe the Mother goddess in labour) and during that night offered, through lunar reflections, a description of the divine birth, concluding with moonset on the mother's breast.

We also have shown how at August and at the Winter quarter days (Martinmas and Candlemas), sun and moon rose or set in alignment with the axis joining the two sacred springs – a circumstance which gave the Avebury district a particular suitability for the celebration of a Four Quarters religion.

Referring to the ancient British tradition, MacNeill confirms that 'this division of the year into quarters, each of which began with a festival, is well known, much taken for granted, and hitherto little studied'.[4]

Consistent with this scheme, we intend to demonstrate that the Avebury henge was built to provide a communal May festival wedding ring, shaped as a living image of the goddess as Bride, pictured in union with her male consort.

The temple was designed to reveal the shape of the Great Goddess, on a scale big enough to be occupied or 'known' by large worshipping congregations who re-enacted her transformation, while, in the distance, monuments representing her body at other seasons looked on, awaiting their turn. At the henge we can understand why, in British folk custom, the corn dolly known as the Hag is also called the Maiden.

As in the fairy tales, the ultimate truth was not the dramatic differences between her monumental forms, but their fundamental identity. The ugly old woman *was* the beautiful princess, and the thread which passed from autumn to spring, by way of winter, was *one* thread, though variously coloured. So, in the Avebury Cycle, the goddess's serpentine energy ran throughout

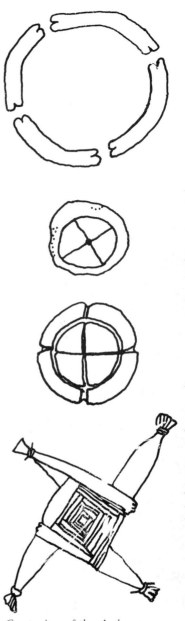

Comparison of the Avebury henge plan (top), a late Neolithic carved stone found at nearby Windmill Hill (centre), and an incised sandstone ball from Uisneach, Ireland ('The site of the primal unity'), reveals a similarity of design. The underlying theme is suggested by St Brigid's rush cross (bottom), inherited from the pre-Christian goddess of the four quarters of the year.

The living stones. The Avebury megaliths, taken from the surrounding hills, were regarded individually and collectively as alive.

her personality – the grass 'string' found inside the Silbury mound became the 'dead' snakes of the long barrow ditches, and the coiled Sanctuary serpent, which was in turn unleashed in the avenues to couple at the henge.

The living monument

All the henge stones were thought to be alive, both individually and as the cells of a larger organism:

A large number of stone circles in Cornwall, Dartmoor and elsewhere are said to represent maidens, transformed into stone. The belief that standing stones turn round, or go to a neighbouring stream to bathe or drink when they hear the clock strike twelve, is very widespread, and so intimately connected with prehistoric stones that it may well be a garbled form of very early belief. All these traditions, along with many others which relate that the stones grow, dance and speak, suggest the idea of primitive man investing them with properties of living beings.[5]

Even in Stukeley's day, the Avebury Diamond stone at the north entrance to the henge was believed to turn round at certain times.[6] The entire structure was

originally conceived as alive, an organism drawing its life from the vital spirit of the landscape.

Therefore, when the medieval authorities tried to kill off nature worship at the henge, they sent, not for a man with a sledge hammer, but for a surgeon with a metal probe, perhaps because the stones he touched were regarded as parts of a living body which had to be operated upon, killed and then buried.

The life of the henge came from the living land. Among primitive peoples everywhere, landscape is still recognized as a divine functioning body. So it was in classical antiquity. Scully found, in his study of major temple sites in ancient Greece, that they grew up around holy places where the deity's presence had been previously recognized in the natural topography. The temple served to amplify and render more accessible the sacred qualities of the *genius loci*.[7] This principle operated at Avebury.

The water triangle
H. Bayley suggested long ago that the Avebury temple may possibly owe its situation to the felicitous

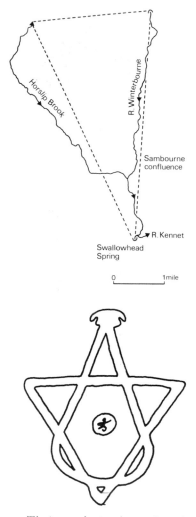

The inverted triangle, a universal female symbol, is formed at landscape scale (top) by the sources of the two Avebury streams with Swallowhead, prime source of the Kennet. The same symbol appears in the yantra of Radhika, (above), with seed syllable at the centre of triangle and U-shape.

symbolism of the surrounding landscape.[8] 'The henge', as A. C. Smith writes, 'is placed at the junction of two infant streams which go to form the river Kennet.'[9] This water-meet lies some 370 yards from the west causeway.

Henges, as many workers have observed, are usually sited close to running water, and so we find the greatest of all henges enjoying a position near the centre of what might be called a water triangle.

The sources of the Winterbourne and Horslip brook define the top corners of this triangle. After flowing down to the confluence of Avebury, they run together for a mile to the spectacular Swallowhead birth spring, which forms the bottom tip of the triangle. Here the headwaters give up their name to a new river, the Kennet. Their pre-birth task has been accomplished. They are the streams which meet and conceive a new entity from their two long river strands twisted together, and then give way to the Kennet and its monumental equivalent, the Silbury Mother goddess.

This reading is confirmed by the line running from Avebury confluence to Swallowhead, which passes directly over the Silbury summit.

In prehistoric symbolism, the spot near the centre of an inverted triangle, such as the Avebury tributaries make, is usually associated with conception. Thus in the Great Goddess's imagery handed down to modern times through the Indian Tantric tradition:

'There is in existence, at the first stage of creative evolution, a dot inside a downward pointing triangle. The dot at the centre indicates the invisible first principle, the self-originated seed of Being and Consciousness.'[10] The Horslip confluence corresponds to that dot.

The inverted triangle was the chosen containing shape throughout the ancient world because it also described the female pubic triangle.[11] From Old Stone Age European carvings onwards it was therefore, in Eliade's phrase, 'the archetype of universal fecundity'.[12]

When the land was regarded as the body of the Goddess, and fertility (as always) depended on water, it would have followed naturally that the twin headwater streams should be equated with her two-lobed uterus.

References equating the sacred rivers of Mesopotamia to the goddess's genital passages are well known, and the clay tablet from Neolithic India, showing a river gushing from a goddess's womb, is closely paralleled by the fragment from the Roman Frieze of the Seasons at Bath.

Choosing the site

The Avebury meadow at the point of confluence was until recently called Sambourne.[13] In archaic English *sam* meant 'to bring together or join in marriage, friendship, and to assemble a number of people'.[14]

Yet if the Sambourne confluence offered the natural point for weddings and seed planting, at the head of the

(Above), the inverted triangle: goddess figurine, c. 3000 BC, from Mesopotamia.

The generative goddess with natural spring, once a universally accepted embodiment of the deity, survived into the Roman period in Britain. (Left), the goddess Sul at Bath (Aquae Sulis). (Above left), the Celtic goddess on a Roman tile from Caerleon, holding dolphins, symbols of fertility, and rising from a fountain, which also forms her vulva.

127

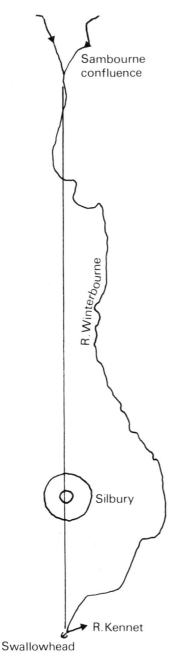

Sambourne
confluence

R. Winterbourne

Silbury

R. Kennet

Swallowhead

From the Sambourne confluence, hard by the Avebury marriage henge, the Cycle's river flows down the Winterbourne to the Swallowhead spring, while the Sambourne-Swallowhead sightline passes over the Silbury birth-mound summit.

Horslip-Winterbourne vagina, to reach that spot one had to penetrate the river goddess's vulva, which in local river features was epitomized by 'that most abundant spring called Swallowhead', a mile further south. Swallowhead, Stukeley found, retained its sanctity among the villagers into the eighteenth century, and provided the primary natural focus for the entire Neolithic cycle.

The henge designers were therefore faced with a difficult choice. If they built their wedding ring at Swallowhead they would seem to reject Sambourne, and vice versa. What was to be done? With a typically Neolithic solution they rejected neither and chose both, by siting their ring *at* Sambourne, while *shaping it* like a greatly enlarged version of the Swallowhead model, 'true fountain of the Kennet'. As with the other monuments in the group, the length of the Swallowhead feeder, 65.25 ft (SH-K1), and that of the nearby Waden feeder, 400 feet (WS-K2), were employed as the basic linear modules in setting out the temple.

By constructing an architectural version of the sacred birth spring close to the Sambourne confluence, the community were able to draw it into juxtaposition with the water triangle nucleus. This made a very efficacious pairing of water images evoking the physiological sequence which runs from penetration at the vulva (Swallowhead) to the place of conception (Sambourne). Given a belief in sympathetic magic (and all societies with the exception of our own *do* believe in sympathetic magic), one can imagine the advantage perceived in conducting marriage rites within an architectural version of the birth spring, large enough to accommodate a national gathering, on ground adjacent to the confluence.

Stukeley came very close to this understanding when he wrote:

The whole temple of Abury may be considered as a picture, and it really is so. . . . The plan on which Abury is built is . . . the Circle and the Snake. The Circle meant the supreme fountain of all being.[15]

But he did not add: As locally revealed in the Swallowhead fountain. The final clause is missing because he belonged to the modern world, where the sense of real identity with the land was fast dissolving, especially among the educated classes. His generalized poetic metaphor had lost contact with the ground, a state vividly summed up in his most unprehistoric dictum, 'A symbol is an arbitrary sensible sign of an intellectual idea'.[16]

To fit this idea, he rejected the sensible evidence presented by the peculiar shape of the henge bank, and drew it, drastically changed, as a true circle.

On one level he was justified in making this alteration, because whatever other considerations were satisfied by the odd shape, the henge is simultaneously *experienced* as a ring – a ring bank and a ring ditch, surrounding a ring of stones, evoking notions of endlessness.

Yet the fact remains that the henge bank is not a true circle, but rather a great U-shape, with the terminals of the U joined by the two relatively straight sections of bank and ditch that lie on either side of the western entrance. This arrangement produces two distinct corners in the northwest and southwest – 'an ill-shaped monument' in Aubrey's opinion, resulting, he could only suppose, from primitive incompetence. For 'although the form of a circle was aimed at by the Britons, yet they did not succeed in rendering it perfect'.[17]

One need look no further than the perfectly drawn inner circles, embraced by the U-bank, to see the weakness of this argument and the need for a more positive Neolithic explanation. The U-shape model can be seen today at the curving arc of exposed chalk, 15 feet across and 4 feet high, which surrounds the Swallowhead spring.

We have shown earlier, and in *The Silbury Treasure*, how at each seasonal stage in the Cycle the goddess made use of the Swallowhead image. The architectural images of death goddess (West Kennet long barrow) and pregnant goddess (Silbury) flanking the sacred spring, incorporate its shape into their own forms, (barrow west chamber and Silbury top terrace).

The Neolithic involvement with Swallowhead is also shown in a number of little chalk models, found nearby at Windmill Hill. Model C.9, for example, is engraved with parallel lines around its back wall, probably simulating the chalk strata around the springhead, while its flat floor (also matching the springhead facts) is incised with broader lines, combining a reference to flowing water with the well-known stylized treatment of pubic hair offered on decorated woman-pots of the same period.

Smith refers to C.9 as a ritual vessel; but whereas such an object could easily be moved about during the

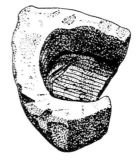

The Windmill Hill chalk 'cup', known as C.9, may be a possible model of the sacred spring. Comparable, 'non-functional' Neolithic objects have been found in Sussex.

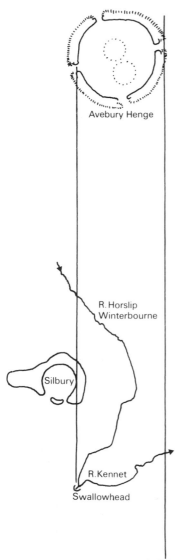

Avebury Henge

R. Horslip
Winterbourne

Silbury

R. Kennet

Swallowhead

West Kennet
long barrow

North-south lines unite the henge, west and east causeways, with two of the other monuments, Silbury and West Kennet long barrow.

rites, the same cannot be said of the architectural U-shapes. With them, a decision had to be made concerning the best permanent orientation.

The henge's orientation

In the case of the henge *and* the Silbury U-terrace, the axis chosen ran from east-north-east (70°) to west-south-west (250°), and at Silbury this corresponds to the 250° setting position of the vital Lammas full moon, signalling the start of harvest. Full moon and Swallowhead created harvest together. We can see the viewing terrace (but not the bulk of the Hill) from the henge, and it could be argued that the distant prospect of the Silbury viewing terrace provided sufficient incentive for the May henge orientation to follow suit, thus establishing a vital spring-moon collaboration. To this motive should be added the fact that the full moon of the May quarter day *also* sets at 250°. They are the only full moons in the year which do so.

But if that accounts for the 'tilt' of the henge towards the southwest, we still need to know why the monument was not built *around* the Sambourne confluence, rather than 1100 feet to the east, especially since the line joining the confluence to Swallowhead (measuring 4800 feet, or WS-K2 × 12), passes directly over the top of the pregnant mother image, Silbury Hill, erected two-thirds of the distance along this sight line.

Here we could refer to the very marshy condition of the Sambourne field in spring – an annual swamp beyond the power of architectural control. By moving a mere 1100 feet to the east the builders found firm ground on solid chalk.

They also found there a way to affirm the unity of the henge goddess with her winter and harvest modes. On the site selected, the monument becomes part of the three-in-one godhead arising from Swallowhead, because the henge east causeway, cutting the base of the great U-ditch, lies due north of another previously constructed Swallowhead image, the West Kennet long barrow's west chamber. Similarly, from the henge west causeway, a parallel sightline due south touches the Silbury squatting goddess at her moat vulva, before passing on over the actual Swallowhead spring.

So the three key monuments were carefully sited in a north-south strip of country, a mile in length, its width established by the east-west distance between spring and barrow chamber, and repeated by the henge span.

In making this arrangement, the north-south line was not an abstract concept, but the very tangible direction where every full moon reached maximum altitude to an observer on the ground, and where every day the sun was at its highest. All this celestial energy was drawn into the plan of our greatest Neolithic achievement – a composite working image where Avebury henge played the part of head, Silbury the womb, West Kennet long barrow the anus, and the spring itself the female cleft, with each building incorporating the spring-vulva image, in a mode fitting the part.

Identification of head with womb, as represented in the henge architecture, remained an orthodox view for at least the next 2000 years. (Left), the Avebury Headstone, and (above) the Baubo goddess from Priene, Asia Minor, fifth century BC.

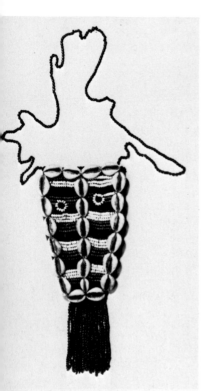

Cowrie shells on the loincloth of a Chagga (Tanzania) woman repeat the shape of the genital organ and also resemble eyes – an idea taken up by the two little rings of beads.

This implies that the henge in its entirety was planned as a double image, which could be read both as an enlarged vulva, suitable for May marriages, *and* as a great head, where the inner circles functioned as eyes – a possibility which is entirely consistent with the employment of two-way images at the other monuments.

The head-genital ambivalence is copiously recorded in classical literature. For the Romans the head contained the seed, the very stuff of life and the life soul associated with it. The Latin word for brain (*cerebrum*) is cognate with *c(e)reo* – I beget. According to Onians, this explains why 'the source of a stream [such as the Kennet] was called its head'[18] (e.g. Swallowhead).

This attitude is also well known from surviving 'primitive' communities in other continents, as witnessed by the Chagga pubic shield with eye decoration from East Africa.

Ditch as moat

In comparing the natural chalk wall around Swallowhead with the structure of the henge bank, certain similarities emerge. The Swallowhead enclave exhibits a massive vertical wall of Melbourne rock about 4 feet high, rising from a flat floor of greenish plenus marl (a clayey layer which causes the water to emerge at that point), and capped by a sloping deposit of loose rubble-like material called coombe rock, with soil on top. All these features are reflected at the henge.

Between 1908 and 1922 H. St George Gray made several cuttings through the Avebury ditch,[19] temporarily removing a twelve-foot-thick deposit of silt to reveal the very same geological formation which is exposed naturally at Swallowhead – the Melbourne rock.

Quarried from the ditch base, large blocks of this material had been used to make the lower courses of the surrounding bank, followed by layers of finer chalk rubble interspersed with seams of soil, so that the bank structure eventually bore some resemblance to the geological sequence around Swallowhead. The treatment is also reminiscent of the striped layering developed in the West Kennet long barrow and in the core of Silbury Hill – three contemporary deposits.[20]

But the real value of the henge bank lies in the bottom of the ditch for, when Gray had cleared out the last of the modern silt, he found himself standing on the

Excavation of the silt from Avebury ditch (1922) reveals that it was filled with water at the appropriate season of the year.

flat Neolithic ditch floor, which was a 'soft, smooth, palish green-grey . . . poor chalk'.[21]

Poor chalk perhaps, but the best water divide on the Downs, acting as a partial barrier to the vertical percolation of underground water. When prevented from moving downwards, water flows sideways, and lo! the mighty Swallowhead became gloriously wet. Avebury's hidden secret is water. And not just any water, but the very same underground saturated layer which is tapped at Swallowhead, and which flows into Silbury ditch.

To find this sacred water, the henge's flat ditch bottom, averaging 13 feet in width, followed the rise and fall of the gently undulating marl layer[22] which never rose more than 7 feet above the bed of the nearby confluence.

In 1922 Passmore recognized the significance of this very small disparity, when he wrote, 'One can say without fear of contradiction that in late Neolithic times, the (subterranean) water level was at least ten feet higher than today'.[23]

The geologist Professor H. L. Hawkins supports this statement.[24]

We can be sure that whenever there was water at the confluence, there was water in the henge moat. In a normal year, both would be dry in autumn, following the sinking of the water table as a result of heavy summer evaporation on this sensitive, permeable chalk land – a water retreat into the underworld which even the plenus marl layer could not check.

But by April fresh streams met at the Sambourne confluence, and new water sparkled in the moat. The monument at Avebury, or Aubury as it was known in the seventeenth century, was built to create New Water, and in the oldest European language, the Neolithic Basque tongue, *Urberri* means New Water! True to the cyclical nature of mythical reality, the Aubury water was new not only in 2600 BC but every spring.

The moat's part in the henge ritual is indicated by the stepped treatment of the inner rock face, leading in some places up to the enclosure or down to the moat: 'The section dug in 1938 . . . showed the upper part to rise in a series of broad, shallow steps; several deep antler pickmarks were preserved in the vertical faces of the steps'.[25]

This points to the same careful treatment as was given to the Silbury moat, where revetted steps and a flat bottom were also discovered. Gray found that the steepness of the Avebury bank caused debris to fall into the water, but this was not allowed to clog up the moat. There were 'indications that it had been frequently cleaned out in prehistoric times'.[26]

The river references
Recent work at the Marden henge in the Vale of Pewsey, Wiltshire, has revealed seasonal waterlogging to a depth of one to seven metres, and also proved that the south side of the enclosure was formed by the river Avon itself.[27] This serves to strengthen the possibility that, at Avebury, lengths of the Winterbourne and Kennet running to and from Swallowhead were woven symbolically into the architectural imagery.

Local precedent is found in the ragstone walling 'rivers' at the West Kennet long barrow, running to and from the west chamber, at Lanhill barrow, Wiltshire, and further afield in Welsh and Orcadian monuments. At the Avebury henge they are represented perhaps in the western part of the henge plan, where they provide the stretches of moat on either side of the west causeway, and serve to link the terminals of the U design, to complete the moat ring, while keeping the U-shaped bridal image (the main body of the trench) well above what, Gombrich asserts, was the necessarily low threshold of recognition:

'In an erotically charged atmosphere, the merest hint of formal similarity with sexual functions creates the desired response.'[28]

The henge was the goddess of love, described formally. As with all primitive societies, where 'the invariable point of departure is naturalism',[29] the description was based on the natural appearance of spring and river, and of the two ends of the female body. The search was for a comprehensive symbol 'which could represent the radical archetypal element in which specific diversities met'[30] – (in this case head and genitals), combined to offer the right wisdom, and the right place to conceive.

The sun and moon circles

But to be effectively comprehensive, the two main celestial bodies had to be incorporated as well. So the henge North and South Circles, and the features they contain, were probably intended as a reflection of the sun and moon. For, as Rice Homes puts it, 'our Neolithic forefathers, like other savages, saw sun and moon as living beings'.[31] Stukeley was right to label the inner circles 'Solar' and 'Lunar' on some of his Avebury plans.[32]

Eliade outlines the intellectual principle involved:

Clearly man's integration into the Cosmos can only take place if he can bring himself into harmony with the two astral rhythms, 'unifying' the sun and moon in his living body. The unification of the two centres of sacred and natural energy aims, through the technique of mystical physiology – at reintegrating them in the primal undifferentiated unity.[33]

The belief in sun and moon as the eyes of a divine body was carried from the Neolithic to the nineteenth century by a people who, according to Professor O'Riordain, however much altered by Iron Age warriors, 'are basically the people of the Neolithic and Early Bronze Age',[34] namely the Irish.

A superhuman female, holding within the great circle of her body two smaller orbs, 'do expresse Eternitie' in Peacham's Minerva Britanna, *1612, a late form of the henge image, and carrying a related meaning.*

The motif of two balls within a hoop (head) was 'still carried on May Day by the Irish peasantry. Suspended within a hoop, the two balls represent the sun and moon, and are sometimes covered with gold and silver paper,' wrote Lady Wilde, who witnessed the ceremony.[35] In miniature then, the Avebury plan swung and swayed along country lanes to enter modern times.

Sun and moon, like river sources, and women, were not abstract concepts. They were living things, believed because seen and experienced by particular people in particular places.

The value of the Avebury henge rested firmly on its combination of tangible images, known and loved. By drawing them together in a manner appropriate to the season, the population was able to see and enter their goddess at her wedding.

'It seems likely from the presence of avenues that processions played a certain part in the ceremonial',[1] wrote Professor Clark, in his review of British henges.

The Avebury henge was built to receive two winding processional ways of exceptional splendour, each defined by 100 pairs of standing stones – the Beckhampton and West Kennet avenues, which enter the monument by the west and south causeways.

As Stukeley appreciated, the avenues form an indispensable part of the henge image.[2] They contributed what Scully has recently called 'the cosmic snakes, earth molded, rising up from the river bottoms'.[3]

In Parts One and Two we traced the progress of the annual serpent from death in the long barrow ditches to resurrected hibernation during the Candlemas quarter, when ploughing and preparation of the seed bed were synchronized with the separate incarceration of male and female adolescents for a period of instruction and initiation rites. These rites, it was suggested, took place

The Brides' route to the May wedding, along the West Kennet avenue, passes a flowering may tree.

in the Sanctuary temple and its lost male equivalent. At these two sites, sexual libido was generated, eventually released in late April, and represented in the archetypal form of male and female serpents.

The Beckhampton avenue

The West Kennet avenue snake (with its serpentine procession of brides) proceeded to the south entrance of the henge. But whereas the West Kennet avenue has always retained enough stones above ground to place its existence beyond dispute, the same cannot be said of its counterpart, which had lost all but one of its regular members by 1730. In Victorian times, following two articles by the Rev. W. C. Lukis, it became fashionable to discuss the Beckhampton avenue as a figment of Stukeley's 'serpents on the brain' imagination.[4]

Stukeley's account is based on his own fieldwork and supported by maps and drawings. He says:

'In the year 1722, I found out this other [avenue] extending itself above a mile from the town of Abury. It goes towards the village of Bekampton.'[5] He counted over 30 stones remaining, some in pairs, and estimated that there were once '100 stones on a side 4000 cubits in length', matching exactly the West Kennet avenue, even in respect of longitudinal and transverse intervals between the stones.

It began under Cherhill Down, near Fox Covert, 'there in a low valley, near a fine group of barrows, at a like distance from Avebury town as Overton Hill'[6] (the site of the Sanctuary). From there it wound to the west of Beckhampton (near the present roundabout):

'Mr Alexander told me he remembered several stones standing by the parting of the roads under Bekhampton, demolished by Richard Fowler.'

Then to the Longstones – two exceptionally large megaliths (only one of which seemed to have been incorporated into the line). Thanks to the intervention of the Anglican curate of Avebury, 'with difficulty they were saved by applying from the farmer (Fowler) to the landowner'.[7]

They survive to this day, and are now known as Adam and Eve. Adam is 16 feet high and weighs 62 tons. He fell down between 8 and 9 a.m. on 2 December 1911, and was re-erected the following August. Immediately in front of the stone socket, Cunnington found a human skeleton and fragments of a late Neolithic beaker, reminiscent of those found against some West Kennet avenue stones.[8]

The Eve stone, 10 feet high, is perhaps the sole survivor of the Beckhampton avenue, the 100 paired megaliths which originally matched the West Kennet avenue on the other side of the henge.

Stukeley's drawing of May, 1724, shows several stones on either side of the Cove 'thrown down and half buried'.[9] Farmer Griffin broke nearly 20 stones in this part of the avenue, which continued '. . . through farmer Griffin's yard, thro' one barn that stands across the avenue, then by another which stands on its direction. Two stones and their opposites still lie in the foundations.'[10]

Approaching Avebury Trusloe, he found the marks of buried stones 'yet to be seen in the corn and others used for a new footbridge'[11] over the Winterbourne, just below the confluence. From conversations with villagers like Reuben Horsal, he dated the removal of stones from the Avebury village street (1710, 1714, 1702) and noted 'two stones [still] lie by the parsonage gate', and one lay in the floor of the house by the churchyard. Here in 1968 two of the avenue megaliths were found. They lay 'just buried under the surface' immediately north of the Bath Road, where they were

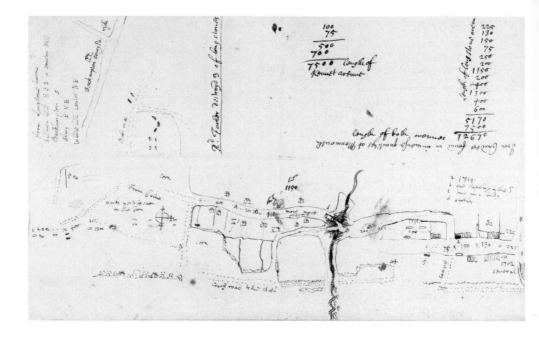

The Beckhampton avenue, as recorded in Stukeley's field notebook, 1722. Reading from left to right across the bottom, the avenue runs towards and through Avebury Trusloe, then, crossing the Winterbourne, it goes up the Avebury village main street to join the henge.

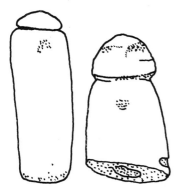

Neolithic phalli: carved chalk from Windmill Hill, and carved bone from the Trundle, Sussex.

spotted and photographed by Major Vatcher during GPO cable-laying operations,[12] and it is now certain that the Beckhampton avenue was as real as the West Kennet avenue.

The Wedding can now take place, especially since the Beckhampton avenue-serpent has a Best Man in the form of a whole collection of contemporary phallic images, including four carved chalk phalli from the nearby Neolithic camp on Windmill hill, and a ten-inch-long stone phallus, buried in a ritual pit at the Dorset henge of Maumbury rings'.[13]

On a bigger scale, the tall, thin, vertically set megaliths within the avenues and henge are acknowledged by Keiller, V. Gordon Childe and others to be phallic in intent.[14] In the avenues, they are often paired off against a broad, diamond-shaped 'female' stone, where 'the stones appear to represent male and female symbols and so suggest that 'the monuments were dedicated to a fertility cult'.[15]

There is nothing passive about any of the Avebury monuments, but nowhere in the cycle is dynamism more plainly stated than in the colossal encounter of the stone avenues at the henge. They complement the Winterbourne-Horslip meeting, while at the same time bring to the centre of the water triangle energies from the two flanking springs at Beckhampton and Waden Hill, with which they have been identified.[16]

The coupling serpents

The avenues were needed at the henge broadly for the same reason that serpents were brought to the temple of the ancient goddess, Bona Dea in Rome, whose festival was celebrated on May 1st.

The avenue snakes, equal in length and girth, wind their way towards a circular marriage dais, which lies between them. They are a summary of the total life force of bride and groom. In this, they resemble the most popular form of painted icon found in the Roman household shrines, known as Lararia. These were painted on plaster, sometimes in conjunction with a U-shaped recess. At Pompeii alone, Boyce has recorded over 90 instances where confronted serpents crawled up a kitchen wall – often in the smartest villas.[17] The altar over which the serpents met sometimes contained an egg. In many instances the serpents' tails spring from the ground or from a circular plate equivalent to the Sanctuary. Incorporated into the design one often finds a goddess: Luna, the Roman moon goddess, has been identified; so has Isis-Fortuna, and we may suppose that the Avebury henge made sense to some Roman visitors for whom the snakes and wedding ring theme served as a closely related purpose.

To the Romans the domestic snakes were 'the male and female forms of the family or clan's power of

The snakes' wedding, a Roman Lararia from Pompeii. The goddess Luna, horned and horn carrying, is in attendance on the left.

141

In the snake's jaws. Part of the South Circle, with two stones of the Great Circle beyond. The most distant stone, beyond the fence and to the right, belongs to the West Kennet avenue, the snake's throat.

continuing itself by reproduction. At every wedding, a bed, the lectus genialis, was made for the genius and iuno of husband and wife and its presence in the home was a sign of matrimony,'[18] while in many parts of medieval Europe, 'snakes were placed under the marriage bed – the virtue of them was to help conception'.[19]

As in the Avebury Cycle, these snakes came from water: 'Before the wedding day, a Bride Bath took place in a holy river or spring. For this purpose a lutrophoros was used – a special two-handled tall vessel'[20] – snake handles, meeting at the vessel's open mouth, through which the winding springwater would enter the body-pot.

Another similarity is that the Lararia serpents were not regarded as *portraits* relating to one generation, but as passing, on death, to their successors.[21] This helps to explain why the Avebury monuments were still receiving active veneration in AD 1300, long after the Neolithic peoples had vanished.

Eventually, in adapting to modern times, the genius had to give up its body, and now appears in dictionaries as 'high intellectual ability measured by performance on a standardized intelligence test, i.e. 140+ or even 180.'[22]

Opposite.
The continuing identification of male serpent with phallic club (above), and female serpent with deep bowl and hibernation basket – equivalent to the Sanctuary – appears on a fourth-century Roman diptych, used for carrying love letters.

In vestigial forms, both the spirit and the iconography of avenues and henge were maintained at English rural weddings until about 1750, where silk stockings took on the role of the avenue snakes, and a shallow bowl, or posset of sack, stood for the henge-vulva. The newly married bride and groom sat up in bed, while their young friends gathered round. Then, according to the writers of *The West Country Clothier Undone*, '. . . sack posset must be eaten and the stocking flung'.[23] The stockings, shed by the married couple prior to getting into bed, were suffused with the warmth and energy of the imminent vital moment. The onlookers took them up:

'The bride's stockings were taken up by the young men and the bridegroom's by the girls; each of whom, sitting at the foot of the bed, threw the stockings over their own heads endeavouring to make them fall on the bride or her spouse.'[24]

The girls aimed for the man's head (Peacock says his nose), the boys for the woman's. If either landed, it was a sign of their own speedy marriage. Then, 'when one of the young ladies flings the stockings full in the Bason it is time to take the posset away, which done, they last kiss round, and so depart,'[25] leaving the couple alone.

In remote areas of Britain, such as the North Yorkshire moors, a variant of the stocking rite was recorded as late as 1891: 'Only a week or two since, the bride gave two ribbons to be run for.'[26] And to this day a reference to the coupling of the two serpents may still perhaps be detected in the two ribbons traditionally stretched over the front of the bridal car outside the church or the registry office.

The henge and the serpents' union

Of all the world's animals, none has featured more consistently in human fertility symbolism than the snake, irrespective of whether the culture ascribes a positive or negative value to carnal knowledge.

Campbell and Eliade have shown that the Neolithic snakes signified 'the divine world-renovating connubium of the monster serpent with the naked goddess in serpent form',[27] and Coomaraswamy reminds us that 'the transformation of a hideous and uncanny bride represents a universal mythical pattern underlying all marriage, and is in fact the mystery of marriage'.[28]

The serpent image retained a double relevance during human coitus, because the snake's 'phallic suggestion is immediate, and as swallower the female organ is also suggested; so that a dual image is rendered which works implicitly on the sentiment.'[29]

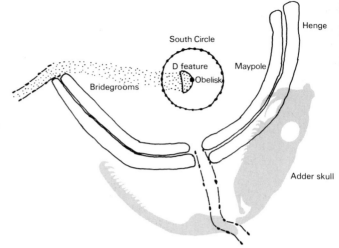

Plan of the West Kennet, female, avenue, with henge jaws open to receive the temporary male extension of the Beckhampton, male, snake, whose tip is the Obelisk Maypole within the D feature. Compare the extensible jaws of an adder.

Nor did the serpent's contact with the human life cycle end there, because 'the ancients thought these animals brought forth by the mouth, [to] exert their mighty power by the mouth only. Horus Apollo says a serpent is the symbol of the mouth. The ancients concluded this [the snake] to be the most divine of all animals . . . whom they affirmed to be the creator of the world.'[30] In the Neolithic world, 'the Snake or Dragon are one and the same Lady of the Land'.[31]

Therefore, when we move across the south causeway from the West Kennet avenue, we may be entering the female snake's open mouth – the upper jaw being the southeast bank, ditch, and corresponding quadrant of the outer stone ring, with the lower jaw being described by the southwest segment of the same ensemble. Thus the female genius came to the place appointed for copulation with her jaws ajar and 49 stone teeth showing, ready to swallow down the phallic extension of the male Beckhampton avenue.

The equating of snake and dragon *teeth* to human seed passed into the literature of classical times, which also stressed the sexual importance of the jaws that produced them.[32] At Avebury the female teeth (southwest sector) are noticeably bigger than the stones in the restored northwest sector.

It was these mighty lower-jaw tooth-stones which the barber-surgeon was extracting when he was killed. He died trying to turn the devouring female into a toothless worm, still leaving erect the first stone in the Great Circle to confront the young women as they crossed the south causeway.

The Devil's Chair

This huge sarsen, 14 feet wide and 13 feet high, has never been disturbed. It is a portal stone, and physical portals are often psychological thresholds, where truths emerge which elsewhere are seen less clearly. The stone is known locally as the Devil's chair,[33] and it *is* a chair. At a convenient height, 1 foot 6 inches above the ground, is a well defined natural ledge, wide enough and deep enough to make a comfortable seat. A sitter could be incorporated into the stone, in a natural alcove forming an inverted U-shape, 8 feet high and 4 feet wide, in the top end of which there was (and is) a large hole giving a view of the sky.

Until the 1930s the stone continued to hold a seasonal sway over the fortunes of adolescent Avebury girls, for the Devil's Chair was also known as the

The Devil's Chair, 14 feet wide, showing the seat within the U-shaped alcove, with natural vent above. Used by Avebury girls as late as c. 1900, it is placed where the West Kennet avenue meets the Great Circle.

Wishing Stone 'on which it is traditional for girls to sit on May Day Eve'.[34]

May Day Eve, the eve of the spring quarter day, was the moment in the Avebury Cycle chosen for the avenue snakes to meet – a coincidence giving point to Randall MacIver's dictum: 'Any reconstruction of a primitive culture uninformed by a knowledge of folk life would be blind in one eye and very shortsighted of the other.'[35]

The Devil's Chair is the only Avebury stone with a top aperture. It may have been selected because the pourings, whether natural or controlled, simulated the emission from Swallowhead, and baptized the initiate seated below as a true part of the Swallowhead stream and recipient of the divine liquid,[36] enabling the primary life symbol to be *joined* rather than merely observed.

The Devil's Chair also suggests that there was a place in the cosmic Avebury grandeur for the individual. The 'loss of individuality', so often advanced by modern writers as the price paid by a primitive person for the group ethos, would not be experienced as a penalty if the individual felt the society as literally One Body; so when a single initiate moved forward in the long line to take her place in the Devil's Chair, the whole Avebury civilization lived through her.

Lodged in the henge bank near the south causeway is a massive post hole, 5 feet in diameter at the top. When excavated in 1939, the remains of a prehistoric timber core were found in the base. Dr Smith has suggested that it may have had a ritual or symbolic significance;[37] perhaps it represented the serpent's eye.

Standing alone, 65 feet within the snake's Great Circle jaws, aligning with this 'Eye post', and the centre of both the inner circles, is the remaining stump of a stone called the Ringstone. This megalith was entire and erect in 1724, when Stukeley called it 'an odd stone not of great bulk. It has a hole wrought in it.'[38]

Perforated stones are known as adderstones in British folk custom, where 'according to tradition, they were generated by snakes who at certain times of the year congregated in large numbers, coiled into a living ball, and while so united, emitted saliva which hardened into stone. Their use as luck-bringers is not yet entirely extinct; when carried in the pocket they prevent eye troubles.'[39]

The Avebury Ringstone was set up deep within the monumental female snake's mouth, and may represent a perforated adderstone of a corresponding size.

Consistent with the arrangement and purpose is the certain knowledge that, in the neighbouring Cotswolds, holed megaliths of the Ringstone type were regarded until recently as 'having the power to promote fecundity in the newly married'.[40]

In Welsh tradition, the nomination of May Eve as the chief time for snakestone formation fits the Avebury festival, while the Ringstone gives massive substance to the Welsh saying, that people placing their heads together in loving conversation are 'blowing the gem'.[41] The Avebury henge is where the snake heads meet. There, in the architecture, we find them making love:

'The ancient writers had to say that in the copulation, the male (serpent) did insert his head into the throat of the female, and there emitted his seed.'[42]

But if the Avebury Ringstone/snakestone was the result of a symbolic sexual encounter, we need to show that the male snake, the Beckhampton avenue, did in fact extend its head into the female jaws. This leads us to the site of the tallest pillar stone in the entire monument, which Stukeley called the Obelisk. It once stood within the jaws, and close to the centre of the South Circle.

'*The Viper when he doth engender, loe,*
Thus downe the female's throate, doth put his head . . .'
A seventeenth-century version of the serpent copulation myth, which may be traced back to the Neolithic. In the foreground, the female is shown dying as it gives birth.

The D feature

The Obelisk, 'prostrate' in the eighteenth century, was most unlikely to have fallen by accident, since its very shape ensured stability.[1] The eighteenth-century burning pit where it was finally destroyed was 21 feet long, but no *single* stone would have been big enough to satisfy the female snake's appetite. Vast though it was, the Obelisk was dwarfed by the jaws and required support. And for that we should look at the group of stones, (culminating in and including the Obelisk), which archaeologists refer to as the D feature.

The D feature, restored in 1939, is perhaps the seasonably extended head of the Beckhampton snake-phallus, placed deep within the inner South Circle, which in turn is encompassed by the female jaws. Significantly, it was the second target of the medieval anti-paganism drive, its twelve stones being toppled

The holed stone IV of the D feature, lying on a direct line between the west (male) causeway and the Obelisk (indicated by the ribbed concrete marker). The natural hollow leading into the body of the stone may have been the object of ritual penetration.

View of part of the D feature
with the South Circle stones
behind, and, beyond, the back of
the Devil's Chair.

and buried at that time, though six were subsequently
dug up and burnt, probably in the eighteenth century.

The medieval attack on the D feature was extremely
systematic. Although most of the stones are relatively
small, (only 3 to 6 feet high when erected), all were
buried with great care, indicating that to the destroyers
they had a vital *collective* role in making the phallic
terminal knob, 80 feet wide, from which the curved
section of the 'D' swells out to meet the Obelisk at its
eastern extremity.

The Avebury henge was not sculpture in the sense of
being a finite, completed object. Instead, it was
brought to completion at *the right time* by human
participation. Only when a double column of young
men poured across the west causeway, and joined the
male avenue to the D feature on the May quarter day,
was the architectural image of sexual union achieved.

The distance from the west causeway to the Obelisk
is 900 feet – a living serpent phallus in scale with the
surrounding female organ (the wet moat), simultaneously describing Swallowhead and open-mouthed
snake.

The entire column could be seen by a spectator on the surrounding bank, and the angle made by this gigantic penis relative to the body of the Beckhampton avenue would contribute to the naturalism of the working image.

Thus, in Maytime completion, the Avebury henge illustrated 'the almost universal reverence paid to the images of the sexual parts, regarded as symbols and types of the generative and productive principles in nature, and of those gods and goddesses who were the representatives of the same principles'.[2]

When Christianity rejected this heritage, it passed naturally to the Devil. Beelzebub concludes the Winter Mumming play by presenting the emblems of the May marriage – the phallic club and the female dripping pan.[3]

Just as the Devil's Chair, set up in the female snake's throat, enabled the women to identify with the stones, so stone *IV* in the D feature may have provided a similar opportunity for the men. This sarsen lies on a direct line between the west causeway where they entered, and the Obelisk which was their probable destination.

The stone is only 5 ft 3 in. tall and 4 ft 4 in. broad – small enough to embrace. On the outer face there is a rounded concavity, running up into the stone, at a convenient height and angle for ritual penetration. Once again we are reminded that 'the hard and fast distinctions that Western thought has come to make between the inanimate and the animate'[4] did not then apply.

The androgynous godhead

In the sexual energy generated at the May festival, male and female 'lost themselves' in each other. That was their aim and it was everywhere expressed in a blurring of sexual distinction, with the ultimate union, bisexuality, being exhibited in the ritual. At the Padstow May Day ceremony, the club or Teaser pushed under the circular horse's body is both obviously phallic and clearly bisexual, being equipped with a strongly patterned female emblem strapped to the shaft, while the receiving female horse has a complementary phallic nose.

By the time the Beckhampton avenue reaches the west causeway, its commitment to bisexuality is already secure, because there it performs in the river imagery as a male emission from the *female* Swal-

Neolithic androgynous figurines from Windmill Hill (top), and from the bell Track, a wooden avenue which led across the Somerset marshes.

The Padstow (Cornwall) hobby horse is, like the henge image, brought to completion and life by human agency at the annual May Day ceremony. The bisexual motif is seen in the phallic nose of the female 'horse', while the Teaser, the phallic club, carries a female emblem.

lowhead destined to re-enter the larger version of the Swallowhead, i.e. the eastern half of the henge.

In Neolithic thought, maleness was an aspect of the universal being, or vessel, which was regarded as female. How could it be otherwise, if she truly encompassed everything? An architectural expression of this view is often found at Indian temples, where the overall form displays the feminine creative shape, based on the womb cell which contains the Lingam or male element.

In Europe, as Giedion asserts, 'this androgynous godhead . . . persisted throughout the many thousands of years from the Aurignacian period into Neolithic times'.[5]

Among the carved chalk objects found at the Windmill Hill Neolithic camp, within sight of the henge, is a figurine referred to as C.11, dating from before 3000 BC. A deep vertical groove defines the division between the thighs, and there is an irregular groove above the buttocks. Above this level swells a big globular form with no suggestion of arms or head, and no indication that they were ever broken off. On the other hand, it fits perfectly the Neolithic bisexual deity. The same combination is displayed again in figurine C.9, also from Windmill Hill, which has a deep U-shape carved into its realistic phallus shaft.

Bronze Age goddess (Denmark) with bearded male head.

English stay busk love token, sewn down the front of a young woman's dress, 1783. The traditional images – phallus, eye, flowers, inverted triangle, and heart – are all brought together.

The Avebury connection between copulating serpents and human bisexuality is reflected in Ovid's story of the wise man, Tiresias, who 'knew both sides of love'. For once, with a blow of his staff, he had outraged two huge serpents mating in the green forest; and, wonderful to relate, from man he was changed into a woman for seven years.[6]

Remote in time and implausible though this androgynous figure might seem, Aristophanes in Plato's *Symposium* was premature in pronouncing it dead:

Original nature was not like the present, but different; there was man, woman and the union of the two having a name corresponding to this double nature, which had once a real existence but is now lost, and the word androgynous is only preserved as a term of abuse.[7]

In fact this strange being, the ultimate Neolithic reality, continues to stalk through the European folk drama enthusiastically portrayed by men dressed as women.

British folklorists recognize as the most potent figure glimpsed in our tradition a woman-man, sometimes called Dirty Bet, alias the chief character in the midwinter sword dance, alias the boy-girl character who is involved in the vital ritual marriage embedded in the East Midland Wooing plays.

The dying embers of European folk performances indicate that, far from being emasculated in the Neolithic world, male attributes of physical zest and conceptualizing power were probably stretched to the limit in the course of presenting the year's greatest works, the acts of the Great Goddess. In a harmonious civilization, men *show* what women *know*.

The Obelisk

The Avebury henge action brings us back to the biggest stone, set at the head of the D feature within the South Circle (or left eye of the Goddess) – the Obelisk, which we may see as a concentration of the phallic image *and* as an embodiment of the tall Bride-Goddess, previously noted in the form of Waden Hill. We have come to the Maypole.

What helps us to recognize it as such is that, after the great stone was toppled and broken up, the villagers erected a wooden Maypole in its place and very close by. A cluster of several post holes dug for this purpose were found in 1939, and older inhabitants could recall dancing there on May Day.[8]

Part of the Solar Temple since the central obelisk 10 July 1723.

The *21-foot Obelisk (above),
drawn by Stukeley, once
functioned as a Maypole, and
after its destruction it was
replaced by a traditional wooden
Maypole of the type shown left,
where ring garlands, added to the
pole, are a stylized version of the
May Wedding bride and groom to
be seen in the painting hanging
from the window on the right.*

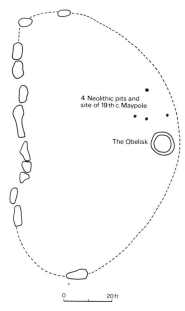

4 Neolithic pits and
site of 19th c. Maypole

The Obelisk

0   20ft

Plan of the D feature,
terminating in the
Obelisk/Maypole.

The abiding quality of the Maypole was well understood, and not least by its opponents, such as Thomas Hall, a Warwickshire pastor, who wrote in 1661:

The Rise, Root, and Original of May-Games is evil, Ergo they cannot be good. For if the fountain be bitter, the streams cannot be sweet. 'Tis a robbing God of His honour and giving it to a whore.

Who are they that delight in the Fool's filthy speeches, lascivious gestures and the man's wearing of the woman's apparel, but the profane of the world?

These men's actions do virtually and interpretively thus speak: 'O Goddess Flora, be thou our helper, the Earth is now adorned with fruits and flowers, O do thou keep them from barrenness and blasting . . . on thee we do depend, and thine honour do wee celebrate at this season of the year.'[9]

The flowery image of the communal May wedding, set within the great ditch and bank, once hung about the Neolithic Obelisk.

Indeed, there is good reason to believe that *all* Neolithic henges were designed for the May wedding. Of the Stanton Drew henge (Somerset), Stukeley wrote:

This noble monument is vulgarly called the Weddings; and they say 'tis a company that assisted at a nuptial solemnity thus petrified. Other Circles are said to be the Company dancing, and a separate parcel of stones standing a little from the rest are call'd the fidlers, or the band of musick.[10]

He went on: 'I have observed that the appellation of Weddings, Brides and the like, is not peculiar to this place, but applied to many others of these Celtic monuments about the land.'

Since marriages are made to be consummated, we can assume that love-making took place somewhere within the Avebury enclosure, and where better than under the shadow of the Obelisk?

Keiller found a group of four Neolithic pits lying a few feet from the base of the great stone. Their placing was 'unlikely to have been fortuitous'. They were 'readily distinguished' from the modern Maypole sockets 'by their oval shapes and smoothly rounded sides',[11] and they were filled with a fine, dark brown soil, which contained neither bone, flint, pottery nor burnt twigs. What were they for? The Ndembu tribe of Central Africa may provide a possible explanation of the soil in the four pits:

A senior female practitioner removes a piece of black alluvial soil from below the arch of the river source (which was built

The Spring Wedding stone, Maltegard, Denmark, c *2000* BC. *The marriage takes place within a plaited ring. The man offers his energy to the woman, who is also the hole in the ground.*

to symbolize the man-woman union). This earth is put in the village shrine, and after the bridal night, the soil is rubbed into the bride and groom, and fragments of it are scattered on the threshold of every hut in the village inhabited by a married couple, and means 'that the couple now love one another properly and the instructress wishes to join all the married people in the village with that same love'.[12]

We still use something similar ourselves, for the same purpose, and call it wedding cake.

Lovemaking in the fields as a means of promoting their fertility has been a persistent custom in many parts of Europe,[13] and at the root of these practices is intertwined the identification of woman with plough-land, phallus with plough, and sexual intercourse with working the land.[14] Conception and birth were seen in these terms. If water was involved, so too was the land.

'Maidens have their field in their own body':[15] thus a Finnish proverb summarizes a widely held belief, and it follows reciprocally from this that the Avebury field was the body of the Bride-Goddess, and a pit dug there would be the concentrated epitome of 'the womb of the Earth'.[16]

The henge earth was regarded as *the* Bride, held in common by all the young men just as, today, the Akamba of East Africa make love to a common Earth Wife prior to human marriage:

'A small hole is scooped out of the ground, and each of the initiates in turn has to ejaculate into the hole which represents the vagina.'[17]

The North Circle Cove's surviving horn, the only stone in the monument running up to a sharp point, was originally matched, according to Aubrey, by a similarly shaped stone on the right, forming a three-sided figure. The horns of consecration (opposite) found at Mallia, Crete, represent another version of the schematized bull horns, one of the basic images of Old European religion.

Distantly related to this behaviour was the pouring of libations of milk and whisky into the ground at eighteenth-century Scottish May Day ceremonies.[18]

The mating which perhaps took place in the Avebury South Circle was noted by the goddess for, as we have seen, the circle represented her left eye. She looked to the future, and like the Voice from the Well in George Peele's *Old Wife's Tale* (1595), was heard to murmur:

> Comb me smooth, and stroke my head;
> And every hair a sheaf shall be,
> And every sheaf a golden tree.[19]

The North Circle ox

Turning now to the concentric northern circles and the Cove, we find no local traditions to draw on. King Charles II commanded Aubrey 'to dig at the bottom of the [Cove] stones, to try if I could find any human bones, but I did not doe it'.[20] Two hundred years later, A. C. Smith did do it, and instead of human skeletons he discovered 'many bones of ox'.[21]

The ox image pervades the New Stone Age and the Avebury Cycle. Ox bones were found in the core of Silbury Hill; carved ox phalanges lay in the West Kennet long barrow chambers; from the long barrow's

forecourt ox the goddess arose at Candlemas; ox bones covered the sacrificed youth in the Sanctuary; an ox skull lay in the West Kennet avenue ritual pit. Everywhere the Great Goddess went, the ox was bound to follow, because 'its sacrifice incarnated the fecundity of the earth'.[22] In every sense, the ox was the chief power in Neolithic farming – providing meat, hides, milk and the strength to plough the land for cereal cultivation. The Cove ox bones reveal the operation of that impulse common to all religions – the sacrifice at the right time of what is most highly valued.

There is plenty of British evidence to link ox sacrifice with May Day. In Elizabethan England, the Maypole was preceded into the enclosure marked out for the May fertility rites by 'six young maidens, leading a fine sleek cow, decorated with ribbons and flowers, its horns tipped with gold'.[23]

English youths 'delighted' in blowing 'large cow-horns' on May Eve, keeping John Aubrey awake all night at Oxford.[24] On May Day in Wales, it was customary 'to throw a calf into the fire when there was any disease among the herds'.[25] And in nineteenth-century Ireland the ox continued to hold an important place in May Day ceremonial; the cattle were still

Stylized stone oxen from the circles of Aquorthies, Midmar, and Ardlair, where the architectural image, recumbent, is the dominant feature of the circles.

The Dorset Ooser.

singed along the back with a wisp of straw and driven through the hot May Fire embers.[26]

Now throughout the Avebury Cycle we have seen how the chief characters in the religious drama have been rendered as architectural images. So where, by the Cove ox bones, may we find the architectural ox? The answer may lie in the form of the Cove itself. The three stones were probably recognized as the horns and skull of the divine ox.

The head stone is 16 feet broad. The horns (one of which fell in 1713 and was broken up)[27] were both 8 feet wide and 16 feet tall. The surviving horn is now the only stone running up to a sharp point in the entire monument, and if not worked into this shape,[28] it was presumably selected for a place of honour *because* of it.

Professor Gimbutas writes: 'The schematized bull horn represents one of the basic philosophical ideas of Old European religion.'[29] Passed on to Minoan Crete, the stone 'horns of consecration' poke into the sky at Knossos, Palace of Minos, where they were regarded as 'the symbol of the active power of the earth's motherly form, traceable from the Neolithic period'.[30]

At the Cove, 'the Bull became the altar of its own sacrifice',[31] which in many instances may have involved castration rather than death, since the clear evidence of plough teams at work in the vicinity 'implies a knowledge of castration'.[32]

The North Circle participants, then, possibly included bullocks and heifers, entering via the north and east causeways – some to be killed, some castrated, some mated, and all to be blessed in the new fire. On this interpretation the North Circles would have a function complementary to the South Circle, and, (when we consider the high esteem in which cattle are often held by primitive people), equally sacred.

The nature of the relationship between the Avebury people and their cattle may have approximated to that of the Nuer tribe (Sudan), where 'the largest and finest ox is regarded as guardian genius, and they refer to this beast by the same name as they assign to the conception of a Supreme Being. . . . Married Nuer women use cow names among themselves. When a boy is initiated his father gives him in sign of his manhood an ox or a bull calf which will later be castrated.'[33]

The youth now enters through this ox into a new kind of relation with God, the guardian spirits of his family and lineage and the ghosts of his ancestors . . . this ox is a direct means of communication with the spirit world – a point of

158

meeting with a sacramental character. The ox-name of the youth is taken from the particular physical attributes of the ox. Even after the ox has been sacrificed, bartered for wedding, or died, the man retains the name.[34]

Tantalizing fragments exist in the British oral tradition which indicate that here too the ox role was formerly mimed by a man:

> *My name is Captain Calf-tail, Calf-tail.*
> *And on my back it is plain to be seen.*
> *Although I'm simple and wear a fool's cap*
> *I'm dearly beloved of a Queen.*[35]

A comparable degeneration from the 'once triumphant horn of plenty, fertility and power, to that of a symbol of scorn' is identified by Dewar in the horned mask known as the Dorset Ooser.[36]

The harmonizing of acts performed on cattle and people is revealed by an Irish account of a 'custom on May morning at sunrise to bleed the cattle and taste the blood, mingled with milk. Men and women were also bled and their blood sprinkled on the ground.'[37]

The Neolithic stone ox, lying within a stone circle, can still be seen at Arbor Low henge, Derbyshire (Central Cove) and at several Scottish sites including

Under this possible image of a recumbent ox, cut on the Cove horn stone, quantities of ox bones were found.

Midmar, Sunhoney, Aquorthies and Ardlair. In Scotland, the ox trunk was apparently laid recumbent – a stone 'always large, often impressively so',[38] flanked by two upright members (head and tail) and with two 'leg stones' set at right angles to the body.

In almost all the Scottish examples, the ox head and foreleg lay closer to the centre of the circle than the hindleg and tail.[39] This preference may be related to the Bryn Celli Ddu discovery, where the carcass of a real ox was buried 'with its head twisted round towards the entrance of the tomb', and therefore towards the centre of the small henge which lay beneath that barrow mound.[40]

The massive scale of the Avebury Cove ox head is combined with smaller images of the complete animal. On the southwest face of the 'skull' stone, a pattern of natural bumps and crevices creates an image of a sitting ox calf, which may help to explain the selection of this particular stone from the large number available.

The inner surface of the same Cove stone appears to carry an engraved ox head design and a carved drawing of a whole beast, lying on its back with legs extended, immediately above the spot where ox bones were deposited in the ground. Prehistoric art and real cattle were never far apart. Nor is it easy to separate the Neolithic ox from the Great Goddess, for they were interchangeable terms. Holy Cow was holy in the ancient world because she was God.

In Egypt the Great Cow was the goddess Nut.[41] Similarly, the Cretan goddess was symbolized by a pair of horns, [42] and the rhyton, the ritual vessel shaped like a bull's head, got its name from Rhea, Great Goddess of the Earth,[43] whilst Taurica Dea, otherwise known as the goddess Artemis, was identified with a bull symbol. When Greek and Roman authors referred to Juno as 'ox-eyed' they meant exactly what they said. To them, the Great Goddess had the eyes of an ox, just as the Avebury henge goddess held the image of her own ox head in her north eye Cove.

The Cove's surviving horn stone contributes notably to the ox-as-goddess theme. A huge pair of her natural stone eyes can be seen rising from the ground on the outer face, in that slanting manner previously seen rendered on West Kennet avenue stone 25S and subsequently employed in the boring of 'eyes' into many Bronze Age pygmy cups. (The diagonal possibly refers to the course of the rising sun and moon.) On the Cove horn the lower 'eye' is half buried, while the

upper is entirely visible, measuring 3 feet across. The sarsen between and around these eyes is heavily pitted, whereas the 'eye rings' are notably smooth and raised above the generally rock level. A lithological accident had given them a higher quartz content, but can we avoid the conclusion that this striking configuration was specially selected to form part of the ox centrepiece, matching the long goddess-with-eye motif, which stands out so dramatically on the West Kennet forecourt ox leg, stone 44 (see p. 59).

The goddess's eye motif and the Cove horns. The ascending eyes, with the lower partly submerged in the turf at the left hand corner, parallel the eyes on stone 25S in the West Kennet avenue (p. 86), and on many Bronze Age pygmy cups, such as the one (opposite) found in a neighbouring barrow. Like sun and moon, the eyes come up from below.

The world garden

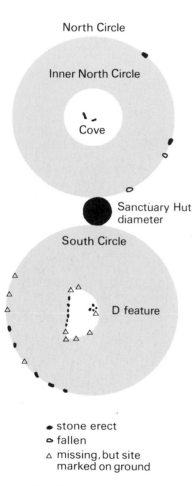

North Circle

Inner North Circle

Cove

Sanctuary Hut
diameter

South Circle

D feature

- stone erect
- fallen
- △ missing, but site
  marked on ground

Plan of the two inner circles of the henge separated by a 65-foot gap – the precise diameter of the Sanctuary – shows careful reference to other monuments in the complex.

The love sacrifice

The more we look at the henge circles, North and South, the more suitable they and their settings appear for the May marriage, yet the greater seems their integration with the surrounding monuments.

This is partly a matter of common proportions. For example, the North and South Circles at the henge are set 65 feet apart, so that the Sanctuary hut and the Silbury fence (primary mound) would both fit exactly between them, while the inner North Circle shares a 130-foot diameter with the outer ring of the Sanctuary.

At every Neolithic feast there was a place set for Death, and within the Avebury henge Dr Smith found evidence for 'the close relationship between death and fertility'.[1] She specifically refers to the similarity in form of the South Circle D feature to the long barrow façade, which have in common a 65-foot run of continuous stones set in an 80-foot span. As Professor Clark rightly says, 'The idea that life proceeds from death . . . may easily have been combined with fertility cults.'[2]

This correspondence was partly based on a fact of life clearly understood in British folk songs, where the decline and fall of the male member is a standard theme:

As I was walking out one morning, I met a buxom lass
Going to a dairyman, she had a field of grass,
It grew between mountains, at the foot of a spring,
She hired me to cut it down while the birds did sweetly sing.

With courage like a lion I entered in the field,
I'll mow your meadow down before that I do yield,
Before I'd mowed a rood of grass my scythe it bent and broke,
She said, My man, you must give in, you're tired of your work.[3]

Evidence of the most extreme form of human sacrifice may be contained in the prehistoric urn full of human bones found in 1880 by Mr Pratt, buried within the henge South Circle.[4] The death of a young man is faintly echoed in the Scottish May custom recorded in 1794 at Callender, Perthshire:

A big oatmeal cake is cut up into portions, one being blacked with charcoal from the fire. The pieces are then put into a bonnet, and everyone, blindfolded, draws out a portion. Whoever draws the black bit is the devoted person who is to be sacrificed to Baal, whose favour they mean to implore, in rendering the year productive of the sustenance of man and beast, although they now pass from the act of sacrificing and only compel the devoted person to leap three times through the flames.[5]

These ceremonies often took place within a henge type enclosure dug afresh annually on the moors:

'They cut a table in the green sod of a round figure, by casting a trench in the ground of such circumference as to hold the whole company.'[6]

The Celts called the May festival La-Bel-Taine, meaning the Day of the Sacred Baal Fire, and in Ireland the sacred fire was lit at Tara (a temple strongly resembling the Avebury plan). This act reflected the natural quarter day bonfire – sunrise at 70° east of north – the direction in which the Avebury Cove horns point. We should also recall that, seen from Swallowhead, this sunrise appears over the Waden Spring confluence K2, creating a prophetic enactment of the only other occasion in the year when this occurs – the longed-for August 8th quarter day, the start of harvest.

The henge and Silbury

The henge looked forward to harvest, and in the monumental cycle that meant Silbury Hill.

The Silbury top terrace repeats the henge shape. It was raised to that pregnant height from below ground, which may explain Atkinson's 1968 discovery of a curious ring ditch lying concealed *beneath* the chalk hill, which had a maximum diameter of 400 feet (WS-K2 × 1) – a very appropriate figure, because both the Lammas *and* the May Day full moons, seen from Silbury, rise over the 400-foot-long Waden stream. The 400-foot ditch '*completely buried beneath the present* [chalk] *mound*, was not even suspected until the new tunnel cut through it in 1968, just at a point where it ends at a causeway or entrance gap'.[7]

The Avebury henge also has causeways or entrance gaps. The hidden Silbury 'henge' is 20 feet deep and has vertical unweathered sides.[8] This means that it was refilled almost immediately on digging, with the same careful network of radial and concentric walling, and with fine rubble packed into the interstices, as was used through the chalk mound. The great Hill-Womb-Eye therefore rose directly from a symbolic Avebury ditch,

Avebury henge	feet	Silbury	feet
Bank diam.	1302 (SH-K1 × 20)	Height of Hill	130.25 (SH-K1 × 2)
Central area diam.	1104 (SH-K1 × 17)	Length of moat	1104 (SH-K1 × 17)
Gap between inner circles	65 (SH-K1)	Wattle core fence diameter	65 (SH-K1)
Ringstone to S. Circle circumf.	65 (SH-K1)	West causeway width	65 (SH-K1)
Centre Cove to S. Circle burial	520 (SH-K1 × 8)	Chalk mound diameter	520 (SH-K1 × 8)
Obelisk to Cove	400 (WS-K2)	Hidden ditch berm diameter	400 (WS-K2)
S. causeway post to centre 4 pits	400 (WS-K2)		
Diam. of bank NW to SW corners	1302 (SH-K1 × 20)	Diam. top terrace, NW to SW corners	130.25 (SH-K1 × 2)

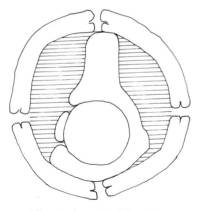

The Avebury Wedding Ring compared with the Silbury Harvest Goddess. Common measurements reveal the underlying identity of Bride and Mother-to-be.

helped also by the central wattle fence which was the same diameter as that of the Sanctuary hut. Silbury grew from the accumulation of springtime images.

That is why the long axis of the Silbury moat (the squatting mother image) exactly matches the maximum diameter of the area bounded by the henge moat – 1104 feet.

In referring to the Silbury long axis, we should recall that its east-west alignment corresponds to sun and moon positions at the equinoxes, when night and day are of equal length – a concern for balance also demonstrated at West Kennet long barrow, and by the Sanctuary's location east of Swallowhead. Between them they cover the 10° span of the lunar equinox, the long barrow axis denoting 85°N. (lunar north stand-still), and the Swallowhead-Sanctuary line marking 95°N. (the lunar south extreme) – important evidence for the lunar commitment running through the Cycle.

Consistent with this pattern, we find that the centre of the henge lies due east of the Horslip-Winterbourne confluence. Furthermore, the distance *between* the confluence and the henge, reading along the axis, is 1104 feet, or the length of the Silbury long axis again!

South Circle Neolithic pits, with modern markers, were dug near the Obelisk, from which can be seen the top of Silbury Hill (at left of the telegraph post). A visual link between Maypole and Pregnant Mother.

Here is the mathematics of maternity, where multiples of the chosen river lengths define the east–west equinoctial pivot.

The maternal aspect of the English May festival was kept up in some districts till the late nineteenth century.

'A large china doll in a blue frock was arranged in a sitting position on a little ledge in the centre front of the garland [a bell-shaped, light wooden frame of graduated hoops, four feet high, covered with flowers],' making the 'Mother Earth shape known from corn dollies'. The china doll was known as the Lady. It was understood that the 'garland was her garland, carried in her honour'. Her human counterpart was an older girl, nominated as the Mother.[10]

From the Avebury obelisk, one can plainly see the top of the Mother Hill Silbury, showing above the sloping head of the Waden Hill daughter. To underline the connection, a solitary stone, formerly 9–10 feet high, was erected within the henge South Circle, in a direct line between the Obelisk and the visible Silbury summit, and at a distance from the Obelisk of 130.5 feet, a distance which *precisely equals the height* of Silbury Hill.

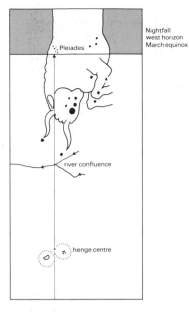

Nightfall
west horizon
March equinox

Pleiades

river confluence

henge centre

Taurus rising over Avebury.

The constellation Taurus rose due west of the henge at the time of the spring equinox in 2600 BC, forming a starry counterpart to the Cove, and perhaps recognized as such by the Avebury builders:

'In all the ancient Zodiacs, Taurus is the beginning sign, and marked the vernal equinox from about 4000 BC to 1700 BC.'[11]

Since Taurus moves backwards into the sky, the first part of the constellation to appear is the star cluster known as the Pleiades. In 4000 BC, when the farming communities of Britain were achieving cultural identity, the only stars in the group visible at dusk on 21st March were the Pleiades, including the brightest member, Alcyone.

Consequently Alcyone, riding high on the Bull's back, was widely adored as the centre of the universe and the start of all things. Alcyone, the greenish-yellow star, became the first star in the systems of lunar mansions, which all predate the solar zodiacs. Alcyone was also the Central One of the Arabs, Temennu, (the Foundation Stone) of the Babylonians,[12] and in 2600 BC, when Avebury's construction was being considered, the Egyptians were watching for Alcyone to herald the start of spring.[13]

As the year 2600 BC approached, the movement of the stars relative to the solar year caused equinoctial attention to run to the Bull's head, defined by the Hyades star cluster, where it probably focused on the great red giant, the first magnitude star Aldebaran, the Bull's eye.[14] The importance of the star in connection with the henge, and in particular with the Cove, lies in the practice, found throughout the ancient world, of seeing recurrent stellar events as living images, the counterparts of happenings on earth.

The garden

In sum total, the human design practised annually at the Avebury henge made a new world, and made it according to a standard mythological pattern. 'Myth' says Kerenyi, 'is the story of beginnings',[15] and the oldest mythical beliefs state that 'the world not only originates from, but consists of, and returns to water, on which the earth floats'.[16] Following the dissolution or flood, the new earth, 'conceived by primitive man as a flat disc, rose up through the waters from the floor of the universe', and upon emerging continued to be 'encircled by waters, unmeasurable to man, and extending to a junction with the sky'.[17]

Hence the importance of the deep Avebury moat, and the primary quality of the events staged in the henge (world-island) which the moat enclosed.

Knowledge of this idea comes to us by many paths, including that of garden symbolism, for as Wilkins says: 'The history of the miniature world-garden in the world-lake has been traced back to the temenos of the primitive spring fertility rites.'[18]

The medieval clerical authorities, while tearing up the rosary of sacred stones surrounding the Avebury world-island, could not prevent the old image seeping into their own picture of the Virgin Mary in the Rose Garden, consummating the mystic marriage with Christ.[19]

The same continuity is expressed in the anonymous medieval poem, *I Sing of a Maiden*:[20]

The Garden of Paradise is here a Christian version of the henge's world-island, with the serpent-dragon, bottom right, not worshipped but dead.

> *I sing of a maiden*
> *That is makeless,[21]*
> *King of all kinges*
> *To her son she chose.*
>   . . .
> *Mother and maiden*
> *Was never none but she;*
> *Well may such a lady*
> *Godes mother be.[22]*

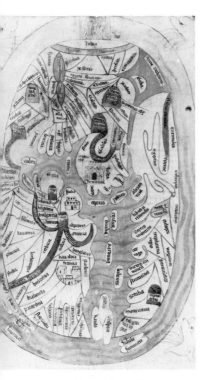

The world as island. In the moat-ocean of Higden's fourteenth-century map, analogous to the deep Avebury moat, Adam and Eve appear at top with the serpent.

She *chooses* God 'as one might a lover, and God is both her lover and her son'.[23] The mystery of the unified male Trinity is here seen patterned upon the Neolithic triple goddess.

The poem also presents the paradox, typical of the Age of Myth, whereby the positively ordered, endless sequence of necessary acts is suffused with a mysterious tranquility. Careful preparation, and the rhythmic gradualness of the action, are essential to the engendering of this quality. In the Neolithic, 'a smooth transition from one phase to another spelled happiness'.[24]

Proper arrival brought absolute completeness. Thus, in one view, the two avenue snakes merged in the henge ditches to form the sum of all snakes, the single ultimate serpent, 'biting its own tail, which symbolized the earth, surrounded by the world river',[25] and perhaps recreated on the henge bank in the following manner, as described by an observer of Irish customs:

'The circular serpent-dance has been practised from the remotest antiquity. At the great long dance held on May Day, all the people held hands . . . and simulated the sinuous curves of the serpent.'[26]

In England, the transformation of a pair of snakes into a single ring is the principle accomplishment of the Abbot's Bromley Horn Dance, Staffordshire, which is enacted every year.

The serpent in the world garden reminds us that, although Christians may have expelled themselves from Eden with their masochistic belief in Original Sin, 'there was the plain fact, supported by theologians and repeated by geographers and voyagers that the original Garden of Eden, spun bud of the world,' still existed though closed to all men by 'thunderous waters, a high wall, and a gate of flame'.[27]

The annual marriage

An attempt to reconstruct the proceedings at the Avebury Wedding involves trying to establish the Neolithic concept of marriage and of conception.

Stone Age people who have survived into modern times display a very wide range of customs and beliefs on these subjects, so we cannot graft bits of anthropology onto the henge in the name of a monolithic orthodoxy which does not exist.

Yet it would be equally foolish to overlook what primitive peoples *do* have in common in their attitude to sex and marriage, since these general rules throw some further light on the Avebury practices. Professor Evans

The serpent dance, of extreme antiquity and widespread distribution. Terracotta figurines from Palaikastro, Crete, c. *1400* BC.

Pritchard, in his *Position of Women in Primitive Societies*, offers a convenient summary:

(1) There is plenty of lovemaking, but no romantic love.
(2) There are no unmarried adult women.
(3) Every girl finds a husband, and she is usually married at what seems to us rather an early age.
(4) Polygamy is always permitted, and in varying degrees practised.
(5) Custom also enables widows to remarry without difficulty.[28]

Traces of these patterns persisted in the remoter parts of Ireland till the eighteenth century, and led many English visitors to misinterpretations, as in Wood-Martin's statement that 'very little attention was paid to the tie of matrimony'.[29]

But the same writer hastens to correct the impression of total randomness:

'The rude and unpolished part of the people who despised the discipline of the Church nevertheless very religiously observe their matrimonial contracts for the space of ONE YEAR, and think they may then lawfully dissolve them.'[30]

One year! In one year the corn dolly turns from Maiden to Mother to Hag, with the procession of the seasons and the farming year. The Neolithic goddess lived on a yearly cycle, and gave every incentive for the Neolithic population to order all aspects of their lives, including matrimony, on the annual pattern. (Conversely, there would be a pronounced disinclination to enforce lifelong monogamy against the grain of the yearly myth.)

The fullest written accounts of Irish yearly marriages relate to the great gatherings held at Teltown, Co. Meath. Teltown was known by the local inhabitants as 'the oldest place in Ireland except Tara', and was named after the legendary queen, or goddess, Tailtiu. There, among the Neolithic monuments, 'Man and Woman joined hands by blind chance, and were obliged to live with each other for a year and a day'.[31]

O'Donovan makes it clear that large numbers of men and women were involved on these occasions.

The principal monument on the site, Rath Dubh, resembled a henge: a circular area 112 paces in diameter, surrounded by a ditch, beyond which (until removed in the early nineteenth century), stood a massive concentric embankment.[32] Like the Avebury henge, it lay close to a river, and while the Avebury river leads towards Silbury, the ancient name for the Teltown river was Selesig.[33] At the end of a year:

It has been said that in pagan times those who contracted a Teltown marriage might cancel their contract if so disposed, by simply marching up the nearby mounds (the knockans), and turning their backs upon one another.[34]

The monument makes and breaks the marriage, the active arbiter of human destiny. Perhaps these coincidences permit a provisional connection between Teltown and original Avebury behaviour.

Conception

The Teltown water focuses attention once more on the water in the Avebury ditch, reached with such immense labour, impelled by the ancient belief that human life had its origin in water.

The human foetus was believed to have 'begun life in water'. Even today, 'there are people in Europe who believe children "come" from pools, springs and rivers . . . before being thrust by magic into their mothers' wombs'. Sometimes the agency of water animals (fish, frogs, swans) is invoked in the transference process, whereas 'the human father merely legitimizes such children by a ritual (including copulation) which has all the marks of adoption'.[35]

In West Meath the lack of emphasis on paternity was retained until well into the nineteenth century. All married women called themselves by their maiden

names, and in order to establish a two-way relationship with the life-holding water, 'a plaine countrey bride' in eighteenth century England 'must weep shoures upon her marriage day – by vertue of mustard and onions if she cannot naturally dissemble'.[36]

For the embryos to rise from the curving Avebury moat and become implanted in the young women, the new crescent moon was an encouraging catalyst. This belief endured well into historical times: 'No couple chuses to marry except with a growing moon,' wrote the minister of South Ronaldsay in 1795.[37]

The first quarter moon, shaped and growing like ox horns, thin as the henge moat, hung over the ceremonies in a state of Becoming (as distinct from the full moon's Silbury achievement).[38] Of the Avebury monument we may say with Eliade: 'These waters and snakes achieve that paradox of being, at once themselves and something other – in this case the moon.'[39]

Far from being a special case, the connections remained orthodox throughout antiquity, and are plainly stated in the Orphic Hymns:

(To the Moon)
Here, Goddess queen, diffusing silver light,
Bull-horn'd, and wand'ring thro' the gloom of Night,
Female and male, with silv'ry rays you shine,
and Now full-orb'd, now tending to decline.
Mother of ages, fruit producing Moon. . . .

The world garden as it appears on the twelfth-century porch of Great Rollright church, Oxon. Surrounded by chevrons (symbolizing water) and mythical beasts, and containing the all-engulfing serpent, budding solar flowers, and embryos of life, it offers a working magical image comparable to the henge. Under this portal, marriages took place.

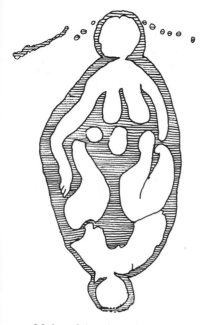

Male and female combine to form the cosmic egg. Old Stone Age union of two engraved figures from Laussel, Dordogne, France.

(To Proserpine)
All-ruling Virgin, bearing heavenly light,
Horn'd, and alone desir'd by mortal kind;
O vernal queen whom grassy plains delight,
Sweet to the smell, and pleasing to the sight;
Whose holy form in budding fruits we view. . . .

In Celtic tradition the May quarter day was often called Luan (New Moon) Lae Bealtaine,[41] and the tradition of women calling out to the growing horns was carried on in the last century on the Berkshire Downs:

New Moon, new moon, I hail thee!
By all the virtue of thy body
Grant this night that I may see
He who my true love is to be.[42]

So when today's Sudanese women raise their arms in the spring fertility Cow Dance, they hold up the snakes, the ox horns themselves, *and* the horns of the crescent moon all together, and all at once.[43]

The wedding dance
We can be sure that dancing played an important part in the Avebury ceremonies, if Neolithic Africa is any guide:

Dancing takes to a large extent the place which prayer occupies in (modern) European religions, representing the power of supernatural influences which enfold them, the ecstacy of joy in life, of youth and strength and love – all the deeper and more poignant feelings, so far beyond expression by mere words.[44]

In the Middle Ages, English villagers still knew something of this, for 'there was always one leader of the dance, generally a woman, who marked the time with a little bell'.[45] 'The woman who leadeth the dance be said to have the devil's bell on her for the Devil, hearing the sound, is easy in his mind and saith: "I have not lost my cow, she is safely mine." '[46]

The dance went on, the Great Carole or Round Dance being accompanied by the praises sung to the magical hawthorn Tree-Woman,[47] and to the Sacred Lady of the well or spring.

The last tinklings of this Avebury Maytime snake could have come from a little eighteenth-century rumbler bell found in the ditch during excavation.

Who danced around the bank? Probably the entire congregation, with the exception of those men and women who were snaking their way up the two avenues. By midnight, the two snakes' heads, we may speculate, had crossed their respective causeways, and begun the South Circle rites.

For the Brides, the rites probably included the Devil's Chair ceremony, and a descent by the carved steps into the embryo-filled moat. (This immersion finds its parallel in the former custom of pulling a rope – snake? – through a stream, and then through a field at the May festival.) Around the bank the dance rippled on and on, while the Beckhampton men moved in procession to meet the D feature, the Obelisk, and a woman each, while maintaining the shape of the overall figure.

By dawn, perhaps the virginal blood on the South Circle grass was balanced by blood and flame from the North Circle oxen and a rising solar fireball. Absorbing power from the sacred vulva-ground, the lovers bestrewed the grass, eventually to arise and wash their faces in the dew.

Belief in the special efficacy of May Morning dew was general in Britain till *c.* AD 1650. Thomas Henshaw's 'Observations and Experiments upon May Dew', reported in the *Philosophical Transactions of the Royal Society*, 1665, indicates something of its former life-giving properties:

From wedding to birth: Two coupling figures on the left, a mother and child on the right. In this sculpt from a Catal Hüyük shrine, c. 5900 BC, the male appears as the goddess's consort and as her son. This may be one of the earliest representations of the hieros gamos, *the sacred marriage.*

If put into a long narrow vessel of glass, a substance like boiled white starch, though something more transparent, if his memory (saith he) fail him not . . . and from a pretty quantity of this gelly . . . a large Mushroom grew.

Other tubs of May dew spontaneously generated 'hog lice, millepedes, spoonfuls of green stuff, an innumerable Company of small Flyes . . . and from another Gallon jarre-glass, with a wide mouth . . . little insects with great heads, somewhat resembling Tadpoles.'[48]

With that experiment the wedding goddess prepared to depart, leaving the world to science.

But the people in the henge looked to the south, and saw the top of Silbury Hill peeping above the head of Waden Hill. Then the women, maidens no longer, knew that the long goddess could turn into the broad-hipped pregnant goddess, and that they would carry her child, because they were Swallowhead, they were Avebury, and in time, they would be Silbury Hill.

PART FOUR
The Composite Goddess

Why then, O Man, know thy selfe, and
know all things. . . . Thou hast thy Body, a
Booke of Nature, and carriest a little Modell
of the greater World continually about thee.

Samuel Purchas, *Microcosmos*, 1619

One and half miles northwest from Avebury henge, an isolated hill called Windmill Hill swells out of the chalk plain. Stukeley described it as 'a pretty round apex, the turf as soft as velvet. The air here extremely fragrant'.[1]

Despite its modest height, the view from the top is extensive. Beyond the subdued landscape comprising the middle distance, opulent downland, whose colour changes with the farming year from green to gold to fawn, can be seen rolling around the horizon to reach a high climax in the southern escarpment (950 + feet), beyond which, out of sight, lies the Vale of Pewsey.

Much closer to hand, and easy to pick out, are the Avebury henge, the stone avenues, the Sanctuary, the West Kennet long barrow, and Silbury Hill. But the earliest signs of Neolithic activity on Windmill Hill predate the West Kennet barrow by 500 years, and Silbury by over 1000 years. In fact, the site has given its name to the earliest Neolithic culture of southern England, and is the largest such camp in the country.

Windmill Hill may be said to preside over the pre-Kennet, and is lodged, visibly and uniquely, between the tributary horns. It offered a natural grandstand and commentary position, and archaeological remains left behind over a 4000-year period testify to heavy use.

The pit goddess

The earliest structure created on Windmill Hill of which evidence has been found is a curious cluster of 32 pits. They were dug c. 3700 BC,[2] and were originally about 5 feet deep and 3 feet broad – very substantial holes.

British archaeologists tend to classify holes as either *post holes*, once housing structural uprights, or *storage pits* for corn or other foods.

Because the Windmill Hill pits are so close together, and contain no traces of wood or packing stones, no one has attempted to explain them as post holes. Instead, Smith writes: 'They are best interpreted as storage pits . . . the relative dearth of archaeological content seems to indicate that most of them were

(Pages 174–175) The landscape goddess, Mother Earth, was a working reality for preliterate farming peoples. A glimpse of its truth may be seen in this airview of the downs, with the summits of Rybury (centre) and Clifford's Hill crowned by Neolithic earthworks.

refilled with clean material as soon as they went out of use for storage.'[3]

But this is incompatible with the known fact that the material in at least 12 of the pits was anything but clean. Pit 7, for example, contained dogs' faeces and an ox horn core, while pit 33 (the system of numbering follows Dr Smith's, with pit 4 the first of the group) held a complicated deposit unsuited either to functionally defined food pits or to sterile in-filling.

What seems to emerge is a purpose more in keeping with the site's generally accepted role as a cult centre – the cult of the Earth Goddess, controller of the farming year.

Windmill Hill is capped with a thin layer of Upper Chalk, and the pits pass through the bottom strata of this formation, thereby cutting precisely the same section as did the deeper holes at the Sanctuary. There, 'green-coated nodules were very noticeable at the bottom of the deeper holes'.[4]

Green stones! An extraordinary subterranean crop, which may well have been regarded as fruit from

Windmill Hill, showing the excavated parts of the three rings of the causewayed camp, c. 3250 BC, which predates Avebury henge by more than 600 years. The Neolithic Square Enclosure, returfed after excavation, lies in the right foreground. Bronze Age barrows appear on the left.

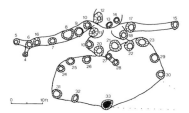

The pit goddess.

underground. For us to call a stone a fruit would be whimsical, to say the least, but we are concerned here with Neolithic attitudes. In this context, as Eliade shows, there was no division made between vegetable and mineral:

If Earth is a living, fecund Mother, all that she brings forth is at the same time organic and animated; not only men and trees, but also stones and minerals. If the Earth is likened to a Mother, all things that she carries in her bowels are homologous with embryos, or living beings in the course of gestation.[5]

Indian mineralogists still refer to emerald in its matrix as an embryo called 'The Rock is Born',[6] and in Britain the green stone silinite was 'supposed to give the faculty of prediction . . . [because] this stone followeth the moon'.[7]

Many contemporary figurines testify to the fact that, when the Neolithic Mother gave birth, she squatted on the ground and raised her arms (the upturned legs and the pulling arms are a stylization of a woman in labour).[8] Precisely this image is created by the pattern of pits on Windmill Hill.

Her head is formed by pits 12, 13 and 14;[9] her extended right arm by pits 4, 5, 6, 16, 7, 8 and 9; her left arm terminates at pit 15; her shoulders and breasts are defined by pits 10, 11, 12, 17 and 18; her great spreading haunches are described by 22–33, with the 'vulva', pit 33, being given unique attention. Pits 34 and 35 complete the lower figure.

The image has a maximum dimension of 65 feet (pits 5–35) – which it will be remembered, is SH-K1 × 1! This suggests that the Swallowhead-Kennet module, so central to the measurements of the Avebury monuments, was already in use in 3700 BC. And further inspection seems to indicate that the entire design was drawn up using simple fractions of the SH-K1 module.

The central axis of the pit goddess, running through vulva and face, is a due east-west line, and so provides a local model for the east-west Silbury goddess alignment, constructed over a thousand years later.

Apart from posture and orientation, the pit goddess declares her preoccupation with birth processes in other ways. For instance, her pear-shaped vulva, pit 33, is both the largest and the most fully furnished of all the pits, containing 31 sherds of Windmill Hill pottery (probably from two vessels), 2 worked flint flakes, 2 hammerstones, a disc of sarsen, and 14 sarsen balls weighing a total of 12 lbs.

This collection of rounded sarsens may represent a symbolic harvest child, on the verge of being born. Similar sarsen balls were also found beneath the silt of the Silbury pregnant Mother. In terms of the topographical deity, pit 33 is equivalent to the Swallowhead birth spring, and source of the Kennet (Cunnit).

Granted the special treatment of pit 33, it is still hard for us to think of holes in the ground as parts of an intended effigy. But there are many examples (the Uffington White Horse, for instance) of sculptural forms cut *into* the rock. Even nearer to hand, the quarry around Silbury Hill, which forms the watery body of the goddess (see *The Silbury Treasure*), is evidence that, to the people of the Neolithic, holes were well able to express a positive version of the deity. In fact, the Silbury Mother is the ultimate development of a long tradition of subterranean sculpture.

A desire to be close to the earth pervades all the Avebury work, and finds an echo in the English peasantry's belief, surviving into the nineteenth century, 'that Death and Birth came more easily if the dying man or the mother was laid directly upon the ground. . . . Where the floor was of beaten earth, the mother was often laid upon it in the last stages [of labour] so that she might draw strength from there.'[10]

'Within every yoni, every active World-as-Woman, is buried the lingam, the phallus, without which there would be no energy to inflate her pattern,'[11] says Rawson, and we have seen how the general principle applied to the Avebury henge, where the goddess incorporated maleness.

The same bisexuality is displayed at the Windmill Hill pits, where the squatting goddess seems to have a penis, defined by pits 27 and 28. The terminal pit 28 contained worked flints, and both holes are smaller in diameter than those arranged on the surrounding hips, to which they are as firmly attached as the Obelisk/D feature is to the henge.

The phallus appears again as part of a design carved on a small chalk slab less than 3 inches wide, usually called the Windmill Hill amulet. Buried in an adjacent ditch, and dating from *c.* 3250 BC, the chief lines show a remarkable similarity to the pit goddess layout. The vulva, hips, thighs, trunk and right arm are clearly defined. At the junction of trunk with left hip, a double line describes the phallus.

The vulva, strongly emphasized, is shewn as a slender version of pit 33, and repeats the Old Stone Age

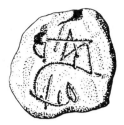

The Windmill Hill amulet, found near the pit goddess complex (after I. F. Smith).

sign for the female orifice listed by Leroi-Gourhan.[12] The figure's head is more lightly engraved than the body, but is present nevertheless.

The amulet shows a miniature version of the squatting goddess, used within yards of the pit goddess, and dropped into the earth at about the same time that the long barrow chambers were being constructed to the same plan.

The square enclosure

Almost all the themes taken up in the Late Neolithic monuments of Avebury and surroundings make their first appearance on Windmill Hill. Such is the case with the ox motif, which we have seen already, massively stone built across the West Kennet long barrow forecourt, *c.* 2600 BC, and at the Avebury Cove. The forerunner was probably a design, identical in scale and brilliant in conception, which was created, *c.* 3700 BC, at the hilltop feature known as the 'square enclosure'.

This enclosure lies 652 feet (SH-K1 × 10) from the head of the pit goddess, on a bearing 110° azimuth, and is defined by a ditch one foot wide and one foot deep. Its antiquity was confirmed by the discovery during excavation of early Neolithic potsherds, 23 pieces of oolitic limestone of the type used in the long barrow walling, and fragments of a coiled clay-daub lining to an internal hole (No. 51) closely resembling the treatment of the West Kennet avenue holes.[13]

Eleven shallow holes were enclosed by the trench. From the central hole, No. 52, a circle with a radius of 16.3 feet, 6 megalithic yards, or $\frac{\text{SH-K1}}{4}$, was probably used in setting out the overall design. In detail, the layout reveals a scrupulous adherence to the Swallowhead-Kennet module, the following fractions being employed:

Enclosure lengths	feet	meg. yards	river unit	times used
Trenches	32.65	12	$\frac{\text{SH-K1}}{2}$	4
Inter-hole distances (1)	16.325	6	$\frac{\text{SH-K1}}{4}$	9
Inter-hole distances (2)	24.4	9	SH-K × $\frac{3}{8}$	9

The measurement $SH\text{-}K_1\over2$ occurred 7 times in the nearby pit goddess, often on important lines joining terminal pits (hand or foot) to the vulva; here at the square enclosure, $SH\text{-}K_1\over2$ forms both the sides of the square and diameter of the circle which they contain.

And how familiar a length is $SH\text{-}K_1\over2$ for anyone who has made the journey through the Avebury Cycle: 32.65 feet is the diameter of the important double-posted D ring at the Sanctuary, the width of the long barrow forecourt, and the width of the Avebury Cove from horn to horn.

The last two features raise the stone ox into view, and should we be astonished to discover the same animal described by the pattern of square enclosure holes? There it lies in the ground – long-horned (holes 56–59),[14] big-nosed (49), wide-eyed (52 and 53), and massive-shouldered (48, 50 and 51). But a good Neolithic ox, seen frontally, requires a blaze, rosette, or ritual skull wound on the forehead, similar to the ritual pole-axe perforation dealt to the ox skull found in the Windmill Hill ditch.[15] The square enclosure provides this with the pear-shaped pit 54.

The white cow haunted the British imagination long after Neolithic society had vanished under patriarchy – hence the Irish folk belief:

'Sometimes on the 1st May, a sacred heifer, snow white, appeared among the cattle, and this was considered to bring the highest luck to the farmer.'[16]

Similarly, the white bull led by a woman to the medieval shrine at Bury St Edmunds was supposed to promote human fecundity.[17]

In Giraldus Cambrensis' account of the Donegal kingship ritual, where white ox was replaced by sacred white mare, the human-animal fusion, reminiscent of the square enclosure image, comes to life once more:

At Kenet Cunil (Co. Donegal) . . . the whole people of that country being gathered in one place, a white mare is led into the midst of them, and he who is to be inaugurated . . . comes before the people on all fours, confessing himself a beast. . . . The mare being immediately killed, a bath is prepared for him from the broth. Sitting in this, he eats of the flesh.[18]

In Neolithic times the white ox represented the Great Goddess in bovine form. Similarly, the square enclosure animal *was also the divine woman, squatting in the birth position, with arms raised.* To see her, one has only to move around the enclosure from the east to the west.

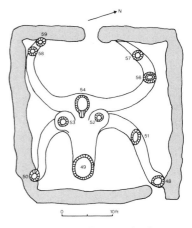

The Square Enclosure oxhead, c. 3700 BC. The 11 pits within this otherwise inexplicable site may have acted as supports for a renewable oxhead structure, 30 feet long. (Below), viewed from the west, oxhead becomes squatting goddess with arms upraised in the orante manner.

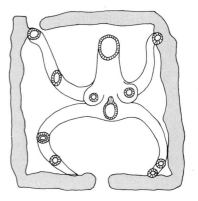

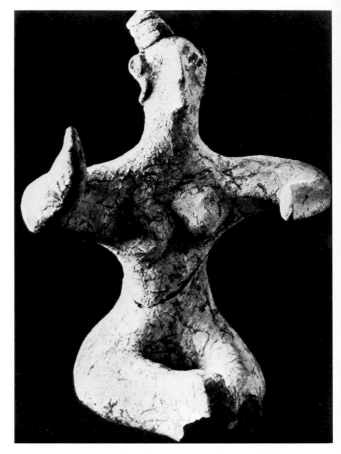

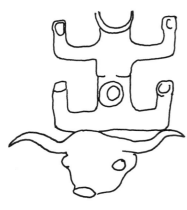

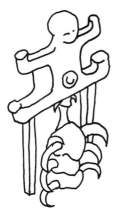

The horns become thighs, shoulders become arms, nose becomes head, eyes become breasts, and forehead blaze becomes vulva. Head and vulva, holes 49 and 54, are by far the largest, and their common long axis leads westwards between the thighs through the only certain causeway across the enclosure ditch, the point of exit from the figure of the achieved birth.

On this green Wiltshire hill we see that 'the horned altar represents the Mother Goddess herself', as it did at Gournia, Crete.[19] In ancient Egypt the Queen Mother was described as 'the cow who bore the bull',[20] while the European ox divinities, capable of human form, constituted an entire class (the Tauriformii).[21] The ox's warm breath, streaming over the Bethlehem manger, carries the same old truth, that the holy mother of God was once a cow.

During the last 5000 years a two-foot thickness of chalk has been dissolved by chemical solution from the surface of Windmill Hill, so any original shallow markings between the square enclosure holes, describing the curves of the ox-woman, would have been obliterated. It is equally possible that the inter-pit shapes were regularly traced only in highly ephemeral material, such as leaves, or blood, according to seasonal requirements. The white cow, and the mother in labour, were sunk permanently into the fabric of human life, yet perhaps not continuously revealed in full form, for just as the Irish cow was seen only occasionally, so the enclosure pits provided an empty and meaningless pattern until, through ritual conducted at the right time, the scattered holes coalesced for a while into a divine double image.

The Silbury Hill breast, so vital to the Late Neolithic harvest, lies on a direct line between the centre of the enclosure and Swallowhead, and this choice of site probably indicates a connection between the square-enclosure image and the Silbury form of the goddess (which was also conceived as an invertible image).

Placed on the southeast shoulder of Windmill Hill, rather than on the summit, the enclosure image is equidistant from the Swallowhead and Waden springs, and at a range of 11607 feet, or WS-K2 × 29. Moreover, this line from the enclosure to the Waden spring incorporates the Sambourne confluence of the Winterbourne and the Horslip brook – a circumstance which might be deliberately indicated in the structure of the enclosure trench.

The trench is in fact *two* trenches (two causeways divide the square), and the pits representing the left and right upraised hands of the goddess hold this pair of ditches aloft, perhaps showing the double waterways to the world. But this is not to deny that in orthodox mother goddess figurines the streams thus held aloft are also snakes. At the square enclosure, the snake-stream ditches are born between the goddess's legs, and run to her wrists.

The causewayed camp
Nearly 500 years after the pit goddess and the square enclosure had been laid out on Windmill Hill, an additional structure was created there. Since its discovery in the 1920s this structure has been called a 'causewayed camp' and is the largest known example in the world. It consists of three roughly concentric and approximately circular ring ditches whose mean diameters and average depths are, respectively, 1200 feet and 7 feet, 660 feet and 5 ft 6 in., and 280 feet and 3 ft 2 in.

The ditches were dug in sections, and gaps (causeways) varying in width from a few inches to 25 feet were left between one sausage-shaped trench and the next. The causeways, everyone agrees, indicate no defensive function for the enclosure, but rather, in Professor Cunliffe's phrase, 'a place where the community would meet in a group to worship the gods'.[22]

Which gods? Professors Berciu, Gimbutas, Campbell, and Glob (to name but a few) tell us that in Neolithic Europe 'the gods' means the Great Goddess, who steered the annual cycle through the seasons. And British interpreters of the Avebury monuments have approached close to the recurring mythic truth in their insistence that Windmill Hill *was* used for seasonal rites 'for a population of a fairly wide area, . . . [with] ceremonies performed to ensure agricultural fertility and celebration of harvest. . . .'[23]

Here we should recall that the outspread arms of the hilltop squatting pit goddess (pits 4–15) are physically incorporated into the innermost causewayed ring, indicating that it was she who made the year revolve.

The cyclical nature of the Earth Goddess worship 'required the throwing of objects into the ditches, and their deliberate burial by pushing some part of the inner bank over them. This process took place a number of times until the banks had been almost completely removed.'[24]

Over and over again the divinity's mythical life cycle was acted out through sympathetic sacrifice, and in the process, between *c.* 3250 BC and *c.* 2000 BC, the deposits were laid, implying (in Smith's view), not only Harvest festivals, but also 'initiation ceremonies and the exchange of seed corn and weddings.'[25]

As a result, 'an enormous quantity of archaeological material,'[26] including whole oxen, carved stones, axeheads and wheat grains, pottery and crab apples, venison and grinding stones – images of winter, spring and summer, were gathered in natural companionship. This collection is wholly consistent with the concerns of the later monuments, arranged at the foot of the Hill.

We may suppose that these later monuments took over some of the functions of the causewayed camp, and in recent years archaeologists have seen in the ditch and bank structure a prototype for the henge.[27] But the evidence also unmistakably points to continuing ritual use of the camp through to the Bronze Age and beyond.[28] (Important traces of Iron Age eye goddess worship have been found on the hill.)

Mother Earth

The progressive clearing of the woodland cover, which accompanied agricultural work from 5000 BC onwards, gradually revealed the land forms to full scrutiny. Standing on Windmill Hill in 3500 BC, the farmer could see the bare and majestic downland around the Kennet headwaters, much as we see it today. A tract of over 50 square miles is unified in a single net of converging valleys, wet and dry, with a general slope down to the Kennet from Hackpen Hill in the north, and from the high escarpment overlooking the geologically distinct Vale of Pewsey, in the south. This chalk crest forms the natural climax of the Kennet country, culminating at 964 feet in Tan Hill.

Tan Hill is the dominating feature of its thyme-scented and lark-haunted world. There is something brooding, con-templative, maternal too – yes, and protective – in that great swelling outline, that smooth and tender rounded slope, those massive, never changing proportions.[1]

That is how it struck a *Times* reporter in July 1920, and there is plentiful archaeological evidence to suggest a comparable reaction from mid-Neolithic Man, for whom, apparently, Tan Hill functioned as the maternal head to this huge, visibly coherent tract of chalk country. East and west stretch the escarpment 'arms',

Part of the chalk escarpment overlooking the Vale of Pewsey.

and a great torso and squatting legs are arranged naturally around the two springs.

To understand how such a tract of landscape could ever have been regarded as a goddess image, it is necessary to recall that *all* the earth's surface known to Stone Age farmers, ancient and modern, was viewed anthropomorphically. 'Mother Earth' was no poetic fancy, but a universally acknowledged working truth.

What the landscape around the Kennet headwaters provided was a particularly vivid, medium-scale version of this Mother Earth reality, inspiring a particularly vivid architectural response. No fewer than 27 monuments of the fourth millennium BC (including Windmill Hill camp) were arranged around the periphery of this topographical squatting goddess image, in order to define it more clearly.

Each monument can be read both as a contribution towards the composite goddess and as a monumental image in its own right. It was *within* this long established outline that the Late Neolithic ensemble was eventually to be sited.

Before examining this great chain of mid-Neolithic monuments in detail, there is more to say about the topography as a triple watershed.

From the chosen landscape body, rivers run to three different seas. The principal waterway, the Kennet, flows east to the North Sea. The head and right arm provide the headwaters of the Hampshire Avon, which feeds into the English Channel, while from the left hand (Kings Play Down), streams run westwards to the Bristol Channel and the Irish Sea.

Moreover, these facts remained part of a confused oral tradition, recorded by John Aubrey in 1648, wherein the three streams' sources were said to be located at Tan (St Anne's) Hill itself:

It is at the foot of St Anne's-hill . . . yt three springs have their source and origen; viz. the south Avon which runnes to Sarum and disembogues at Christes Church in Hampshire; the river Kynet . . . which disembogues into the Thames, and on the foot of the north side rises another . . . that runs to Bristowe into the Severne.[2]

Whether one takes Aubrey's version or the literal truth, it seems that the primary landscape figure of mid-Neolithic Britain was in contact with the three seas, sending her water to the margins of Britain.

For thousands of years after Neolithic society had been submerged under a wave of warrior-patriarchs and male sky gods, the concept of 'Kingdom' frequently retained a strong female characteristic:

'The country [was] a woman. A union between the king and the goddess of the land was an essential part of the royal ritual in ancient civilizations of the Near East.'[3] Similarly, 'The kings of Ireland were men who showed favour to, or were accepted by the Lady, who personified the realm.'[4]

This woman was of immense antiquity, pre-dating the emergence of modern Ireland from beneath the primordial waters: 'The woman who settled Ireland before the flood, as eponym of Ireland . . . is to be identified with the land that would emerge from the waters'.[5]

The goddess of Ireland *was* Ireland, and seen in this context Neolithic personification must surely also have applied to the larger British Isle, whose full-length portrait was similarly drawn in profile by the coastline,[6] and subsequently appeared as the female Britannia on the reverse of many Roman and modern British coins of the realm.

The head and arms of the composite goddess lie in the present-day parishes of Bishops Cannings and All Cannings. Thus the shared second name helps to link the image from side to side, and perhaps also from end to end, because Cannings was spelled Kening in AD 1212, and the name leads inexorably back to the river.[7] Wet or dry, the valley arteries belong to the same White Goddess who may be remembered in the name Albe (White) Cannings, a thirteenth-century form of All Cannings, where her head rests.

The monumental chain
When introducing his account of the West Kennet long barrow, Piggott wrote: 'The barrow is a member of a group of chambered and unchambered tombs concentrated in the Avebury region,' distributed in a 'rough ellipse', spaced around the headwaters of the Kennet and its junction with the Winterbourne (at Swallowhead), and 'related to the southern escarpment of the chalk overlooking Pewsey Vale'.[8]

In fact these proposed subgroups merge without a break to form the single concentration to which he alludes. Victorian antiquarians like Thurnam and A. C. Smith established by excavation that all these long barrows were built in the New Stone Age. Recent dating techniques have refined this conclusion,[9] and have shown that construction belongs to the fourth millennium BC, with units being added to the pattern over a period lasting several hundred years.

Concerning the relation between barrows and camps, Piggott writes: 'Wiltshire long barrows are the products of communities which also made and used causewayed camps, and are chronologically contemporary with these sites.'[10]

The concentration of three causewayed enclosures in one area is itself unique, and again serves to emphasize the unparalleled importance of the goddess's outline, to which they contributed.

Incidentally, the idea is sometimes advanced that causewayed camps and long barrows functioned mainly as emblems of territorial division.[11] This may or may not be true in other parts of the country, but in this instance the 21 barrows are far too closely set to make sense in such a role.

The composite goddess's intention might be brought into question if it could be shown that long barrows, other than those listed, once existed in locations which would render the profile untenable. But what is so striking about the known distribution is the clarity of the group. There seem to be no other barrows at a few miles' distance whose inclusion might confuse the figure. Piggott comments, for example, on the absence of a long barrow 'on the commanding bluff crowned by the Iron Age hill fort of Oldbury Castle'.[12]

The international tradition

In pointing to the extraordinary nature of the composite goddess achievement, we are not implying that comparable chains of buildings, consciously organized into a pictorial system, did not exist in other countries. On the contrary, it is known that 'Egyptian priests were convinced that the holy places of Egypt were linked together . . . by physical ties, sacred stones, earth and so forth'.[13]

Of Great Goddess temple complexes in Minoan Crete, Vincent Scully writes:

The landscape and the temples *together* form the architectural whole. The formal elements of any Greek sanctuary are firstly the specifically sacred landscape in which it is set, and secondly the buildings that are placed within it. . . .
In Greek architecture, the actions of buildings and landscape were fully reciprocal in meaning as in form . . . [showing us] the miracle of reconciliation between men and earth.[14]

Of the standard landscape elements in these compositions, Scully lists, firstly, 'an enclosed valley of varying size, in which the palace is set. I should like to call this the Natural Megaron.'

The Winterbourne-Kennet valley precisely fulfils this role.

Secondly, 'a conical hill, on axis with the palace, north to south'.

In the Wiltshire composite goddess, the Windmill Hill three-ring 'palace' lies due north of the conical Rybury Hill, which was specially regarded during the same period, while the Late Neolithic additions repeat the palace-cone relationship, in that the Avebury temple lies due north of Silbury.

Finally, Scully notes as a recurring feature 'a profile (of mountains or hills) some distance beyond the mounded hill but on the same axis. . . . [These] create a profile which is basically that of a pair of horns, but it may also suggest raised arms.'[15]

The Tan Hill escarpment, 4–5 miles south of Avebury-Silbury, fits the description perfectly.

As to *why* creation cones should rise in the south relative to 'palaces', the south, we have noted, marks maximum altitude of sun and moon, and it may have been considered that the land sympathetically swelled up in its symbolic conical essence.

The urge to organize large tracts of country into a dynamic image of the deity, by combining topographic and architectural features, is typical of the Great Goddess cult in its mature form. Far from being a freak, the Wiltshire composite goddess should be seen as one brilliant exposition of an international orthodoxy.

In passing one might observe that this common inheritance is possibly reflected in some resemblances between the categories of Greek Bronze Age temple components identified by Scully, and the Late Neolithic assemblages, which make up the composite goddess's internal Avebury organs:

Greece	*Avebury*
Labyrinthine passage	West Kennet and Beckhampton avenues
Open court	Avebury henge
Columned Pavilion	Sanctuary
Pillared Cave	West Kennet long barrow (modified)

To sum up, the human image, underlying the bulk of prehistoric art and architecture, also shaped the communal experience of monumental groups, and entire tracts of country.

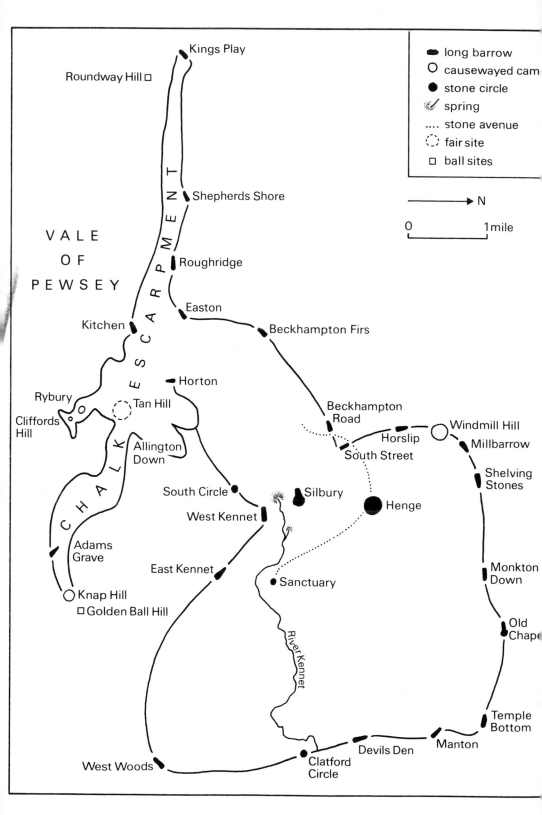

long barrow
causewayed cam[p]
stone circle
spring
stone avenue
fair site
ball sites

N

0   1 mile

Kings Play

Roundway Hill □

VALE
OF
PEWSEY

CHALK ESCARPMENT

Shepherds Shore

Roughridge

Easton

Beckhampton Firs

Kitchen

Horton

Rybury   Tan Hill

Cliffords
Hill

Beckhampton
Road

Windmill Hill

Horslip   Millbarrow

Allington
Down

South Street

Shelving
Stones

South Circle   Silbury

West Kennet   Henge

Adams
Grave

East Kennet

Monkton
Down

Sanctuary

Knap Hill

Golden Ball Hill

Old
Chape[l]

River Kennet

Temple
Bottom

West Woods

Clatford
Circle

Devils Den   Manton

English archaeologists who deny this in the name of knowledge should watch more television – programmes like Granada's 'Vanishing World'[16] – to hear the living voices of prehistoric people in the Sudan, New Guinea, and Amazonia, saying loud and clear, as a statement of fact: 'This low-lying swamp is our Mother's groin; this dry upland her head.'

Whether or not they build monumentally, these vestigial peoples live with

... an image of the world which has taken aeons to form, where certain features, the archetypes or dominants, have crystallised out in the course of time. They are the ruling powers, the gods, images of the dominant laws and principles, and of typical, regularly occurring events in the soul's cycle of experience.[17]

The fourth dimension

To list the parts of the composite goddess is easier than to convey the quality and vast scale of the image. Stukeley experienced the same difficulty when he started work at Avebury. How, he asked, could he set down the henge in a single drawing?

The whole scope of a piece of paper is taken in at one glance, but a building or other large object exceeding the capacity of the eye, we must necessarily *go round*, step by step. As our wonder continually increases with the survey, so is the notion thereto annexed proportionally more vast as more perfect.[18]

Indeed, even a tiny female figurine that may be held in the hand cannot be viewed entire without the help of the fourth dimension, Time. Top and bottom, front and back, can never be got into a single snapshot.

Like infants engaged in a tactile and visual journey across a mother's body, those who wish to know the composite goddess must undertake a 33-mile walk. Every step is necessary to the gradual accumulation of the knowledge, and to establish rapport with the world of myth which was in slow perpetual motion. As Stukeley remarked, there is no finer ground to walk upon:

I have an infinite number of times remarked the fine breathings ... sweeter than can be imagined, saluting the nostrils most agreeably and recreating the spirits, like taking snuff, tho' fatigued in walking ... [the ground] yielding to the weight of the impressed foot, yet rebounding again with an elasticity which saves half the labour of walking, and I never yet found any sultry heats, but breezes, very inconvenient for drawing as blowing the paper about, and that in the calmest weather I ever found here.[19]

Let us pack up our papers and start to walk.

Opposite.
Map of the composite goddess. Twenty-seven Neolithic monuments emphasize the natural features and contours of the landscape, to form a 33-mile topographic image.

Compared to Britannia, this composite goddess is minute. Yet, as with all deities, her scale is essentially flexible. She is the entire Earth and a handful of mud. Similarly, she is as old as humanity and younger than tomorrow morning. She was here before the first monument was begun and after the last was completed.

(The dimensions are chiefly drawn from Grinsell's Gazeteer in the *Victoria County History of Wilts*, Vol. 1, Part 1, but wherever possible these have been checked against the results obtained from modern excavations.)

Site	GR	Orient.	Approx. dimensions (feet)	Descriptive role
1A Rybury Hill	083638	N-S	520 × 470	Crown for Tan Hill head
1B Clifford's Hill causewayed crescent	084637	N-S	260 diam.	Crown/horns for Tan Hill head
2 Adam's Grave long barrow	112633	SE-NW	130 long axis	Right wrist
3 Knap Hill causewayed camp	122636	NE-SW	650 × 430	Right hand
4 Horton Down long barrow	076658	SE-NW	132 × 36	Breast
5 South Circle	098671	N-S	261 long axis	Navel
6 West Kennet long barrow	104677	E-W	330 × 80	Groin
7 Ritual site G.55	103678		300 diam.	Vagina
8 East Kennet long barrow	116668	SE-NW	344 × 100	Thigh
9 West Woods long barrow	156657	NE-SW	120 × 66	Knee
10 Clatford Circle	061685		65?	Shin
11 Devil's Den long barrow	152696	SE-NW	230 × 130	Shin
12 Manton Down long barrow	151714	SE-NW	65 × 35	Ankle
13 Temple Bottom long barrow	148725	E-W	?	Foot

14	Old Chapel long barrow	129729 NW-SE	100 × 27	Anus
15	Monkton Down long barrow	116723 E-W	90 × 45	Buttock
16	Shelving Stones long barrow	094722 E-W	?	Buttock
17	Millbarrow long barrow	089722 E-W	215 × 55	Buttock
18	Windmill Hill causewayed enclosure	086714	1200 diam.	Hip
19	Horslip long barrow	086705 SE-NW	185 × 75	Hip
20	South Street long barrow	090692 SE-NW	138 × 55	Waist
21	Beckhampton long barrow	087691 NE-SW	225 × 120	Small of back
22	Beckhampton Firs long barrow	066677 NE-SW	135 × 35	Back
23	Easton Down long barrow	063661 E-W	132 × 100	Left armpit
24	Roughridge Hill long barrow	054657 E-W	230 × 100	Left upper arm
25	Shepherd's Shore long barrow	038661 E-W	90 × 55	Left elbow
26	King's Play long barrow	011660 NE-SW	100 × 45	Left hand
27	Kitchen Hill long barrow	066648 NE-SW	107 × 64	Left shoulder
28	Tan Hill Fair, site of	083647		Head

The perambulation

The escarpment arms

By walking eastwards from the Tan Hill head along the crest for two and a half miles, we come to a notable long barrow called Adam's Grave, of which Grigson says:

'Once you are aware of it, you always look for it, and in a way it becomes the determinator of the scene.'[1]

When Thurnam dug into the barrow in 1860, he found three or four skeletons and a leaf-shaped flint arrowhead reminiscent of the one placed on the central axis of the West Kennet long barrow forecourt.[2] According to Lewis Spence, 'All over the world the flint arrowhead is the emblem of rain. The flight of arrows symbolized the rain shower.'[3]

The play of wet and dry contrasts is seen again in the drystone 'river' walling which Thurnam discovered encompassing the Adam's Grave mound beneath the modern turf. Specially imported from the region of Bath, the thin oolite was used to create horizontal courses in the manner of the West Kennet barrow.

Stukeley remarked that 'the neat turn of the huge barrows wraps you up in a contemplation of the flux of life, a passage from one state to another.'[4] The awareness of this flux, which is the subject of the architecture, is intimately connected to the landscape. The crest hilltops are dry. No streams run. We are walking the goddess's arms, which may also be seen as ox horns. Yet their visible connection to the distant Kennet valley is reinforced by a measure of the sacred water source, Swallowhead to K1, running right down the central axis of Adam's Grave, which is 130 feet or Sh-K1 × 2.

Maximum dimensions of the other barrows in the group support the intention: Horton (132 feet), Beckhampton Firs (135 feet), South Street (138 feet), Devil's Den (130 feet), Manton (65 feet), and Kitchen (64 feet).

From Adam's Grave the causewayed camp of Knap Hill, which occupies the position of right hand on the topographical composite goddess, sticks up half a mile

further east. Established before 3500 BC, 'its skyline position may have made it an ideal place for religious and ceremonial functions,' according to Dyer.[5]

The summit enclosure is picked out by a single causewayed ditch, showing strongly on the north side. A carved chalk object found within may well be a Neolithic Mother Goddess. It has two eyes, a rudimentary head, and a deeply excavated belly-cup. Another Neolithic reference to the two eyes might also be intended by the two circular holes dug just outside the north bank. Only 1 foot apart, each was 4 feet in diameter and 2 feet deep, and both contained Windmill Hill pottery.[6]

Immediately beyond the camp 'hand', 'fingers' are naturally suggested by a small plateau, tapering to the northwest, and additionally defined around its edge by the later ditch and bank 'too slight to have been intended for defence'.[7]

On this triangular patch, a more contrived 'finger' was added in Romano-British times, showing once again the continuity of mythical interest. This took the form of 'a long artifical bank or mound that has sometimes been taken for a long barrow',[8] starting from the causewayed bank, and terminating in a

Adam's Grave long barrow defines the right wrist of the landscape goddess's escarpment arm.

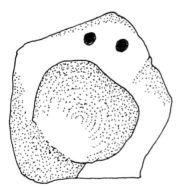

Knap Hill causewayed camp, half a mile east of Adam's Grave. Neolithic ditches and banks, separated by causeways, appear clearly on the side of the hilltop. A probable Mother Goddess figurine (below) was found inside the camp.

circular mound. The overall length was 110 feet. Beneath the circular end, Cunnington found a pit with ash and pottery.

Standing at Knap Hill, one is struck by the dramatic contrast between this downward-thrusting right arm, and the opposite position of the other limb, and inclined to wonder whether they might have had something of the same significance as the raised and lowered arms of the worshippers who carried torches in their procession around Demeter, the Great Goddess of Graeco-Roman times, swinging the life-fire up and down in paired gestures.

Golden Ball Hill – a mystery to place-name experts – stands immediately east of Knap Hill, in the right spot for such a torch or beacon. It may be relevant that, according to a nineteenth-century report, a special ball game was traditionally played by a number of boys on Palm Sunday at the nearby Martinsell Hill:

They take their positions at intervals in a line from the base of the hill to its summit, and using hockey sticks [perhaps formerly ox horns?] knock the ball in succession up the hill until it reaches and passes the summit.[9]

The correspondent does not mention the colour of the balls, but another witness adds: 'Oranges were

thrown down the slopes and boys went headlong after them. Now a few children stroll about the hill on Palm Sunday, but less than forty years ago it used to be crowded.'[10]

A futile game (though apparently preserving some of its original dangers) may be played by children, but it was certainly not invented by them. The awakening springtime ox deity, and the organized human response on which much depended, are perhaps seen here in their last rotations.

We are dealing with a goddess for all seasons. In springtime the young men took their chance around her horns, as in the Minoan bull dance. That this sport may once have been a matter of life and death can also be inferred, perhaps, from the precipitous 500-foot plunge of the composite figure's westerly 'horn tip', significantly called King's Play Down, and the adjoining field of Roundway Hill, where in 1909 'a ball game is played by a number of boys on Palm Sunday'.[11]

The dip-slope torso
Midway between the outstretched horns or arms of the escarpment, we meet the two great lobes of Allington Down, which even to our eyes look like breasts.

The breast-like contours of Allington Down, seen from Tan Hill, with the Kennet valley in the distance.

As Clark says, 'The nude does not simply represent the body, but relates it by analogy to all structures that have become part of our imaginative experience.'[12]

Even without taking note of the frequent hill-breast identification, inherited through place names like the Paps of Jura, we still 'feel close to divinity in those flashes of self-identification, when through our own bodies, we seem to be aware of a universal order'.[13]

Beneath the breasts of Allington Down lies Horton Down long barrow. Cursorily excavated by Thurnam, who mentioned skeletons, but gave no details,[14] it is tempting to regard it as just another long barrow, such is their extraordinary concentration in these parts. But the length, 132 feet, falling within two feet of the SH-K1 × 2 figure, gives point to Reed's recent statement: 'The length of a long barrow should have been no less of a planned feature than an elaborate façade.'[15] And even in its present blurred state, we should not forget that 'the form of the finished monument would obviously have been an eminent concern of the builders'. Each of these barrows, while contributing to the overall squatting image, is a version of her alternative long mode.

From Horton, following the outline downwards and north-eastwards, we come to the site of the South Circle, defining the navel of the landscape figure. This was described by Stukeley as 'a very large oblong work, like a long barrow, made only of stones pitched in the ground, no tumulus'.[16]

By 1877, when A. C. Smith arrived to inspect the monument, a recent switch to arable from sheep pasture had caused damage, though many of the stones remained in their original holes, and an oval figure, aligned north-south, with a long axis of 261 feet (i.e. SH-K1 × 4) could be discerned, positioned 'due south of Silbury Hill'.[17]

Deep ploughing and the systematic removal of the sarsens have now obliterated all trace of the monument, but Smith's plan shows an interesting 'neck' created by a bank, forming a stubby northern extension to the work.

Neck and body together form a shape known to archaeologists as the *bouclier-écusson*. Found in a Neolithic context, it is generally regarded as the 'conventional representation of a cult figure, possibly a Mother Goddess'.[18] Boucliers-écussons are well known in Brittany,[19] while, in England, an engraved version was discovered by Newall on the massive Stone 37 at Stonehenge.[20]

(*Top*), a plan of South Circle, situated at the navel point of the landscape goddess, presents an architectural version of a recognized goddess image, which also appears on one of the stones of Stonehenge (below).

198

Here it appears again as the navel of the composite goddess, though it is also an accepted image of the Great Goddess in her entirety, and positioned to point straight at the Silbury Mother Goddess summit.

From the South Circle the way runs down a slope to the 'groin' of the composite figure at the West Kennet long barrow, fashioned at the critical point on the composite goddess anatomy between the two spring-heads, Swallowhead and Waden, the natural working secrets of her landscape body. The barrow, it will be recalled, remained open throughout the mid-Neolithic period.

Emerging into the barrow forecourt, another point of union becomes clear, for this is the place where the mid-Neolithic composite goddess comes into physical contact with the Late Neolithic – the West Kennet forecourt ox.

From the west end of the same barrow mound, a distance of 1600 feet (WS-K2 × 4) separates us from Swallowhead, the vital generative nucleus of the entire figure. Exactly halfway between the two points, and right on line, is the now vanished mid-Neolithic site known as G.55.

I. F. Smith excavated this site in 1965. Although severely damaged by ploughing since Stukeley's day (when, from his drawings, it registered as physically impressive), she found enough evidence in the range of potsherds to prove that it had been 'the scene of activities stretching back over a span of perhaps 1000 years, and the earliest activity could have been related to the construction of the long barrow'.[21]

A number of Bronze Age pits, one containing the dismembered body of an infant, were also found. The circle lies due south of the centre of the Avebury henge. This fact, combined with the similarity of form, raises the possibility that G.55 also functioned as a mid-Neolithic Wedding Ring – a pre-Avebury henge for the May festival.

The legs

Of the 21 barrows on the composite periphery, the longest is the tree-covered East Kennet, 344 feet, which defines the thigh. Indeed, there is no longer barrow in the country.[22] The femur which it describes is also the longest bone in the human body. As Piggott showed in his West Kennet report, the femur was often used in mid-Neolithic fertility ritual. Moreover, the orientation

*East Kennet long barrow,
following the line of the landscape
goddess's thigh, is the longest in
the country and has never been
excavated.*

of the barrow is aligned with the 'thigh' of the
composite goddess, illustrating the general landscaping
policy whereby the long axes of the barrows, instead of
running uniformly east-west, contribute positively to
the profile by aligning with the flow of the overall
image. (Perhaps this is most clearly marked at the South
Street and Beckhampton Road barrows, which are set at
a pronounced angle to each other, and thus emphasize
the junction between back and buttock.)

The East Kennet barrow has never been excavated,
but this 'magnificent and classic example'[23] has sarsens
sticking from its broader east end, indicating a hidden
chamber. The rising midwinter sun (129° azimuth)
joins together, in a single shortest-day straight line, the
east end of this barrow, the West Kennet barrow
forecourt, the Swallowhead spring, the Beckhampton
spring, and the forecourt of the Beckhampton Road
barrow. And the setting midwinter moon occupies the
other end of the same axis. Thus both sun and moon
strike through the composite goddess's vital terrestrial
and underworld organs at the critical moment for
renewal.

The West Woods barrow, which is located at a point
equivalent to the landscape outline's knee, lies in a
copse of widely spaced hardwood saplings. Of the knee
Pliny writes, '[Among] various nations, certain religious ideas have been attached to the knees: it is the
knees that they worship, like so many altars, as it were;

perhaps because in them is centred the vital strength. For in the joint of either knee there is on the foreside of each an empty space which bears a strong resemblance to a mouth and through which, like the throat, if it is ever pierced, the vital power escapes.'

Sir Henry Meux excavated the mound in 1880, and discovered a central cairn of small sarsens overlying 'a dolmen consisting of four uprights (the spaces between which were packed with large flints) and a capstone, all of sarsen.'[24] Inside the chamber, which measured 6 feet by 3 feet, was black matter, but no bones or pottery were seen.

The long barrow is one of many in the group lacking human bodies. Meux's insistence that there were no signs of previous disturbance fits with the discoveries at Horslip,[25] South Street,[26] and Beckhampton Firs barrows, which challenge the assumption that a Neolithic long barrow always held human corpses. Instead, the goddess image-mounds covered between them a much more diverse set of intentions, including the celebration of agricultural processes (at South Street flint sickles were incorporated into the structure), the honouring of the goddess as ox, (at Manton barrow a poleaxed ox lay in a central pit),[27] and the housing of geological offerings from other areas (Horslip, now in a severely denuded state, held greensands, old red sandstone from Mendip, and Jurassic sandstones from the Cotswolds).

West Woods, the knee of the composite goddess, is one of several long barrows in the complex which were not used for human burial purposes.

In a lane from Kennet towards Marlborough 8 huge Stones in a circle fallen down and rudely hewn.

Clatford Circle's 'huge large stones', as sketched by Aubrey in the seventeenth century.

The next monument stood 'in a lane leading from Kennet to Marlborough . . . eight huge large stones . . . rudely hewen . . . in a circle, which never could be by chance,' according to Aubrey.[28] This is the Clatford Circle, known also from Stukeley's drawing, but now gone. Stukeley, like Aubrey, was impressed by the stones' size. One measured $16\frac{1}{2}$ feet by 6 feet. Four neighbouring stones 'may possibly have been the beginning of an Avenue,'[29] he thought.

Clatford is the only point in the 33-mile circumference where Kennet water touches the periphery, and Stukeley's description of the circle's site, 'over against Clatford at a flexure of the river',[30] emphasizes the importance of the river in its design.

Moving north across the Kennet, we enter a deep dry valley called Clatford Bottom. Half a mile in, there stands the chamber of the vanished Devil's Den long barrow, with three massive sarsen uprights and a capstone still in place. Stukeley's drawing shows traces of the barrow mound, and a horned forecourt, which he described as 'four more stones set as wings to [the chamber] and formed an oval cell'.[31]

Of the capstone, a nineteenth-century labourer told A. C. Smith that 12 white oxen had been provided with new harness and set to pull it off, but 'the harness all fell to pieces immediately', and this was 'the work of enchantment'.[32] The White Goddess seems to have lingered on here, in this confused fragment.

The next barrow in the chain stood in the valley north of Manton and was finally removed, not by oxen, but by a tractor in 1952. Corresponding to the composite goddess's foot, it was in a bad state, c. 1870, when Smith noted 'part of the mound . . . and some of the stone which apparently surrounded it are still to be seen'.[33] Piggott's plan of 1947 shows a mound about 65 feet long, a small chamber, and one stone remaining of what subsequent digging proved to be a façade and shallow forecourt.[34] There, three additional stones and an ox skull in a pit were set, reminiscent of the West Kennet forecourt.[35]

Lying less than a mile further north, Temple Bottom long barrow, excavated by Smith and Lukis in 1861,[36] has since disappeared. Colt Hoare described it as 'a stone barrow, having a kistvaen [chamber] at the east end of it . . . the finest example we have yet found . . . excepting the one in Clatford Bottom'.[37]

Treading the route today from West Wood to Temple Bottom, one is struck by the fact that all the

monuments were set in valley bottoms along this part
of the composite goddess's anatomy. By far the greater
part of its length is sunk in deep narrow valleys,
contracting the view in a way quite untypical of the rest
of the perambulation. Here the hills press down on us.

*The chamber of Devil's Den long
barrow. 'Enchantment' was said
to have prevented a nineteenth-
century attempt to tear down the
capstone.*

The haunches

Eventually the shadows part, and we climb, passing a
group of cottages called Top Temple, to a patch of high
downland which until recently was known as Glory
Ann. The fields seen from Glory Ann are speckled with
multitudes of sarsens, like flocks of stone sheep.
Beyond these, far to the southwest, rise the arms and
head of the Great Goddess. We can see the point where
we started. We have travelled seventeen miles and have
come halfway.

In 1723 there stood 'a remarkable thing . . . on
Temple downs called Old Chapel. Lord Winchelsea,
Lord and Lady Hertford and myself were curious in
observing it. 'Tis a large square, entrenched, 110 druid
cubits by 130 [approx. 145 × 170 feet] . . . with one
entrance on the southwest side towards Abury. The

enclosure is made of a vallum and ditch; beyond that, a row of flat stones set quite round and pretty close to one another like a wall.'[38]

On the northeast side of the enclosure Stukeley found a long barrow, likewise set quite round with great stones, with its horned entrance 'a demi-ellipsis consisting of five great stones', touching the side of the square enclosure. Within the head of this barrow was a stone setting resembling the ox figure in the West Kennet forecourt:

'One stone lies flat on the ground along the middle line of the barrow. On each side a flat stone stands upright and two flat stones stand upright as wings to 'em. These stones are generally very large, about ten feet long.'[39]

The Old Chapel temple, near Glory Ann, as drawn by Stukeley in 1723.

Barrow and enclosure together make another version of the bouclier-écusson figure (seen in a slighter form at South Circle), a rectangular contribution to the goddess's architectural imagery, following the Windmill Hill square enclosure pattern.

In practical terms, the enclosure is placed within a few yards of the Ridgeway, the great route from the northeast, and would mark the northward traveller's point of exit from the composite figure.

Possibly linked to this function is the adjacent 'great cavity call'd Balmore-pond, which seems to have some regard to this work. 'Tis a pyriform concavity set with stones on the inside. It answers exactly to the Old Chapel entrance.'[40]

In view of the location of the Balmore hole, one might compare it with one of the seven wonders of the Derbyshire Peak District – the great cavern 'which goes by a name shockingly vulgar',[41] the Devil's Arse Hole.

The composite goddess's haunches are very expansive (following the tendency of the majority of Stone Age female figurines). To describe them, we must walk four miles, passing Monkton Down barrow, crossing the Winterbourne, and on to the sites of Shelving Stones and Mill barrow. At Shelving Stones, Stukeley drew two uprights and a capstone, all that remained of the long barrrow previously recorded by Aubrey.[42] But Mill barrow was still 'a most magnificent sepulchre, a large flat long barrow set around with stones'.[43]

By now, we have reached the steeper end of the Windmill Hill 'hip', and the greatest mid-Neolithic causewayed gathering place.

Remembering the squatting goddess images formed by the pit figures there, we continue on to the Horslip barrow, 'another considerable long barrow of a large bulk, length and height',[44] where Ashbee recently unearthed large quantities of antler, bone and flint, some sarsen (grain) rubbers, and definite evidence that the barrow was visited for over 1000 years, so reinforcing the pattern of mythic recurrence proved at Windmill Hill and West Kennet.

The pottery in the Horslip ditches is entirely compatible with a millennium of visits, showing 'the stratified sequence, with Beaker and Late Neolithic wares in the upper silt'.[45]

The Beckhampton back

We are now approaching the composite goddess's narrow waist, and the critical meeting-place of Horslip brook with Winterbourne, where the henge was eventually built. But our route traces the outer skin, not the internal organs, and so we swing up her spine by way of the South Street and Beckhampton Firs barrows.

The criss-cross pattern of furrows found beneath South Street is 'the earliest archaeological evidence for traction ploughing in Britain'. By harnessing the holy ox power, 'the basic agrarian problems have already been solved'.[46] (Fourth millennium BC.)

The barrows in this part of the figure have a spiney quality. From a strongly defined long axis of wattle hurdling, wattle processes (or vertebrae offshoots) are set at right angles, evoking the pattern of engraved lines found on many a Neolithic long figurine (see p. 25).

The 'back barrow' nearest the Beckhampton roundabout has never been properly excavated, though Merewether's discovery of a Late Bronze Age urn (c. 1000 BC), a secondary interment, indicates the long sacred associations of the mound. These associations are also conveyed by the Saxon name for this part of Avebury parish – Beckhampton, written Backhampton in the fourteenth century.

This derives from the old English word baec, meaning BACK, which raises the possibility that the understanding of the composite goddess survived, like the barrows, into Saxon times. As Gover points out, the

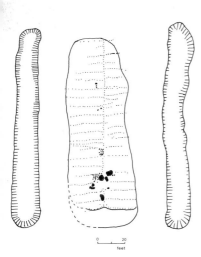

Plan of South Street long barrow, showing the strongly emphasized spine of the long axis, and the 'vertebrae' composed of wattle hurdling set at right angles. The goddess plaque from Antrim (p. 25) expresses the same design in miniature.

name cannot apply to a natural feature, 'for there is no ridge here'.[47]

The lower part of the back was considerably strengthened in *c.* 2600 BC by the Beckhampton avenue, whose route followed the composite outline, entering the henge via the base of her spine – a position corresponding to the bone medically known as the sacrum, and here defined architecturally by the Longstones Cove. In the Tantric tradition the sleeping serpent, Kundalini Sakti, source of resurrection and immortality, rises from that position.

Today, the A.361 road to Devizes runs close to the line for nearly two miles, and is in fact the only stretch where a modern road coincides with the composite figure's form.

In 1809 William Cunnington, the indefatigable barrow digger, now old and sick, was returning to his native Northamptonshire along this road. He later wrote: 'The next morning, on passing Shepherd's Shore into the downs about Abury, I felt much enlivened as if entering the Garden of Eden, [with] Abury, Silbury, etc. all about me. Here the pain in my head and all its gloomy attendants left me . . . and in the further progress of my journey, I felt increase of strength and spirits.'[48] And perhaps the composite figure does describe the Garden before the Fall, for 'there is no theme of guilt connected with the

The Beckhampton long barrow, placed along the landscape goddess's back. No nearby ridge or natural feature explains the name, which derives from the Anglo-Saxon word for back.

[Neolithic] garden. The boon of the knowledge of life is there in the sanctuary of the world, to be culled.'[49]

At Easton Down long barrow, where four skeletons were found by Thurnam,[50] we are on the high escarpment. Extending four miles to the west, a series of monuments delineate the 'left arm' of the composite goddess, with the elbow defined by Shepherd's Shore long barrow, and the hand by King's Play long barrow. The long trudge across the flat expanse of Roundway down to the King's Play site ends in the most spectacular panorama offered anywhere on the composite goddess. Her upward-gesturing fingers seem to lift us into the sky and give us a view westwards deep into Somerset.

Roughridge Hill marks the junction of arm and body. Here there is a Late Neolithic round barrow where Thurnam found ox bones and a beautiful incense cup[51] with a pair of eye perforations. Then, walking eastwards along the crest of Easton Hill, we come to the last long barrow (defining the Kitchen Hill shoulder), and the final mile to Tan Hill, where we began.

Rybury and Clifford's Hill

Standing once more on Tan Hill, the natural head of the composite figure, we see immediately below us the two spectacular knolls of Rybury and Clifford's Hill, projecting into the Vale of Pewsey, and linked to each other and to Tan Hill.

Both knolls are enhanced by Neolithic causewayed earthworks, and together they register as a bold medium-scale image of the squatting goddess with outstretched arms, while simultaneously offering a possible horned crown to the Tan Hill 'head'.

Credit is due to E. C. Curwen[52] for being the first in modern times to notice that the flat summits of Rybury and Clifford's Hill were emphasized by mid-Neolithic causewayed trenching – an observation confirmed by D. J. Bonny's excavation of 1963.[53] Rybury had a complete ring with a long axis of 520 feet (SH-K1 × 8), a figure used later for the diameter of Silbury Hill, the ultimate hill-womb.

Looking at Rybury, the words of R. Mercer come to mind. He speaks of 'the central importance of hilltops to the Neolithic way of life . . . hilltop landmarks become the focal point, or indeed the . . . personification of a newly created (agricultural) landscape'.[54] Newly created from the forest, and then, we may add, newly *recreating*, with the birth of every harvest.

Eye perforations on an 'incense cup' found by Thurnam at Roughridge Hill in the nineteenth century.

Tan Hill Fair

On Tan Hill, every year 'from time immemorial'[1] until
AD 1932, a fair was held. The first written record, a
Charter Roll of 1499, gives the date as 'the feast and
morrow of St Anne',[2] August 6th–7th.

'There can be little doubt', wrote Thurnam, 'that this
hill has been the site of pagan rites far older than
Christianity.'[3] Tan Hill Fair, sited on the composite
goddess's head overlooking Rybury, is a classic
illustration of the well-known pattern:

The first fairs were formed by the gathering of worshippers
and pilgrims about sacred places, and many fairs whose
origin is lost in antiquity can be traced more or less distinctly
to a religious source.[4]

August 6th was old St Anne's Day. The patroness
of confinements, honoured in southern Italy as La
Vecchia Potente (the powerful old woman), was the
moving spirit at Tan Hill Fair, which continued to be
held on August 6th till 1932. In every English village
on that night, a bowl of water used to be placed on a
stool by women, for the purpose of divination.[5] The
last glimmer of this practice can be detected in the Black
Country superstition whereby a bowl is placed outside
the house door to catch a silver coin (moon?) for a new-
born baby.[6]

Confirmation of the fair as a genuine Neolithic
survival is offered by the very inconvenience of the site.
'Far away from any town',[7] exposed and with exceed-
ingly steep gradients on the south, the perverse decision
to keep gathering there was questioned in the *Wiltshire
Gazette* in 1862:

'We do not known whether the Lady Saint, in whose
honour this fair is said to be held, got tired of the annual
revel which has taken place upon her breezy summit for
so many centuries, but certain it is that for the last few
years we have received a soaking for our pains, and
yesterday brought forth a thunderstorm and a gale
which blew down one of the booths and played havoc
among the gingerbread stalls.'[8]

The link between ginger and St Anne is also ancient,
and was known in Elizabethan times. 'Doest thou think
because thou art virtuous there shall be no more cakes

Saint Anne, mother of the Mother of God and patron saint of childbirth, gave her name to Tan Hill, where the Great Goddess was commemorated from prehistoric times with a great harvest fair.

and ale?' Sir Toby Belch asks the Puritan Malvolio (*Twelfth Night*, Act 2, Scene iii), and Feste adds: 'Yes, by Saint Anne, and ginger shall be hot in the mouth, too.' The *Oxford Dictionary* throws light on the connection: 'The word *Ginger* derives from a compound of horn and body.' Big Ann's arms, we recall, were also horns.

Tan Hill used to be called Ann(e)'s Hill.

'Anne's Hill is in reality the correct name of this famous hill, from the name of Anne or Anna.'[9] All the seventeenth- and eighteenth-century maps of the area, starting with Saxton's (1611), give Ann(e); so does John Aubrey,[10] and so does a Devizes baker, George Sloper, in his 1799 Day Book.[11] Tan was Anne.

Maire Macneill, in her examination of August First Fruits ceremonies surviving in Ireland, when the community resorted to hilltops and visited sacred springs, has emphasized that 'a study of the St Anne cult is a necessary complement'.[12] In Wiltshire, too, the connection is apparent. Since Anne's head is attached to a body, 'the strange name Glory Ann, which has been a sore puzzle to antiquarians',[13] becomes strange no longer when applied to her posterior.

The name Ann has been derived from the Greek Annys, meaning Complete,[14] but we may choose rather to look westwards for the origin in the pre-Celtic Irish goddess, Aine, Joy,[15] who was 'none other than the Great Earth Mother, from which the Welsh royal families traced their line . . . the pre-Celtic Ane, mother of the gods',[16] surviving in the Christian St Anne. Anann was the mother of the gods in Ireland', and Ireland itself was sometimes called 'the land of Anann'.[17]

Celtic mythology treats Ann and Bride as 'different versions of the same Mother Goddess figure'. The strength of the original Mother Goddess's concern with birth is reflected in the continuing association between St Anne and parturition, and so it comes as no surprise that she is the shadowy mother of the Virgin Mary, and that local tradition attributes the church below Tan Hill to St Anne, with the daughter Mary being honoured in the neighbouring villages to east and west – Alton Barnes and Bishops Cannings.

The Mother Goddess gave birth every year at the August quarter day, the midpoint between the midsummer solstice and the autumn equinox, August 7th. It was then that, in the annual mythical cycle, she squatted down and brought forth the corn harvest. To prepare the event and to participate in the enactment, a great mid-Neolithic ceremony may well have been conducted annually on the goddess's head on the eve of the birth night, with attention shifting to the vaginal site of Swallowhead-G.55 (and perhaps the Windmill-Hill pit goddess figure) during the final act of parturition, August 7th–8th.

The strong association between harvest birth and full moon, developed so majestically at Silbury in Late Neolithic times, calls to mind the claim of the Cannings parishes (covering Big Anne's head and arms) to be the scene of the first Wiltshire Moonrake. The precise location is said to be the ford on the road to Etchilhampton, but this is disputed by the inhabitants of the neighbouring parish, Bishops Cannings, who insist that the attempt to gather the moon's reflection occurred in a pond there.[18]

It is worth mentioning that these sites form an equilateral triangle with the spot on Tan Hill where a gold U-shaped torc of the Bronze Age was found buried (National Grid References 067604, 043644, and 090645).[19] The torc, ten inches long, combines crescent, vulva U-shape, and snake-head terminals. It was discovered 18 inches below the surface by a labourer digging for flints and, near by, were found a Neolithic quartzite axe, a Bronze Age copper flat axe, a socketed bronze axe, a socketed side-loop spearhead, and some faience beads dated before 2000 BC – altogether an important collection.[20]

The Fair
The nocturnal aspect of the medieval assembly on Tan Hill also serves to strengthen the Neolithic link, the lunar birth connection found at Silbury and internationally. The night attendance waned with the Enlightenment, but Story-Maskelyne retails the tradition of 'shepherds coming in former years . . . at very early hours in the morning, before daylight'.[21]

Brentnall adds: 'Business begins there fairly early in the morning, but in the past it began earlier still, and the last use of the pagan bonfire was to guide drovers to the spot before dawn.'[22]

The emphasis on ox imagery, such a feature of the long barrows, might also have left traces on the Anne head, though the herds of long-horned *Bos primigenius* have gone forever. What remains on the summit is a round dew pond, known as Oxenmere, referred to by A. R. Stedman as 'possibly the oldest dew pond of all'.[23]

Oxenmere on Tan Hill, an artificial dew pond (possibly the oldest in the country) seen during a drought.

*Long-horned draught oxen at
Aldbourne on the Marlborough
downs* c. *1900. The long-horned
ox goddess stood at the centre of
Neolithic agriculture, imagery,
and religion.*

Oxen were specified as being traded at the Fair in the
seventeenth century, and the last flicker of a former ox
sacrifice may possibly be discerned in the custom,
reported by a Minchinhampton horse dealer (who
attended the Fair annually in the late nineteenth
century), that salt beef and beans were traditionally
eaten there. Mr Fred Green of All Cannings, who is
over eighty years old, clearly remembers a woman with
a bucketful of cooked broad beans offering a two-
pronged fork and a prize for the person who stabbed
the most.[24]

From 1825 till its extinction over a hundred years
later, a brief account of the Fair was carried annually by
the *Wiltshire Gazette.* These terse statements combine
talk of prices, the quality and numbers of animals on
show, the prevalence or absence of disease in the flocks,
and the shortage or abundance of fodder. Farming
matters – the life, livelihood and common experience of
Victorian and Neolithic Wiltshire people – flow on and
on, without fundamentally changing.

We learn of the extraordinary distances that people
and animals still travelled on foot to reach the site; of
drinking, horse play, dancing, thieving, occasional
brawls, the combination of business and pleasure, and
the prevalence of bartering as distinct from cash
transactions. Although the mythical and cosmological
dimension is absent, there are moments when the sense
of expectancy in the face of the annual corn harvest is
registered with awe – the voice of a people dependent
on the living land in its relationship with the capricious
elements of wind and rain. Something of the rhythmic
dynamism of prehistoric existence springs improbably
from the grey columns of print:

July 28th 1825. Advertisement

St. Ann's Hill Fair. Commonly called 'Tanhill'. Notice is hereby given that the Coops, standings and rope Fences will be erected on Fri. 5th Aug. next, the day before the Fair. . . . To prevent disturbances, the Magistrates will appoint several special constables to attend during the Fair.

1823 There was full 20,000 sheep penned. Horned cattle included excellent Devonshires and Scots oxen.

1848 The show of horses very large. Much business especially in good carthorses. In the nag department, the usual amount of fun and jockeyship which peculiarly characterises Tan Hill was displayed. The victims as yet remain unknown.

1849 Some sales of horses, but chopping and changing were as usual on Tan Hill mainly the order of the day.

1850 As night advanced, a terrific fight ensued on the Hill, among a number of blackguards who usually infest this Fair, and many broken heads were the consequence.

1856 Two large droves of horses from Wales and Ireland which met customers at £20 and £35 each. The pleasure fair seemed quite full of holiday folk, the harvest not having yet commenced in this locality. We may say that the corn in the valley below seemed quite to laugh and sing, and it will be fitting for the sickle the early part of next week.

1860 The Gypsy Tribe always abound at this Fair and offer amusements such as throwing at snuffboxes etc.

1865 The Vale beneath the Hill presented a splendid appearance. Covered as it was on Monday with sheaves of ripened corn, the vale furnished a sight which no-one could behold without feelings of thankfulness and delight.

1902 Tan Hill Fair Day is regarded here as a 'Feast' day, and there was much festivity on this occasion. Mr Jenkins engaged the Alton band, and dancing was kept up till ten o'clock.

The Fair continued to be held through the First World War, and in August 1920, the aforementioned correspondent of *The Times* filed his impressions:

In the 4 seasons, there is one morning and one morning only when vehicles and pedestrians concentrate towards its smooth slopes. From a very early hour droves of sheep and solitary wayfarers may be discerned approaching across the downland. Some of them coming 20 or 30 miles have been travelling all night.

The Auctioneer stands in a 'little house on wheels'. Beer and cider is sold. The old barn is a speck on the hilltop, but thrown open once a year it becomes the scene of a grand luncheon for leading farmers and officers of the fair.

Meanwhile, gigs, bicycles and even motorcars carry a number of rubicund bucolic gentlemen accompanied by wives and daughters to the site for a day's outing. There also are drovers, tramps, sheep dogs and policemen, for Tan Hill is a rough-and-tumble institution.

The sale begins about 10 o'clock but the number of sheep offered is nothing like so great as in times past. A recent feature has been the uncommon number of motorcars 'parked' beside the downland track. The Auction is over by noon, yet . . . among the rag-tag and bobtail, drinking goes forward far into the afternoon.

All are gone long before sundown.[25]

The last Tan Hill Fair took place on 6 August 1932, when Frank Cowdrey of All Cannings was 30. Only ten years before, he had helped erect a new barn on the summit, to act as a store for the hurdles used to pen Fair livestock. The fact that he was asked to use pine instead of a hardwood for the chief timbers bears out the feeling current in the area that the Fair was dying.

By 1930, cattle lorries had largely replaced droving, And that's what caused the trouble, you see. August 6th 1932 was a very wet day and the lorries got bogged down in the mud. A lot of them never made it up from Beckhampton. And that was the end of the Fair. They never tried again [recalls Mr Cowdrey, who was present].

In this manner Ann lost the human and animal performance conducted on her head for more than 5,000 years.

But for seven years more the Fair continued at a new site, three miles further north in the Kennet valley, where motor access was still possible even in a rainstorm. The field selected lay between Silbury and the Swallowhead spring. The Second World War killed off this last flicker of activity.

Mythical repetition
Standing in the Kennet-side Fair field, with Silbury so close, the question arises as to why the Late Neolithic peoples felt it necessary to build Silbury when they had inherited a working image in the composite goddess, and a medium-scale version in the Rybury-Clifford's Hill figure, not to mention the square enclosure figure on Windmill Hill. Was Silbury a laborious repetition?

The answer is partly 'yes', and that is because the very essence of the mythical impulse is working repetition. Repetition was both natural and necessary and, from the human standpoint, the indispensable means of achieving union with the godhead. What the godhead had originally provided in the landscape body was acknowledged first by the distribution of long barrows on the divine members, and then in the Silbury figure.

'This is the way of all ancient cultures,' writes Rees. 'Life is meaningful inasmuch as it is an imitation or re-enactment of what the gods did in the beginning.'[26] And Eliade writes, 'Reality is acquired solely through repetition or participation.'[27]

But of course, in the act of repetition Silbury also concentrated and enhanced the divine image.

'Silbury is the marvaillous hill ... every way between the downs we are of a sudden saluted with its deep green vast circumference.'[28] And to that circumference we should add the body moat, whereby the ultimate synthesis of celestial and underground events could be *seen*, rather than merely inferred.

Silbury, Sanctuary, the avenues, and the Avebury henge, collectively possess the concentrated energy of a microcosm, epitomizing the Great Goddess as she turns through her annual gyration. What a stroke of genius it was to encourage the outward flow of this force through bringing the inner monumental image-world into contact with the composite goddess at the West Kennet barrow. Acting as tomb to the inner circle, and vulva to the more diffuse outer figure, the barrow raised the life and death opposites into happy accord.

But these interlocking truths have now been erased by progress of a different kind, while the spring of Swallowhead has shrunk into non-meaning, and is now no more than a little black hole in the white rock. The Kennet signifies nothing.

The contemporary cycle

'Well, you know or don't you kennet or haven't I told you every telling has a taling, and that's the he and the she of it. Look, look, the dusk is growing! My branches lofty are taking root. And my cold cher's gone ashley.' says Anna Livia Plurabelle to herself in *Finnegan's Wake*, as she moves towards extinction in Dublin Bay.[29]

St Ann's Hill, or Tan Hill as it is now known, is the southern culmination of the Marlborough downs. A gentle descent of three miles leads to Silbury, as Stukeley's drawing shows.

Yet for her, and for us, to come to the end is to find the beginning. The world, swept bare of Neolithic intentions, is here now, ready to accept a new human response.[30] And how can one fail to respond to the particular beauty and strength of this countryside, its limbs, dressed and undressed by passing shadows, glittering with flints, harebells, and Chalk Blue butterflies?

We can walk from Tan Hill down the long sloping trunk and, descending the dry valley from Beckhampton Penning, become suddenly aware that the torso is animated by a sound of running water, the first on all the Downs. It comes from beneath the willow trees. There is Swallowhead, with transparent sparkling blood flowing from her deep cavity. For us, as for Stukeley, 'It runs pretty strong now out of the solid chalk, and the water is altogether clear . . . and admirably soft.'[31]

The most important aspects of the past are also the most important present realities – day and night, sun and moon, summer and winter, rain, soil-covered rock, and the animal and vegetable life cycles.

For more than a thousand years the Avebury Cycle revealed as common knowledge the union of this external environment with the internal environment of the human body, and perhaps the experience of such fusion is the best and most sensible reward of *every* good rationale. We therefore live in hope that our own science, having followed its distinctive route, may eventually itself arrive at this unity, and pronounce it to be reasonable.

Meanwhile, the Avebury Cycle provides a glimpse of the Mother we have lost.

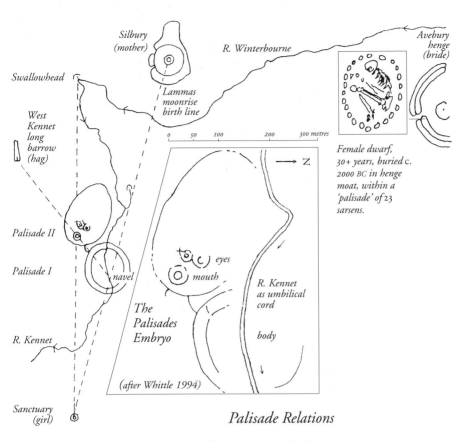

Female dwarf, 30+ years, buried c. 2000 BC in henge moat, within a 'palisade' of 23 sarsens.

(after Whittle 1994)

Palisade Relations

In the years since 1987 traces of two more Avebury monuments have been discovered. These enclosures, Palisades I and II, lie together in the Kennet Valley between Sanctuary and Silbury.

A. Whittle's excavations have shown Palisade I to be, in his words, 'a sacred precinct in the style of other Late Neolithic sites'.[1] Beneath water meadow turf he found a near-circular ring ditch with a maximum diameter of 230 metres,[2] surrounding another of maximum diameter 180 metres.

The two rings were composed of close-set post holes, from which oak timbers up to 40 centimetres thick had risen to an estimated height of 6 metres in the outer and 8 metres in the inner circle. Standing open to the sky these massive colonnades were, in Whittle's view, neither domestic, nor, considering the low-lying site, defensive in purpose. Radio carbon dating shows the 'temple' to have been built around 2,000 BC, with a presumed lifespan of several centuries.

Right through the middle of this edifice, and forming its West-East axis runs the river Kennet. Since recent work by J.G. Evans has shown that circa 2,000 BC, with a rising water table, the Kennet was flowing strongly from Swallowhead, with evidence of seasonal valley flooding,[3] the possibility arises that Palisade I was *intended* to embrace and incorporate the holy stream in this narrow part of its valley. Although streams may wander from side to side of their flood plains, the precision with which the Kennet currently bisects the monument suggests that this was the original plan. But whether running *through,* as in Palisade I, or *alongside* as with the adjoining Palisade II monument, the river appears to complement the enclosures.

These structures may have addressed the water goddess, because she held the secrets of life, including those of human conception – a belief which saturated Antiquity world-wide as Eliade has proved (cf. p. 170). Then, *water,* rather than men, was held to make women pregnant and Palisade I may have provided another version of an Avebury-henge immersion ritual, involving waters of divine fecundity, offered here in more convenient abundance.

The *henge's* water, by contrast, lay at the base of a sheer 10 metre deep south causeway cliff, where devotees had to be lowered by rope. In 1914 Gray found two artificially cut 'shutes' for ropes at opposite corners of the causeway's east face, indicating a 'down' and 'up' system. The sacred pool in the trench bottom (see photo, p. 133) was edged by a path worn concave by young feet, circa 2,500 BC,[4] as the initiates waited to be hauled up to the Wishing Stone – a slow and hazardous procedure.

How pleased the maidens of a later generation must have been, on *their* Beltaine journey, to have diverted from the West Kennet Avenue by a mere 100 metres in order to enjoy instead the life-giving waters of Palisade I, before perhaps continuing to the Avebury henge for other time-honoured reasons.

To facilitate the transfer of henge power to Palisade I, quantities of sarsens (many more and much bigger than required for engineering stability) were packed around the wooden post holes as if the Avebury goddess were working at the roots of the new Maypoles, reminding them of their obelisk prototypes (cf. p. 153).

As with materials, so in matters of location cross-references abound. Although Palisade I's excavation is incomplete, the care with which it was sited in relation the older monuments is already plain. Its riverine entre (map reference SU 111682) falls on the line from anctuary centre to Silbury summit, and is intervisible ith both. Thus Palisade I offers a second May-festival nk to the February-August chain. In addition it lies quidistant (750 metres) between Sanctuary and West-Kennet-long-barrow forecourt, and so brings the hag mage into the fourfold cycle. Each monument sails to s special purpose on a raft of relationships – some of hem hidden. For example, within every Palisade oak, the alternate hard-soft, winter-summer, tree rings testify o the hag's annual transformation into maiden, while opious foundation deposits of pigs' bones laid around he Palisade posts, evoke the goddess in pig form, nown in Neolithic Europe since the 6th millennium C,[5] and stressing the fluid nature of her metamorphoses *etween* the species. At Palisade I, as in Ireland, the pig eity may also have facilitated transactions from magic nderworld to surface plain and back.[6]

When considering the mysteries of the earthly and he human womb, Palisade I worshippers could see, less han a kilometre off, the Silbury mound arising from he moat body of the goddess. This high hope, this ndispensable promise of an August fruition, filled eye nd heart.

Thus Whittle, regarding Palisade I, writes: 'Memory f earlier activity must have influenced the scale of hings, with a desire to emulate the achievements of ncestors [out] of respect for ancient tradition.'[7] Motivated by continuing veneration of the Silbury harvest goddess, the designers of Palisade I ensured that ts maximum diameter would correspond. At 230 metres t repeats exactly the maximum North-South breadth of he Silbury moat effigy, measured from buttock to knee, s she squats in labour.

Turning to Palisade II, the near-neighbour and ontemporary of Palisade I, its extended oval form was designed to point at Silbury Hill. Moreover the 336.5 metre long axis of Palisade II exactly matches the East-West axis of the Silbury moat-hill figure. From the base f her wet thigh to the tip of her water head she also measures 336.5 metres, along that 90°–270° equinoxial unrise to sunset line.

Together Palisades I and II were following where the Avebury henge had already led, for, as we have seen, the henge's central area also has a long axis of 336.5 metres cf. page 164). The Palisades stayed loyal to this Avebury-Silbury relationship, and repeated it twice over.

Cries from the Underworld

*Mace head, Knowth, Ireland,
c. 3000 BC. Ht 8 cm.*

(top)

*Folkton drum, Yorkshire,
2000 BC. Found in a child's
grave. Ht 9 cm.*

*Shouting tomb giant. Barclodiad
y Gawres, Wales. 3rd millenium BC.
Ht 90 cm.*

Whittle's evocation of ancestral influence appears t
hold good on the ground well beyond the point of me
coincidence. Here is the tangible *Ge*-ometry of a livin
Ge, or *Gaia*, consistent and persistent, speaking throug
her interwoven elements.

The discovery that Palisades I and II approach t
within twenty five metres of each other, and were joine
across this short 'neck' by at least one cross-ditch, rais
the possibility that they were initially envisaged as bod
(I) and head (II) of one gigantic wooden effigy. Adding t
the impression, two eyes and an open mouth may be see
in the three double-ring wooden structures located at th
'face' end of enclosure II. Is this figure the supernatura
May Queen, wearing her high-turreted crown, while he
body, spanning the river, gushes with divine secretions?

Or may we see in 'I plus II' the perfect harvest child i
embryo, floating in water meadows, still attache
by the Kennet's umbilical cord to Swallowhead and th
underworld womb? Such archetypes, common to a
humanity, are still available to us if only we choose t
recognize them.

To the very end, it seems, Neolithic civilization was a
intensification of Nature, perceived as sacred, in whic
people, along with their entire animal, vegetable an
mineral worlds, experienced a state of harmon
personified by the goddess of changes.

Fresh evidence of their achievement keeps passin
through our hands, even if a largely reductionis
Archaeology typically reduces it to dust. Meanwhile
Kennet water continues to flow from Swallowhead
through the hidden Palisades, around the Sanctuary spu
towards a far-off confluence with the Thames. A
Battersea, where the combined river goddesses are joine
at every tide by their salty sister, the trio were given fin
items of Bronze Age and Iron Age metalwork as votiv
offerings, whilst from Roman Londinium's bridg
comparable tributes in gold and silver icons were paid t
Nature's eternal stream on behalf of the new city growin
on its banks.[8]

Modern London, by contrast, does not expect civi
lization to operate in sacred synthesis with the natura
order. But our delusions of independence are provin
ephemeral. The present hydrocarbon orgy is alread
melting ice-caps, and rising seas reaffirm relationship
that we have neglected. Meanwhile, Avebury stands a
evidence that Nature and Culture *can* be happily marrie
and offers us the hope that new harmonies are waiting t
be imagined, and to be sung.

Chapter References

Introduction

Fawcett, T., *The Symbolic Language of Religion,* 1970, p. 130.

Atkinson, R. J. C., *Stonehenge,* 1956, p. 167.

Daniel, G., *A Hundred Years of Archaeology,* 1950, p. 323.

Lévi-Strauss, C., *The Savage Mind,* 1966, pp. 15 and 269.

Stukeley, W., *Letters and Diaries,* Surtees Society, 1885, vol. 3, pp. 245–7.

Ibid., vol. 1, letter from R. Gale to Stukeley, 1743, p. 359.

Bachofen, J. J., letter to Henry Morgan, quoted in V. W. Turner, *The Ritual Process,* 1969, p. 2.

Barfield, O., *Poetic Diction,* 2nd edition, 1952, p. 206.

Lee, D. D., *Religious Perspectives of College Teaching,* 1951, p. 7.

Eliade, M., *The Two and the One,* 1965, p. 206.

Bachofen, J. J., *Myth, Religion and Mother Right,* transl. R. Manheim, 1967, p. 49.

De Graeve, F., in *New Catholic Encyclopaedia,* 1968, vol. 10, p. 183.

Brinton, D. G., *Religions of Primitive Peoples,* 4th impression, 1915, p. 18.

Lévi-Strauss, *op. cit.,* p. 210.

Bachofen, *op. cit.,* p. xii.

Schelling, F. W., *Einleitung in die Philosophie der Mythologie,* 1856, p. 124.

De Graeve, *op. cit.,* p. 183.

Roe, D., *Prehistory, the Modern Approach,* 1970, p. 223.

Leach, E. R., in *History of Technology,* ed. C. Singer, 1954, vol. 1, p. 114.

Byrhtferth's Manual, AD 1011, in *Early English Text Society,* no. 177, 1929, vol. 1, pp. 13–15.

Altizer, T. J. (ed.), *Myths and Symbols,* 1969, p. 16.

Coomaraswamy, A. K., in *Speculum,* 1945, vol. 20, p. 402.

[23] Bachofen, *op. cit.,* p. 76.

[24] *Ibid.,* p. 76.

Chapter 1
The Winter Eve corn dolly

[1] 3132 feet = 1152 megalithic yards = Swallowhead-Kennet module (SH-K1) × 48, or SH-K1² × 2.

[2] Macneill, F. M., *The Silver Bough,* 1957, vol. 3, p. 12.

[3] Rees, A. and B., *Celtic Heritage,* 1973, p. 87.

[4] *Ibid.,* p. 89.

[5] Thom, A., *Megalithic Lunar Observatories,* 1971.

[6] Newham, C. A., *The Astronomical Significance of Stonehenge,* 1972.

[7] Jackson, G. F., in *Shropshire Folklore,* ed. C. Burne, 1883, p. 380.

[8] Lambert, M., *A Golden Dolly,* 1969, p. 24.

[9] In Scotland.

[10] In Wales.

[11] Frazer, J. G., *The Golden Bough,* 1912, vol. 7, pt. 1, p. 167.

[12] Banks, M. M., *British Calendar Customs, Scotland,* 1934–41, vol. 1, p. 150.

[13] O'Rahilly, T. F., *Early Irish History and Mythology,* 1946, p. 82.

[14] *Ibid.,* p. 82.

[15] Maclagan, R., in *Folklore,* 1896, vol. 7, p. 78.

[16] Frazer, J. G., in *Folklore,* 1896, vol. 7, p. 51.

[17] Macrury, Rev. J., *Trans. Gaelic Soc. of Inverness,* 1894–6, p. 147.

[18] Maclagan, quoted in Banks, *op. cit.,* p. 71.

[19] *Ibid.,* p. 71; see also Macneill, *op. cit.,* vol. 2, p. 128.

[20] Macneill, *op. cit.,* vol. 3, p. 12.

[21] Powell, T. G. E., *Prehistoric Art,* 1966, pp. 107–8.

[22] Baldwin Smith, E., *Architectural Symbolism of Ancient Rome,* 1956, p. 3.

Chapter 2
The long barrow goddess

[1] Fowler, P., Regional Archaeologies, *Wessex,* 1967, p. 22.

[2] Dyer, J., *Southern England, an Archaeological Guide,* 1973, p.353.

[3] Piggott, S., in *Antiquity,* 1958, vol. 32, p. 235.

[4] Aubrey, J., *Monumenta Britannica,* 1665–93.

[5] Stukeley, W., *Abury Described,* 1743, p. 46.

[6] Colt Hoare, R., *Ancient Wilts.,* 1821, vol. 2, p. 96.

[7] Long, W., in *Wilts. Arch. Mag.,* vol. 4, 1858, pp. 342–3.

[8] Thurnam, J., in *Archaeologia,* 1860, vol. 38, p. 409.

[9] Piggott, S., *op. cit.,* p. 236.

[10] Piggott, S., in *Victoria County Hist., Wilts.,* ed. R. B. Pugh, 1973, vol. 1, pt 2, p. 312.

[11] Piggott, S., in *Antiquity,* 1958, vol. 32, p. 236.

[12] Stukeley, W., *op. cit.,* p. 46.

[13] Thurnam, J., *op. cit.,* p. 410.

[14] Piggott, S., in *Antiquity,* 1958, vol. 32, p. 237.

[15] Colt Hoare, R., *op. cit.,* vol. 1, p. 92.

[16] Colt Hoare, R., *Modern Wilts.,* 1826, p. 54.

[17] Colt Hoare, R., *Ancient Wilts.,* 1821, vol. 2, p. 110.

[18] *Ibid.,* p. 21.

[19] Gimbutas, M., *The Gods and Goddesses of Old Europe,* 1974, p. 205.

[20] Thurnam, J., in *Archaeologia,* 1869, vol. 42, p. 205.

[21] Dalton, G. I., 'The Loathly Lady', in *Folklore,* 1971, vol. 82, p. 130.

[22] See Grinsell, L. V., in *Folklore,* vol. 48, p. 245. There is *one* giant per barrow. This resolves Grinsell's unnecessary dilemma as to how the many Neolithic skeletons found in each,

'average stature only five feet six inches', could be called giants. In fact it was the emanations from these Neolithic *children* of the goddess – the corpses – who came to be known as the Little People or Fairies, haunting the imaginations of later and taller generations, particularly on Winter Eve, when they were said to emerge from the gigantic tomb body, their mother, and ride across the country.

23 Jackson Knight, W. F., in *Antiquity*, 1932, vol. 6, p. 450.

24 Cyriax, T., in *Archaeological Journal*, 1921, vol. 28, pp. 205–15.

25 Wall, D. R., in *New Catholic Encyclopedia*, 1966, vol. 3, p. 767.

26 Phillips, C. W., in *Archaeologia*, 1935, vol. 85, pp. 43–88. 'In a number of Wiltshire examples the pits were covered by a conical mound of black earth. At Tilshead and Winterbourne Stoke Down, charcoal was found, but no human bones have ever occurred in these holes, and it can only be suggested that they had some important ritual purpose which had to be served in the early stages of barrow construction.' What was the purpose if not to establish the site for the barrow as the domain of the Queen of Death, whose form was created, like Silbury, both above and below the original ground surface?

27 Wilkinson, Rev. J. in *Wilts. Arch. Mag.*, 1869, vol. 2, p. 115. Given the span of corn neck-sickle-barrow allegiance, it matters little whether the object was inserted in Neolithic times (favoured by some authorities) or in the Medieval period (favoured by others).

28 Owen, T. M., *Welsh Folk Customs*, 1959, p. 124.

29 Spence, L., *The Fairy Tradition in Britain*, 1948, p. 81.

30 Hemp, W. J., in *Archaeologia*, 1935, vol. 85, p. 256.

31 Clark, G., *Prehistoric England*, 1940, p. 95.

32 Stukeley, *op. cit.*, p. 46.

33 Colt Hoare, *Ancient Wilts.*, vol. 2, p. 96.

34 Merewether, J., *Proc., Archaeol. Inst., Salisbury*, 1849, p. 47.

35 Thurnam, J., in *Archaeologia*, 1860, vol. 38, p. 407.

36 *Ibid.*, p. 412.

37 *Ibid.*, p. 418.

38 *Ibid.*, p. 413.

39 *Ibid.*, p. 410.

40 *Ibid.*, pp. 413–14.

41 Piggott, S., in *Antiquity*, 1958, vol. 32, pp. 235–6.

42 Avebury Museum display, 1972.

43 Piggott, *op. cit.*, p. 236.

44 *Ibid.*, p. 236.

45 Piggott, S., *West Kennet Long Barrow Excavations, 1955–6*, 1962, p. 61.

46 Woolley, L., and Hawkes, J., *Prehistory and the Beginnings of Civilisation*, 1963, pt 1, sect. 2, p. 340.

47 Grinsell, L. V., *The Ancient Burial Mounds of England*, 1936, p. 32.

Chapter 3
The stone rivers

1 See Hawkins, H. L., in *Marlborough College Nat. Hist. Soc.*, vol. 96, pp. 39–45, for an account of the hydrological mechanism involved.

2 Reader's Digest, *Folklore, Myths and Legends of Britain*, 1973, p. 30.

3 Norberg-Schultz, C., *Intentions in Architecture*, 1963, pp. 125–6.

4 Wall, D. R., in *New Catholic Encyclopedia*, 1966, vol. 3, p. 767.

5 Piggott, *West Kennet Long Barrow Excavations, 1955–6*, 1962, p. 14.

6 Boothby, R., *Journ. Brit. Soc. Dowsers*, 1935, vol. 2, p. 115.

7 Smith, R. A., *Journ. Brit. Soc. Dowsers*, 1939, vol. 3, p. 32.

8 Zevi, B., in McGraw-Hill, *Encyclopedia of World Art*, 1968, vol. 1, p. 637.

9 Piggott, *op. cit.*, pp. 15–16.

10 Wall, *op. cit.*, p. 767.

Chapter 4
Bones and pots

1 Visitors can still enter the tomb, following its accurate restoration by Mr J. Mackenzie of the Ministry of Works.

2 Daniel, G., *Prehistoric Chamber Tombs of England and Wales*, 1950, p. 103; 'The majority of the bones in the burial chambers are disordered, fragmentary, and fractional.'

3 Lynch, F., *Bryn Celli Ddu*, 1970, p. 2.

4 Piggott, S., *West Kennet Long Barrow Excavations, 1955–6*, 1962, p. 23.

5 Wells, L. H., in Piggott, *op. cit.*, appendix 1, p. 81.

6 Frazer, J. G., *The Golden Bough*, 3rd ed. 1955, pt 7, vol. 1, p. 14. See also BBC TV documentary on Mount Hagan peoples of New Guinea, 1973.

7 Rawson, P., in catalogue of Arts Council *Tantra* exhibition, 1971, p. 41.

8 Piggott, S., quoted in J. Campbell, *Oriental Mythology*, 1960, p. 149.

9 Grinsell, L. V., *Belas Knap*, H.M.S.O., 1966, p. 4.

10 Clifford, E. E., in *Proc. Prehistoric Soc.*, 1938, vol. 4, p. 188.

11 For example at Fussell's Lodge long barrow, Wilts., and at Bryn Yr Hen Bobl, Anglesey.

12 Thurnam, J., in *Archaeologia*, 1860, p. 413.

13 Gimbutas, M., *The Gods and Goddesses of Old Europe*, 1974, p. 237.

14 Tegner, H., *Roe deer*, 1951, pp. 11–26.

Taylor Page, F. J., *Roe Deer*, 1962, pp. 1–10.

Thurnam, J., *op. cit.*, pp. 405–21. Thurnam found the roebuck antler in the west chamber, in a black organic level, deposited with the final packing of the tomb. He does not give the precise horizontal location of the antler.

Piggott, S., *West Kennet Excavations*, p. 68.

Onians, R. B., *The Origins of European Thought*, 1951, p. 186.

Thurnam, *op. cit.*, p. 416.

Piggott, S., *op. cit.*, p. 26.

See Davies, W. J., *Hanes Plwyf Llandyssul*, 1896, p. 253.

Jones, F., *The Holy Wells of Wales*, 1954, p. 86.

Pericot-Garcia, L., *Prehistoric and Primitive Art*, 1969, p. 227. Bacon, E., *Archaeology: Discoveries in the '60s*, pp. 112–119.

Sandars, N. K., *Prehistoric Art in Europe*, 1968, p. 155.

Smith, G. E., *The Evolution of the Dragon*, 1919, p. 182.

Neumann, E., *The Great Mother*, transl. R Manheim, 1955, p. 43.

Piggott, *op. cit.*, p. 34.

Ibid., p. 34.

Aubrey, J., *Monumenta Britannica*, 1665–93, pt 2, p. 6.

Thurnam, *op. cit.*, p. 414 and fig. 9.

Gimbutas, *op. cit.*, p. 206.

Smith, I. F., *Windmill Hill and Avebury, a Short Account*, 1959, p. 10.

Leach, E., *Lévi-Strauss*, 1970, p. 35.

Quoted in Kirk, G. S., *Myth*, 1973 edition, p. 72.

Lévi-Strauss, C., *The Raw and the Cooked*, transl. J. and D. Weightman, 1970, p. 46.

Piggott, *op. cit.*, p. 38.

Spence, L., *The Fairy Tradition in Britain*, 1948, pp. 68–9.

Chapter 5
The forecourt ox

Piggott, S., *West Kennet Long Barrow Excavations, 1955–6*, 1962, p. 18.

2 Gimbutas, M., *The Gods and Goddesses of Old Europe*, 1974, p. 236.

3 Murray, J. A., *Oxford English Dictionary*, 1908, vol. 6, pt 2, p. 189.

4 Wright, J., *English Dialect Dictionary*, 1903, vol. 4, p. 44.

5 *Ibid.*, p. 44.

6 Gimbutas, M., *op. cit.*, p. 91.

7 Wright, *op. cit.*, p. 45.

8 Frazer, J. G., *The Golden Bough*, vol. 7, pt 1, p. 286.

9 MacNeill, F. M., *The Silver Bough*, 1957, vol. 3, p. 43.

10 James, E. O., *The Cult of the Mother Goddess*, 1959, p. 45. See also Kendrick, T. D., *The Archaeology of the Channel Islands*, vol. 1, 1928, pp. 21–5. Female figurines with prominent breasts are conspicuous in Aveyron, at the gates of the churchyard of St Martin, as statue-menhirs.

11 Traditional ballad, quoted in Gutch, M., and Peacock, M., *Folklore of Lincolnshire*, 1908, p. 265.

12 Peck, W., *The History of the Stamford Bullrunnings*, (unpaged MS copy, Chapter 3, quoted in Gutch and Peacock, *op. cit.*, p. 265).

13 *Ibid.*, Chapter 4, quoted in Gutch and Peacock, *op. cit.*, p. 266. The bull run took place on November 13. Other English bull runs were recorded at Rochdale and in Derbyshire. See *Folklore*, vol. 7, p. 346.

14 Groenewegen-Frankfort, H. A., *Arrest and Movement*, 1951, p. 22.

15 Piggott, S., *Neolithic Cultures of the British Isles*, 2nd ed., 1962, p. 65.

16 Avebury Museum display, 1972.

17 Atkinson, R. J. C., in *Antiquity*, 1968, vol. 42, p. 299.

18 Thurnam, J., in *Archaeologia*, 1860, vol. 38, p. 413.

19 Merewether, J. *Diary of a Dean*, 1851, p. 12.

20 Campbell, J., *Oriental Mythology*, 1960, p. 164.

21 Gimbutas, M., *op. cit.*, p. 236. See also Levy, G. R., *The Gate of Horn*, 1948, p. 131, for her comments on the typically Neolithic ox-horned tomb entrances where the goddess appears, rising through her gate of horn, before the entrance to the grave.

22 Hawkes, C. F. C., in *Antiquaries' Journal*, 1938, vol. 18, p. 130.

23 Piggott, S., *West Kennet Long Barrow Excavations, 1955–6*, 1962, pp. 55–6.

24 *Ibid.*, pp. 27 and 74.

25 Keiller, A., and Piggott, S., in *Antiquity*, 1936, vol. 10, p. 420.

26 Daniel, G., in *Proc. Prehistoric Soc.*, 1940, vol. 6, p. 140. Compare also the 'perforated stone' which once stood 13 feet north of the entrance to the Fairy Toot long barrow, Nempnett Thrubwell, Somerset. See Bere, T., in *Gentleman's Magazine*, 1789, p. 393.

27 Lynch, F., in *Archaeologia Cambrensis*, 1967, vol. 116, p. 13.

28 Piggott, *op. cit.*, p. xi.

Chapter 6
Approach to the Sanctuary

1 Stukeley, W., in Gough Maps, f. 231.

2 Piggott, S., *West Kennet Long Barrow Excavations, 1955–6*, 1962, p. 71.

3 *Ibid.*, p. 75.

4 *Ibid.*, p. 75.

5 Including Ebbsfleet, Rinyo-Clacton, Fengate and Beaker ware.

6 Carmichael, A., *Carmina Gadelica*, 1900, vol. 1, p. 170.

7 Stukeley, *op. cit.*, f. 231. The stone has now disappeared, and its former location is unknown.

8 Aubrey, J., *The Topographical Collections*, 1659–70, ed. Jackson, J. E., 1862, p. 322.

9 Cunnington, M. E., in *Wilts. Arch. Mag.*, 1931, vol. 45, p. 303.

10 Jackson, G. F., *Shropshire Word Book*, 1879, p. 65.

11 James, E. O., *Seasonal Feasts and Festivals*, 1961, p. 233.

12 See *Catholic Dictionary of Theology*, 1962, vol. 1, p. 319: 'Circa 750–850 AD, the Feast was being propagated widely in the Celtic and Anglo-Saxon missions; presumably to counteract the continuing pagan observances. The missions used a Nativity preface for the Feast, which was linked with the second coming of Christ, and eventually with the Purification of the Virgin.'

Chapter 7
Sanctuary circles

1 Pepys, S., *Diary*, ed. H. B. Wheatley, 1897, vol. 8, p. 49.

2 Aubrey, J., *The Topographical Collections*, 1659–70, p. 322.

3 Stukeley, W., *Abury Described*, 1743, p. 31.

4 *Ibid.*, p. 15.

5 *Ibid.*, p. 31.

6 Cunnington, M. E., in *Wilts. Arch. Mag.*, 1931, vol. 45, p. 300.

7 Avebury Museum display, 1971.

8 Cunnington, *op. cit.*, p. 319.

9 Diameters are based on the large-scale plan in Cunnington, *op. cit.*, p. 320.

10 D ring is given as 32.63 feet, not as 34.5 feet, because the former is found to bisect the double holes of this ring most satisfactorily, as set out on her own plan.

11 Piggott, *West Kennet Long Barrow Excavations, 1955–6*, 1962, p. 15.

12 Newham, C. A., *The Astronomical Significance of Stonehenge*, 1972, p. 20.

13 Cunnington, *op. cit.*, p. 332. Of 160 Sanctuary holes, only hole 11, D ring, and the adjacent hole, E ring, contained iron ore.

14 *Ibid.*, p. 313.

15 *Ibid.*, p. 331. Report on bones by J. Wilfred Jackson.

16 Frazer, J. G., *The Golden Bough*, vol. 7, pt 1, p. 247.

17 Campbell, J., *Oriental Mythology*, 1960, p. 160.

18 Kennard, A. S., 'Non-marine Molluscs at the Sanctuary', in *Wilts. Arch. Mag.*, 1931, vol. 45, p. 333. Snails were also found at Neolithic levels on Windmill Hill and Avebury.

19 Brooks, C. E. P., in *Antiquity*, December 1927, p. 412.

20 Woolley, L., and Hawkes, J., *Prehistory and the Beginnings of Civilisation*, p. 338.

21 Eliade, M., *Images and Symbols*, p. 125.

22 Llwyd, E., in *Philosophical Transactions*, 1713, vol. 28, pp. 98–9.

23 Levy, G. R., *The Gate of Horn*, 1948, p. 149.

24 Rudbeck, O., *Atlantica*, 1695, p. 48.

25 Matthews, W. H., *Mazes and Labyrinths*, 1922, p. 77.

26 *Ibid.*, pp. 71 and 91. At Sneiton, Notts., the proximity of the maze to a spring called St Anne's Well seems to have been considered important.

27 *Ibid.*, p. 91.

Chapter 8
The Candlemas womb-eye

1 Musson, C. R., in Wainwright, G. J., and Longworth, I. H., *Durrington Walls Excavations, 1966–8*, 1971, pp. 368–71.

2 Cunnington, M. E., in *Wilts. Arch. Mag.*, vol. 45, p. 314.

3 Matthews, W. H., *Mazes and Labyrinths*, 1922, p. 9.

4 Renfrew, C., *British Prehistory*, 1974, p. 36.

5 Atkinson, R. J. C., 'Neolithic Science and Technology', in *The Place of Astronomy in the Ancient World*, ed. Hodson, F. R., 1974, p. 128.

6 Wainwright, *op. cit.*, p. 70. For a full account of the oculi motif see Crawford, O. G. S., *The Eye Goddess*, 1957.

7 Cunnington, *op. cit.*, p. 332.

8 *Ibid.*, p. 332.

9 *Ibid.*, pp. 309–10. Musson (*op. cit.*) also accepts that they could have stood together.

10 Rachewiltz, B. de, *Introduction to African Art*, transl. Whigham, P., 1966, pp. 5–7.

11 Cory, H., *African Figurines: their ceremonial use in Puberty Rites*, 1950, p. 26.

12 Frazer, *The Golden Bough*, vol. 1, p. 70.

13 Stukeley, Gough Maps 231, p. 227, where the title, retained by him since *c.* 1725 (see Gough Maps, 231.33r) was incorporated into the engraved Sanctuary plate of 1743, but altered at the proof stage.

14 Jackson Knight, W. F., in *Antiquity*, 1932, vol. 6, pp. 445–8.

15 Campbell, J., *Primitive Mythology*, 1969, p. 62.

16 Aubrey, J., *Monumenta Britannica* 1665–93, pt 1, p. 34.

Chapter 9
The avenue snakes

1 Stukeley, W., *Abury Described*, 1743, p. 102.

2 See Childe, V. Gordon, *Prehistoric Communities of the British Isles*, 3rd edition, 1949, p. 102.

3 Stukeley, *op. cit.*, p. 33.

4 James, E. O., *From Cave to Cathedral*, 1965, p. 88.

5 Stukeley, *op. cit.*, p. 33.

6 Aubrey, J., *Monumenta Britannica*, 1665–93, margin note, made on information from Walter Sloper of Mounkton, pt 1, p. 34.

7 Stukeley, *op. cit.*, p. 30.

8 *Ibid.*, p. 29.

9 Smith, I. F., *Windmill Hill and Avebury*, 1965, p. 185. Stones 35N, 33S, 21N and 4S were still erect.

10 Stukeley, *op. cit.*, p. 30.

11 *Sunday Times*, October 1971.

12 Lommel, A., *Prehistoric and Primitive Man*, 1966, p. 80.

13 Campbell, J., *Primitive Mythology*, 1969, p. 416.

14 Evans, J. D., *Prehistoric Antiquities of the Maltese Islands*, 1971, p. 141. See also Hentze, C., *Objets Rituels, Croyances et Dieux de la Chine Antique*, 1938, figs. 4–8, for futher examples of Neolithic snake imagery.

15 *Larousse Encyclopedia of Prehistoric and Ancient Art*, 1966, p. 192.

16 Mackenzie, D. A., *Scottish Folklore and Folk Life*, 1935, p. 188.

17 *Ibid.*, pp. 188–9.

18 Carmichael, A., *Carmina Gadelica*, vol. 1, pp. 170 ff.

19 Mackenzie, *op. cit.*, p. 192.

20 Keiller, A., and Piggott, S., in *Antiquity*, 1936, vol. 10, p. 420.

21 *Larousse Encyclopedia of Mythology*, 1959 edition, p. 239.

22 *Larousse Encyclopedia of Mythology*, 1968 edition, pp. 228–9. Although Candlemas marked the arrival of the serpent-maiden-goddess, her appearance on that day was only a trial run; Winter was by no means over. See Chamber's *Book of Days*, 1869: 'If Candlemas be dry and fair, half a Winter's to come, and mair.'

23 Smith, *op. cit.*, p. 208.

24 Stukeley, *op. cit.*, p. 57.

25 *Ibid.*, p. 18.

26 *Ibid.*, p. 4.

27 *Ibid.*, p. 59.

28 Stokes, A., quoted in Wolheim, R. (ed.), *The Image in Form*, 1972, pp. 70, 73.

29 Burland, C. A., *Mythology of the Americas*, 1970, p. 109.

30 Schoolcraft, H. R., *History of the Indian Tribes of the USA*, 1847, pt 1, p. 52. See also Brinton, D. G., *The Myths of the New World*, 1896, p. 141. Brinton considered that the serpents' temple in Mexico 'represented the jaws of one of these reptiles'.

31 Worth, R. N., in *Devonshire Assoc.*, 1892, vol. 24, pp. 413 and 414–15.

32 Piggott, S., *The Neolithic Cultures of the British Isles*, 1954, p. 65.

33 *Ibid.*, p. 65.

34 *Ibid.*, p. 65.

35 Atkinson, R. J. C., *Stonehenge and Avebury*, 1968 edition, p. 28.

36 Atkinson, R. J. C., *Stonehenge*, 1956, pp. 57 and 148.

37 Rawson, *Tantra*, 1971, p. 7.

38 Campbell, J., *Occidental Mythology*, 1964, p. 8.

39 See Smith, M., *The British Amphibians and Reptiles*, 1951; also Leutscher, A., *Vivarium Life*, London, 1961; Morris, R. and D., *Men and Snakes*, London, 1965.

40 Charas, M., *New Experiments upon Vipers*, 1670, p. 26.

41 Stukeley, *op. cit.*, p. 31.

Chapter 10
Avenue excavations

1 Smith, I. F., *Windmill Hill and Avebury*, 1965, pp. 186–7.

2 Stukeley, *Abury Described*, 1743, p. 30.

3 Emerson, W., *Nature*, ed. Bohn, 1924, chapter 4, p. 386.

4 Grinsell, L. V., *V.C.H. Wilts.*, 1957, vol. 1, pt 1, p. 310.

5 Quoted in Long, W., *Abury Illustrated*, 1858, pp. 39–40.

6 Thom, A., *Megalithic Lunar Observatories*, 1971, p. 9.

7 NGR 1188 7008.

8 MS. Harley 1686, f. 12a.

9 No other stone hole in the avenue contained this rock.

10 The rock is chalk. The funnels are the result of solution and periglacial subsidence. They mostly measure from 2 to 3 feet in diameter at the mouth.

11 Smith, *op. cit.*, pp. 213–16.

12 *Ibid.*, pp. 210–12.

13 *Ibid.*, pp. 210–12.

14 *Ibid.*, p. 211.

15 *Ibid.*, p. 243.

16 *Ibid.*, p. 211.

17 Cameron Gillies, H., *The Place Names of Argyll*, 1906, p. 7.

18 Gover, J. E. B., *Place Names of Wiltshire*, 1939, p. 295.

19 Smith, *op. cit.*, p. 252.

20 *Ibid.*, p. 236.

21 Eliade, M., *Patterns in Comparative Religion*, 1958, pp. 168–70.

22 Compare the $29\frac{1}{2}$ stones proposed by Newham for the Stonehenge Sarsen Circle, and the 30 dark stones at West Kennet long barrow. N.B. From stone 30N to Avebury henge is a distance of 2,400 feet, or WS-K2 × 6, if the line of the avenue is followed.

23 Parinder, G., *West African Religion*, 1961, p. 39.

24 Lewis, C. T., and Short, C., *A Latin Dictionary*, 1927.

25 *Oxford English Dictionary*, 1933.

26 Eliade, *op. cit.*, 1958, pp. 256–7.

27 *Oxford Classical Dictionary*, 1949, p. 519. Whipping of young women also took place at the festival of Bona Dea, 1 May.

28 Money-Kyrle, R., *The Meaning of Sacrifice*, 1930, p. 124.

29 Keiller and Piggott, in *Antiquity*, vol. 10, 1936, p. 424.

30 James, E. O., *Sacrament and Sacrifice*, 1962, p. 77.

31 Smith, *op. cit.*, p. 210.

32 *Ibid.*, p. 210.

33 *Ibid.*, p. 250. The combination, specifically related to snakes, was displayed in the statue of the American earth and mother goddess, Coatlicue – a skull head, prominent breasts, and a skirt of serpents, from which she took her name.

34 For a full appraisal of both matters, see the works of E. O. James.

35 Douglas, M., *Purity and Danger*, 1970, p. 210.

36 *Ibid.*, p. 209.

37 Atkinson, R. J. C., *Stonehenge and Avebury*, 1968 ed., p. 42. Piggott, in *V.C.H. Wilts.*, 1973, vol. 1, pt 2, p. 325, says there are no grounds for this belief.

38 Talbot, P. A., *Southern*

Nigeria, 1926, vol. 2, p. 803.

39 An interpretation of the design from a Christian viewpoint is given by E. Tyrell-Green, in *Baptismal Fonts*, 1928, p. 58: 'It shows the triumph of grace through the ministry of the Church, set forth by the figure of a bishop slaying the serpent.'

40 Stukeley, W., in Gough Maps, 231, p. 25 reverse.

41 Tatlock, J. S. P., 'The Dragons of Wessex,' in *Speculum*, 1933, vol. 8, p. 223.

Chapter 11
The history of the Avebury henge

1 Aubrey, J., *Monumenta Britannica*, 1665–1693, pt. 1, p. 24.

2 *Ibid.*, p. 25.

3 *Ibid.*, p. 36.

4 *Ibid.*, p. 35.

5 *Ibid.*, p. 32.

6 *Ibid.*, p. 33.

7 Palmer, G., and N. Lloyd, *Archaeology A–Z*, 1968, p. 109.

8 Burl, M. A., in *Archaeological Journal*, Vol. 126, 1969, pp. 1–28.

9 Smith, I. F., *Windmill Hill and Avebury*, 1965, p. 27.

10 Emerson Chapman, D., *Is this your First Visit to Avebury?* 1939, p. 9.

11 Thompson, J. D. A., in I. F. Smith, *op. cit.*, p. 179.

12 Smith, I. F., *Windmill Hill and Avebury, Short Account*, 1959, p. 21.

13 *Victoria County Hist. of Wilts.*, 1956, vol. 3, p. 312.

14 *Ibid.*, p. 105.

15 *Ibid.*, p. 107, Under Baker's successor, John Bale.

16 Weber, M., *The Protestant Ethic and the Spirit of Capitalism*, tr. Talcott Parsons, 1930, pp. 105–6.

17 Stukeley, W., *Abury Described*, 1743, p. 22.

18 *Ibid.*, p. 24.

19 *Ibid.*, pp. 24–5.

20 *Ibid.*, p. 37.

21 Where Stukeley stayed during his many visits to the area 1719–1724, and not to be confused with the present Red Lion. Both the holy female and her circular attribute may be a Christian sign for the pagan surroundings.

22 Stukeley, *op. cit.*, p. 26.

23 *Ibid.*, p. 27, and Tab. XIV, where the stone hole of the recently demolished member is clearly shown.

24 Smith, I. F., in *Wilts. Arch. Mag.*, 1964, vol. 59, p. 181. See also Smith, A. C., in *Wilts. Arch. Mag.*, 1858, Vol. 4, p. 325.

25 Colt Hoare, R., *Ancient Wilts.*, 1821, vol. 2, p. 57.

26 Keiller, A., in *Antiquity*, 1939, vol. 13, p. 223.

27 Smith, A. C., *Guide to the British and Roman Antiquities of the North Wiltshire Downs*, 1885, pp. 139–40.

28 Emerson Chapman, D., *op. cit.*, p. 14.

29 Piggott, S., in *Victoria County Hist. Wilts.*, 1973, vol. 1, Pt. 2, p. 317.

30 Wainwright, G. J., in *Proc. Prehist, Soc.*, 1969, vol. 35, p. 116.

31 Aubrey, J., *op. cit.*, p. 31.

32 Emerson Chapman, D., *op. cit.*, p. 6.

33 See Dyer, J., *Southern England, and Archaeological Guide*, 1973, pp. 314–17, and Haddingham, E., *Circles and Standing Stones*, 1975, pp. 50–54.

Chapter 12
The henge as image

1 Dyer, J., *Southern England, an Archaeological Guide*, 1973, p. 317.

2 Forge, A., *Primitive Art*, 1973, p. xx.

3 Clark, G., in *Proc. Prehist. Soc.*, 1936, vol. 2, Pt. 1, pp. 25–6.

4 MacNeill, M., *The Festival of Lughnasa*, 1962, p. 1. See also Caoimhin o Danachair, in *Journ. Scandinav. Folklore*, 1959, vol. 15, pp. 47–55.

5 Grinsell, L. V., in *Folklore*, 1937, vol. 48, pp. 245–56.

6 Stukeley, W., in a common place book, Devizes Mus., p. 73.

7 Scully, V., *The Earth, the Temple and the Gods*, 1962, pp. 1–4.

8 Bayley, H., *The Lost Language of Symbolism*, 1935, vol. 2, p. 211.

9 Smith, A. C., *Guide to the British and Roman Antiquities of the N. Wilts Downs*, 1885, p. 2.

10 Rawson, P., *Tantra*, 1971, p. 93.

11 See Giedion, S., *The Eternal Present*, 1962, p. 176.

12 Eliade, M., *The Forge and the Crucible*, 1962, pp. 42–3.

13 Gover, J. E. B., *Place Names of Wilts.*, 1939, p. 452.

14 *New English Dictionary*, J. Murray ed., 1914, vol. 8, pt. 2, p. 73.

15 Stukeley, W., *Abury Described*, 1743, pp. 18 and 54.

16 *Ibid.*, p. 151.

17 Aubrey, J., *Monumenta Britannica*, 1665–93, pt. 1, p. 31.

18 Onians, R. B., *Origins of European Thought*, 1951, p. 125. 'We may compare also Ceres, goddess of fertility identified particularly with the seed in the "head" of the cornstalk . . .' Hence perhaps the impetus given to the general belief by the advent of cereal farming.

19 Gray, H. St George, in *Archaeologia*, 1934, vol. 84, p. 122.

20 Passmore, A. D., in *Antiquaries' Journal*, 1922, vol. 2, pp. 109–10.

21 Gray, H. St George, *op. cit.*, p. 122.

22 Sometimes called Belemnite marl, from the bullet-shaped belemnite fossils found there.

23 Passmore, A. D., in *Wilts. Arch. Mag.*, 1935, p. 288.

24 Hawkins, H. L., in *Marlborough College Nat. Hist. Soc.*, 1947–55, No. 96, p. 66.

25 Smith, I. F., *Windmill Hill and Avebury*, 1965, p. 193.

26 Dyer, J., *op. cit.*, p. 25.
27 Wainwright, G. J., in *Antiquaries' Journal*, 1971, vol. 51, Pt. 2, pp. 178–239.
28 Gombrich, E. M., *Meditations on a Hobby Horse*, 1974, p. 6.
29 Rachewiltz, B. de, *Introduction to African Art*, tr. P. Whigham, 1966, p. 48.
30 *Ibid.*, p. 48.
31 Rice Holmes, T., *Ancient Britain, the Invasions of Julius Caesar*, 1907, p. 116.
32 Stukeley, W., Gough Maps 231, c. 1724, Bodleian Library.
33 Eliade, M., *Patterns in Comparative Religion*, 1958, p. 179.
34 O'Riordain, S., quoted in G. Daniel, *Megaliths in History*, 1972, p. 16.
35 Wilde, Lady J. F., *Ancient Cures, Charms and Usages of Ireland*, 1890, p. 102.

Chapter 13
The avenues meet
1 Clark, G., in *Proc. Prehist. Soc.*, 1936, vol. 2, Pt. 1, pp. 26–7.
2 Stukeley, W., *Abury Described*, 1743, p. 18.
3 Scully, V., *American Architecture and Urbanism*, 1969, p. 17.
4 Lukis, W. C., in *Proc. Soc. Antiquaries*, 1881–3, vol. 9, pp. 141, 344.
5 Stukeley, W., *op. cit.*, pp. 35–6.
6 *Ibid.*, pp. 26–7.
7 *Ibid.*, p. 37.
8 Cunnington, M. E., in *Wilts. Arch. Mag.*, 1913, vol. 38, p. 3.
9 Stukeley, W., Gough Maps 231, f. 42k.
10 Stukeley, W., *Abury Described*, p. 36.
11 Stukeley, Gough Maps 231, f. 7v.
12 Avebury Museum display, 1970.
13 Gray, H. St George, *Proc. Dorset Field Club*, 1913, p. 102.
14 See also Daniel, G., *The*

Prehistoric Chamber Tombs of England, 1950, p. 120; and Piggott, S., *Neolithic Cultures of the British Isles*, 1954, pp. 56, 166, 200.
15 Smith, I. F., *Windmill Hill and Avebury, Short Account*, 1959, p. 14.
16 See p. 93.
17 Boyce, G. K., 'Pompeian Lararia', in *Mem. American Acad. in Rome*, 1937, pp. 58–110.
18 *Ibid.*, pp. 58–110.
19 *Encycl. Brit.*, 1974, vol. 4, p. 467.
20 Maundrell, H., *A Journey from Aleppo to Jerusalem*, 1721 ed., p. 61.
21 Zinserling, V. *Women in Greece and Rome*, 1973, p. 27. 'If anyone died unmarried, this vessel was set up on the grave to grant the ceremony to the dead!'
22 *Encycl. Brit.*, 1974, vol. 4, p. 467.
23 Brand, J., '*Observations on Popular Antiquities,*' ed. H. Ellis, 1813, vol. II, p. 91.
24 *Ibid.*, p. 92.
25 *Ibid.*, p. 92.
26 Atkinson, Rev. J. C., *40 Years in a Moorland Parish*, 1891, p. 207.
27 Campbell, J., *Primitive Mythology*, 1969, p. 316.
28 Coomaraswamy, A. K., 'On the Loathly Bride', in *Speculum*, 1945, vol. 20, p. 399.
29 Campbell, J., *Occidental Mythology*, 1964, p. 10.
30 Stukeley, W., *Abury Described*, 1743, p. 57.
31 Coomaraswamy, A. K., *op. cit.*, p. 400.
32 Onians, R. B., *The Origins of European Thought*.
33 'Avebury', *Dep. of Environment pamphlet*, 1972.
34 Liddell, D. M., in *Devon Archaeological Exploration Soc.*, 1930, vol. 1, p. 71.
35 MacIver, R., quoted in I. C. Peate, *Tradition and Folk Life*, 1972, p. 17.
36 Libations of oil and milk

were poured over megaliths in nineteenth-century Scotland. See Grinsell, L. V., in *Folklore*, 1937, vol. 48, p. 251.
37 Smith, I. F., *Windmill Hill and Avebury*, p. 204.
38 Stukeley, W., *Abury Described*, 1743, p. 25. 'Probably designed to fasten the victim in order for flaying it,' he supposed.
39 Redford, E. and M. A., *Encyclopedia of Superstitions*, 1948, p. 12.
40 Grinsell, L. V., in *Antiquity*, 1937, vol. 11, p. 117.
41 Halliday, W. H., in *Folklore*, 1921, vol. 32, p. 263.
42 Charas, M., *New Experiments upon Vipers*, 1670, pp. 1–2.

Chapter 14
Circles and rites
1 Stukeley, W., *Abury Described*, 1743, p. 24. See also Gough Maps 231, f. 16, for a drawing dated 10 July 1723.
2 Westropp, H. M., and C. Staniland Wake, *Ancient Symbolic Worship*, 1875, p. 27.
3 See Kennedy, D., in *Journ. Eng. Folk Dance and Song Soc.*, 1949, vol. 6, p. 5.
4 Keen, S., *Apology for Wonder*, 1969, p. 63.
5 Giedion, S., *The Eternal Present*, 1962, p. 236.
6 Ovid, *Metamorphoses*, Book III, lines 392–402, tr. H. King, 1871.
7 Plato, *Symposium*, 189E, tr. W. R. M. Lamb, 1967, p. 135.
8 Smith, I. F., *Windmill Hill and Avebury*, 1965, p. 204.
9 Hall, T., *Funebria Florae*, 1660, pp. 6 and 16.
10 Stukeley, W., *Itinerarium Curiosum*, vol. 2, pp. 169–77.
11 Smith, I. F., *op. cit.*, p. 201.
12 Turner, V. W., *The Ritual Process*, 1974, p. 59.
13 Eliade, M., *Patterns in Comparative Religion*, 1958, pp. 358–9.
14 *Ibid.*, p. 257.
15 Nyberg, B., *Kind und Erde*, 1931, p. 232.

16 Schmidt, L., in *Antaios*, 1960, vol. 2, p. 205.

17 Evans Pritchard, E. E., *The Position of Women in Primitive Societies*, 1965, p. 84.

18 See Pennant, T., *Tour in Scotland*, 1774, p. 90.

19 Peele, G., Song from *The Old Wife's Tale*, 1595, lines 779–781.

20 Aubrey, J., *Monumenta Britannica*, 1665–93, Pt. 1, p. 31, reverse.

21 Smith, A. C., in *Wilts, Arch. Mag.*, 1865, vol. 10, pp. 209–15.

22 Levy, G. R., *Gate of Horn*, 1948, p. 233.

23 Strutt, L., *Queen-Hoo Hall*, 1808, vol. 1, p. 13.

24 Wright, A. R., and Lones, T. E., *English Calendar Customs*, 1936–40, vol. 2, p. 204.

25 Trevelyan, M., *Folklore and Folk stories of Wales*, 1909, p. 22.

26 Vallencey, C., *Essays on the Antiquity of the Irish Language*, 1772; and Wilde, Lady J. F., *Ancient Cures, Charms, and Usages of Ireland*, 1890, p. 102.

27 Stukeley, W., *Abury Described*, 1743, p. 24: '. . . Of the same shape as its opposite, tall and narrow.'

28 Passmore, A. P., unpublished field notebook, *c.* 1919, Devizes Museum. p. 168. He wrote: 'I have concluded today that the stone is worked.' In the following year he gave his reasons: 'The occurrence of a part of the old brown skin of the stone, this on one side remains as far as it agrees with the shape desired; beyond this, it has been tooled off, leaving an irregular line between the two different surfaces, which is plainly seen on two sides of the stone' (*Man*, 1920, pt. 4, p. 9).

29 Gimbutas, M., *The Gods and Goddesses of Old Europe*, 1974.

30 Nuttgens, P., *The Landscape of Ideas*, 1972, p. 30.

31 Levy, G. R., *op. cit.*, p. 230.

32 Piggott, S., in *Victoria County History of Wilts.*, 1973, vol. 1, pt. 2, p. 288.

33 Evans Pritchard, E., *Nuer Religion*, 1956, p. 194.

34 *Ibid.*, p. 252.

35 Quoted in J. Jackson, *History of the Scottish Stage*, 1793, pp. 410–11.

36 Dewar, H. S. L., 'The Dorset Ooser', in *Dorset Monographs*, No. 2, 1968, p. 2.

37 Wilde, Lady, *op. cit.*, p. 104.

38 Thom, A., *Megalithic Sites in Britain*, 1967, p. 135.

39 *Ibid.*, p. 134.

40 Hemp, W. J., in *Archaeologia*, 1930, vol. 80, p. 195.

41 Note also that Pliny thought that menstruation was promoted by bull's gall (*Nat. Hist.*, Bk. 28, Ch. 27) and that ox dung fumigation promoted parturition in women.

42 See E. O. James, *The Cult of the Mother Goddess*, 1959, pp. 58–9, 60–1.

43 *New Larousse Encycl. Myth.*, 1968, p. 86. See also Baumgartel, E. J., in *Cambridge Ancient History*, 1970, vol. 1, Pt. 1, p. 491.

44 See Keiller, A., *Antiquity*, 1936, (plate II, facing p. 424).

Chapter 15
The world garden

1 Smith, I. F., *Windmill Hill and Avebury*, 1965, p. 250.

2 Clark, G., *Prehistoric England*, 1948, p. 116.

3 Baring Gould Collection, Brit. Mus., L. R. 271, Q. 1. vol. 2, p. 111.

4 Smith, A. C., *A Guide to the British and Roman Antiquities, etc.*, 1885, p. 142.

5 Sinclair, Sir J., *Statistical Account of Scotland*, 1794, vol. 11, p. 620.

6 *Ibid.*, p. 621.

7 Atkinson, R. J. C., *Silbury Hill*, BBC Supplement, 1969.

8 Atkinson, R. J. C., in *Antiquity*, 1968, vol. 42, p. 299.

10 Thompson, F., *Lark Rise*,

1939, pp. 201–6.

11 Robson, V. E., *The Fixed Stars and Constellations*, 1969, p. 63.

12 *Ibid.*, pp. 69, and 119.

13 Lockyer, J. N., *The Dawn of Astronomy*, 1894, p. 418.

14 N.B., by 800 BC, when the precession of the equinoxes had caused the vernal equinox to shift from the Bull's head to the Hyades, the Pleiades were said to *presage* rain, and in Classical Greece were personified as the weeping daughters, or virgin companions of the goddess Artemis. – see Smith, W., *Dictionary of Greek and Roman Biography and Mythology*, 1849, vol. III, p. 412.

15 Kerenyi, K., and Jung, C. G., *Introduction to a Science of Mythology*, tr. Hull, R. F., 1951, p. 9.

16 Burnett, J., *Early Greek Philosophy*, 1920, pp. 40–50. See also *Oxford Classical Dictionary*, ed. M. Cary, 1949, p. 889.

17 'Cosmogonies and Earth', in *Encycl. Brit.*, 11th edit., 1910–11, vol. 7, p. 799.

18 Wilkins, E., *The Rose Garden Game*, 1969, p. 127.

19 *Ibid.*, p. 16.

20 Quoted in Speirs, J., *Medieval English Poetry*, 1957, p. 69.

21 Queenly, divine, unique.

22 The Paradise Woman is described by Lorenzo de Medici in these terms: 'For "Paradise" . . . means nothing more than a most pleasant garden . . . and by this one can affirm that Paradise was where there was a beautiful woman, for here was a copy of every amenity and sweetness that a kind heart might desire.' A. R. Turner, *The Vision of Landscape in Renaissance Italy*, 1966, p. 39.

23 Speirs, *op. cit.*, p. 69.

24 Gimbutas, M., *The Gods and Goddesses of Old Europe*, 1974, p. 91.

25 Cook, S. A., in *Encycl. Brit.*,

1911, vol. 24, p. 677. The snake with tail in mouth is a recurring archetype, still regarded as a zoological reality in certain parts of North Wales. See Smith, G. A., in *Folklore*, vol. 64, 1953, p. 351.

26 Wilde, Lady J. F., *Ancient Cures, Charms, and Usages of Ireland*, 1890.

27 Pearsall, D., *Landscapes and Seasons of the Medieval World*, 1974.

28 Pritchard, E. E., *Position of Women in Primitive Societies*, 1965, pp. 45–7.

29 Wood-Martin, W. G., *Traces of the Elder Faiths in Ireland*, 1902, vol. II, p. 38.

30 *Ibid.*, p. 38.

31 O'Donovan, J., *Ordnance Survey Letters*, Meath, 1836, pp. 4–40 and 53–6, quoted in MacNeill M., *The Festival of Lughnasa*, 1962, pp. 312–16. the May Festival was also the time for divorce, see *Ancient Laws of Ireland*, 1865–1901, Dublin, vol. 2, p. 391.

32 Evans, E., *Prehistoric and Early Christian Ireland*, 1966, p. 177.

33 MacNeill, M., *op. cit.*, 1962, p. 313. For the derivation of Sil, Sel, see Dames, M., *The Silbury Treasure*, 1976, pp. 144–156.

34 Conwell, E., in *Proc. Royal Irish Academy*, vol. 15, 1879, pp. 74–5.

35 Eliade, M., *Patterns in Comparative Religion*, 1958, p. 243.

36 Brand, J., *Observations on Popular Antiquities*, ed. H. Ellis, 1813, vol. 2, p. 91.

37 Sinclair, Sir J., *Statistical Account of Scotland*, vol. 15, 1795, p. 311.

38 See Zehren, E., *The Crescent and the Bull*, 1962, tr. Cleugh, J., p. 104.

39 Eliade, M., *op. cit.*, p. 171.

40 *The Mystical Hymns of Orpheus*, tr. T. Taylor, 1824.

41 MacNeill, M., *op. cit.*, p. 16.

42 Hone, W., *Year-Book of Daily Recreations and Information*, 1838, p. 254.

43 Westropp, H. M., *Ancient Symbol Worship*, 1874, pp. 69–70. In many cultures, the new crescent moon is equated with ARK – the vessel sailing out of the black catastrophe, 'carrying in itself the germ of all things (the new generation of animals, arranged two by two), within the lunar ark of the Cow goddess'.

44 Talbot, P. A., *Southern Nigeria*, 1926, vol. 3, p. 802.

45 Coulton, G. G., *Medieval Panorama*, 1938, p. 97.

46 Vitry, Cardinal J., *Exempla*, 131, AD 1210, ed. Crane, 1878, p. 131.

47 'The Hawthorne Tree', in MS. D. 913 Rawlinson, fourteenth century, quoted in J. Speirs, *op. cit.*, p. 61.

48 Henshaw, T., in *Philosophical Transactions*, 1665, no. 3, pp. 24–6.

Chapter 16
Windmill Hill

1 Stukeley, W., in *Gough Maps*, 231, f. 33.

2 See Avebury Museum display, 1972.

3 Smith, I. F., *Windmill Hill and Avebury*, 1965, p. 24.

4 Cunnington, M. E., in *Wilts. Arch. Mag.*, 1931, vol. 45, p. 311.

5 Eliade, M., *Myths, Dreams and Mysteries*, 1960, p. 169.

6 *Ibid.*, p. 169. The belief in the green, hidden beneath the Earth Mother's outer appearance, may be seen in the seated Mayan goddess, Chalchihuitlicue, otherwise known as Goddess of the Green Petticoat.

7 Smedley, E., *The Occult Sciences*, 1855, p. 358.

8 Mellaart, J., in *Anatolian Studies*, 1963, vol. 13, pp. 61–7.

9 Numbers follow I. F. Smith, 1965. The patch of ground immediately to the northeast may contain more 'head' pits. It has not been excavated.

10 Radford, E. and M. A., *Encycl. of Superstitions*, 1948, p. 147.

11 Rawson, P., *Tantra*, 1971, p. 101.

12 Leroi-Gourhan, A., *Bull. Soc. Prehist.*, 1958, vol. 55, p. 520, fig. 2.

13 See Smith, *op. cit.*, p. 32.

14 Neolithic cattle, *Bos primigenius*, were long-horned.

15 Smith, I. F., *op. cit.*, p. 144.

16 Hedger Walters, R., in *Folklore*, 1899, vol. 10, p. 356.

17 Wilde, Lady, *Ancient Legends of Ireland*, 1887, pp. 102–3. In the opinion of R. Hedger Walters, 'Modern Scottish white cattle are the descendants of cattle required for sacrificial purposes . . . a special breed valued for a definite purpose'. See *Folklore*, vol. 10, 1899, pp. 352–7.

18 Giraldus Cambrensis, 'The Topography of Ireland', in *The Historical Works*, ed. T. Wright, 1863, p. 138.

19 Williams, B. E., *Gournia* 1908, p. 48.

20 James, E. O., *The Cult of the Mother Goddess*, 1959, p. 18–9. See Rees, A. and B., *Celtic Heritage*, 1973, p. 351.

21 'River Gods, so called because represented with the heads of Oxen.' See *Cassell's Latin Dictionary*, 1952, p. 566.

22 Cunliffe, B., *The Cradle of England*, 1972, p. 9.

23 Dyer, J., *Southern England etc.*, p. 357–8.

24 *Ibid.*, p. 357–8.

25 Smith, I. F., *op. cit.*, p. 19.

26 *Ibid.*, p. 7.

27 See Wainwright, G., in *Proc. Prehist. Soc.*, 1969, vol. 35, pp. 112–33.

28 Dyer, J., and L. V. Grinsell, *Wessex*, 1971, p. 76: 'Windmill Hill continued to be used after the henge came into being.'

Chapter 17
The composite achievement

1. *The Times*, 30 July 1920.
2. Aubrey, J., *Natural History of Wiltshire*, 1656–91, ed. J. Britton, 1847, p. 24.
3. Rees, A. and B., *Celtic Heritage*, 1973, p. 74.
4. *Ibid.*, p. 75.
5. *Ibid.*, p. 146.
6. For a smaller 'Island as Goddess' one might point to the 26-mile-long island of Jura, with the Paps (breasts) of Jura 2400 feet high, and the famous (or notorious) whirlpool of Corrievrechan defining the vulva.
7. Gover, J. E. B., *Place Names of Wilts.*, 1939, pp. 249–50.
8. Piggott, S., *The West Kennet Long Barrow Excavations, 1955–6*, 1962, p. 57.
9. See Evans, J., in *Economy and Settlement in Neolithic Britain*, 1971, p. 65.
10. Piggott, S., in *Victoria County Hist. of Wilts.*, 1973, vol. 1, pt. 2, p. 332.
11. See Reed, R. C., in *Arch. Journal*, 1974, vol. 131, pp. 33–57.
12. Piggott, S., *The West Kennet Long Barrow Excavations, 1955–6*, p. 57. However, although all the known long barrows appear to conform to the needs of the composite figure, the small stone circle at Winterbourne Basset, sited two miles beyond the northern periphery, and presumed to be Neolithic, *is* anomalous. Its position may have been related to a source of the river Winterbourne.
13. Perry, W. J., *The Primordial Ocean*, 1935, p. 252.
14. Scully, V., *The Earth, the Temple and the Gods*, 1962, pp. 2–5.
15. *Ibid.*, p. 1.
16. Granada TV, Nov–Jan., 1974–5.
17. Jung, C. G., *The Psychology of the Unconscious*, tr. B. M. Hinckle, 1922, p. 93.
18. Stukeley, W., *Gough Maps*, *c.* 1723, pp. 37–8.
19. *Ibid.*, p. 9.

Chapter 18
The perambulation

1. Grigson, G. in *Country Life*, 8 March 1973, p. 572.
2. Thurnam, J., in *Archaeologia*, 1869, vol. 42, p. 203.
3. Spence, L., *Myth and Ritual in Dance, Game and Rhyme*, 1947, p. 37.
4. Stukeley, W., in Keiller MSS. vol. of *Avebury drawings*, quoted in Piggott, S., *William Stukeley*, 1950, p. 183.
5. Dyer, J., *Southern England, etc.*, p. 328.
6. Connah, G., in *Wilts. Arch. Mag.*, 1965, vol. 60. p. 1.
7. Cunnington, M. E., 'Knap Hill', in *Wilts. Arch. Mag.*, 1911, vol. 37, pp. 49–51.
8. *Ibid.*, p. 51.
9. Collectanae, in *Folklore*, 1909, vol. 20, p. 8.
10. Partridge, J. B., in *Folklore*, 1915, vol. 26, p. 211.
11. Collectanae, in *Folklore*, 1909, vol. 20, p. 81.
12. Clarke, K., *The Nude*, 1960, pp. 356–7.
13. *Ibid.*, p. 357.
14. Thurnam, J., *op. cit.*, 1869, p. 180.
15. Reed, R. C., in *Archaeological Journal*, vol. 131, 1974, p. 33.
16. Stukeley, W., *Abury Described*, 1743, p. 46.
17. Smith, A. C., *A Guide to British and Roman Antiquities*, etc., 1885, p. 23.
18. Atkinson, R. J. C., *Stonehenge*, 1956, p. 32.
19. See sculptured megalith in *Mane-er-Hroeck*, Locmoriaquer.
20. Atkinson, R. J. C., *op. cit.*, p. 31.
21. Smith, I. F., in *Wilts. Arch. Mag.*, vol. 60, 1965, pp. 25–30.
22. The mysterious Dorset Banks, sometimes called back barrows, excepted.
23. In the superimposed Bronze Age bell barrow, Smith found a horn pendant – 'a slightly curved slip of polished horn, 11 mm long and pierced'. *Wilts. Arch. Mag.*, vol. 60, 1965, p. 30.
24. Grinsell, L. V., in *Victoria County Hist. Wilts.*, Gazetteer, vol. 1, Pt. 1, 1954.
25. Passmore, A., in *Wilts. Arch. Mag.*, vol. 42, 1923, p. 366.
26. Ashbee, P., and Smith, I. F., in *Antiquity*, vol. 34, 1960, pp. 297–9.
27. Fowler, P., in *Antiquity*, vol. 41, 1967, pp. 289–91. See also Evans, J. G., in *Wilts. Arch. Mag.*, vol. 62, 1967, p. 124.
28. Aubrey, J., *Monumenta Britannica* MS Bodleian, *c.* 1665–93, Pt. 1, p. 43.
29. Stukeley, W., Field Notes, quoted by S. Piggott, in *Wilts. Arch. Mag.*, vol. 52, 1948, pp. 390–1.
30. Stukeley, W., *Itinerarium Curiosum*, Pt. I, 1724, p. 132.
31. Stukeley, W., quoted by S. Piggott, in *Wilts. Arch. Mag.*, vol. 52, 1948, pp. 390–1.
32. Smith, A. C., *op. cit.*, p. 203.
33. *Ibid.*, p. 198.
34. Piggott, S., in *Wilts. Arch. Mag.*, vol. 52, 1947, p. 60.
35. Piggott, S., in *Victoria County Hist. Wilts.*, vol. 1, Pt. 2, 1973, p. 714.
36. Smith, A. C., *op. cit.*, p. 195.
37. Colt Hoare, R., *Ancient Wilts.*, 1821, pp. 22–4.
38. Stukeley, W., *Abury Described*, 1743 pp. 47–8.
39. *Ibid.*, pp. 47–8. Colt Hoare, *op. cit.*, pp. 22–4, describes his search for the old chapel: 'From hence, I ascend a hill to the NW, directing my course towards a cottage adjoining the trackway, distinguished by the fanciful title of Glory Ann, leaving the vale in which Wick Farm is situated on my right. To NE of Glory Ann, I, with some difficulty, discovered the antiquities mentioned by Stukeley under the name of Old Chapel, a large square intrenched.'
40. Stukeley, *op. cit.*, p. 48.

Mavor, W., *British Tourists*, vol. 4, 1807, p. 108.

Aubrey, J., *op. cit.*, Pt. 2, p. 16.

Stukeley, W., *op. cit.*, p. 46.

Ibid., p. 46.

Ashbee, P., in *Antiquity*, vol. 34, 1960, pp. 297–9.

Piggott, S., in *Victoria County Hist., Wilts.*, vol. 1, Pt. 2, 1973, p. 288.

Gover, J. E. B., *Place Names of Wilts.*, 1939, p. 294.

Quoted in Woodbridge, K., *Landscape and Antiquity*, 1971, p. 228.

Campbell, J., *Occidental Mythology*, 1964, p. 14.

Thurnam, J., in *Wilts. Arch. Mag.*, vol. 4, 1858, p. 324. Oolite slabs were used in its construction, as at Shepherd's Shore and Kitchen Barrow.

See Smith, A. C., *op. cit.*, p. 111, fig. 68.

Curwen, E. C., in *Antiquity*, vol. 4, 1930, pp. 38–40.

Bonny, D. J., in *Wilts. Arch. Mag.*, vol. 59, 1964, p. 185; and *Ibid.*, vol. 60, 1965, p. 127.

Mercer, R., in *Current Archaeology*, vol. 5, 1975, p. 18.

Chapter 19
Tan Hill Fair

1 *Wiltshire Gazette*, 12 August 1875.

2 Quoted by Pugh, R. B., in *Collection Charter Rolls*, 1427–1516, vol. 4, p. 273.

3 Thurnam, J., in *Wilts. Arch. Mag.*, vol. 4, 1858, p. 324.

4 Story-Maskelyne, T., in *Wilts. Arch. Mag.*, 1906, pp. 426–32.

5 Wright, A. R., and Lones, T. E., *English Calendar Customs*, 1936–40, vol. 3, p. 41.

6 See 'Worcestershire Folklore', Worcs. Co. Museum Publications, p. 15.

7 *Wiltshire Gazette*, 7th August 1862.

8 *Ibid.*

9 Smith, A. C., *Guide to the British and Roman Antiquities of the North Wilts. Downs*, 1885, p. 119.

10 Aubrey, J., *Natural History of Wiltshire*, 1656–1691, ed. J. Britton, p. 114.

11 Quoted in *Wiltshire Gazette*, May 1922.

12 MacNeill, M., *The Festival of Lughnasa*, 1962, p. 413.

13 Smith, A. C., *op. cit.*, p. 136.

14 Partridge, E., *Name this Child*, 1951, p. 42.

15 Yonge, C. M., *History of Christian Names*, 1884, pp. 40–2.

16 Baring Gould, S., *Lives of the British Saints*, vol. 1, 1907, p. 164.

17 Cocoran, J., in *New Larousse Encycl. of Mythology*, 1968, pp. 228–9.

18 *Wiltshire Notes and Queries*, vol. 1, 1893–5, p. 573.

19 Etchilhampton Ford (NGR 067604), Bourton Pond in Bishops Cannings (043644) and the gold torc location (090645). These three form an equilateral triangle with sides 16000 feet (WS-K2 × 40), the northernmost side running due east-west, thus creating a north-south axis balanced at Etchilhampton ford – the downward-pointing pubic triangle.

20 Grinsell, L. V., in *Victoria County Hist., Wilts*, vol. 1, Pt. 1, 1954, p. 24; see also, Cunnington, M. E., in *Wilts. Arch. Mag.*, vol. 38, 1914, p. 644.

21 Story-Maskelyne, T., *op. cit.*, p. 431.

22 Brentnall, H. C., *The Marlborough Country*, 1912, p. 109.

23 Stedman, A. R., *Marlborough and the Upper Kennet Country*, 1960, p. 3.

24 Told to Miss J. B. Partridge, *c.* 1900, and quoted in Wright and Lones, *op. cit.*, p. 47. This commercial recreation bears all the marks of cult behaviour in decline, especially since beans have occupied a special place in the magic of growth. Similarly, the salt beef may represent the last shreds of what had once been a ritual meal of the great ox-woman.

25 *The Times*, 30th July, 1920, p. 15.

26 Rees, A. and B., *Celtic Heritage*, 1973.

27 Eliade, M., *Myth of Eternal Return*, tr. W. R. Trask, 1955, p. 34.

28 Stukeley, W., in *Gough Maps 231*, f. 9.

29 Joyce, J., *Finnegans' Wake*, 1950, p. 213.

30 See Sewell, M. F., *The Orphic Voice*, 1960, pp. 40–45.

31 Stukeley, W., *Gough Maps 231*, f. 15.

Chapter 20
The Palisade Enclosures

1 Whittle, A., and Smith, R., in *Current Archaeology*, vol. 118, 1990, p. 363. See also Whittle, A., 'A Late Neolithic Complex at West Kennet, Wilts', in *Antiquity*, vol. 65, 1991, pp. 256–62, and Whittle, A., in *Wilts. Arch. Mag.*, vol. 87, 1994, pp. 151–52.

2 Metric measurements are given in this new chapter, reflecting current practice.

3 Evans, J.G., in *Proc. Prehistoric Society*, vol. 59, 1993, pp. 139–95.

4 Gray, H. St G., 'The Avebury Excavations 1908–22', in *Archaeologia*, vol. 84, 1934, pp. 123–24.

5 Gimbutas, M., *The Gods and Goddesses of Old Europe*, 1974, pp. 211–14.

6 Dames, M., *Mythic Ireland*, 1992, p. 204.

7 Whittle, A., in *Oxford Journal of Archaeology*, vol. 12, 1993, p. 48.

8 Lawrence, G.F., in *Archaeol. Journal*, vol. 86, 1929, pp. 69–73. See also Toynbee, J.M.C., *Art in Britain under the Romans*, p. 95.

Bibliography

Abbreviations: *Antiquity – Ant.; Archaeological Journal – A.J.; Archaeologia – Arch.; Folklore – Folk.; Proceedings of the Archaeological Institute – P.A.I.; Proceedings of the Prehistoric Society – P.P.S.; Victoria County History, Wiltshire – V.C.H.W.; Wiltshire Archaeological Magazine – W.A.M.*

ATKINSON, REV. J. C. *Forty Years in a Moorland Parish*, London, 1891.

ATKINSON, R. J. C. 'Neolithic Science and Technology', in *The Place of Astronomy in the Ancient World*, ed. Hodson, F. R., London, 1974.

——*Silbury Hill*, BBC pamphlet, London, 1968–9.

——*Stonehenge*, London, 1956.

——*Stonehenge and Avebury*, London, 1959.

AUBREY, J. *Monumenta Britannica*, Parts 1 and 2, MSS Bodleian, *c.* 1665–90.

——*Natural History of Wiltshire*, 1656–91, ed. J. Britton, London, 1847.

——*The Topographical Collections, 1659–70*, ed. J. E. Jackson, London, 1862.

BACHOFEN, J. J. *Myth, Religion and Mother Right*, tr. R. Manheim, London and New York, 1967.

BANKS, M. M. *British Calendar Customs (Scotland)*, 3 vols, London, 1937–41.

BARING, A. AND CASHFORD, J. *The Myth of the Goddess*, London and New York, 1991.

BARKER, C. T. 'The Long Mounds of the Avebury Region' in *W.A.M.*, vol. 79, 1984.

BOYCE, G. K. 'Pompeian Lararia', in *Mem. American Acad. in Rome*, 1937.

BRAND, J. *Observations on Popular Antiquities*, ed. H. Ellis, 2 vols, London, 1813.

BRENTNALL, H. C. *The Marlborough Country*, London, 1912.

BURL, AUBREY *Prehistoric Avebury*, London, 1979.

BURL, H. A. W. 'Henges: internal features and regional groups', in *A.J.*, vol. 126, 1969, pp. 1–28.

BURLAND, C. A. *Mythology of the Americas*, New York and London, 1970.

BYRHTFERTH *Manual*, in *Early English Text Society* no. 177, vol. 1, London, 1929.

CAMPBELL, J. *Creative Mythology*, London, 1968; New York, 1970.

——*Occidental Mythology*, New York, 1964; London, 1965.

——*Oriental Mythology*, London and New York, 1960.

——*Primitive Mythology*, New York, 1959; London, 1960.

CARMICHAEL, A. *Carmina Gadelica*, 2 vols, Edinburgh, 1900.

CHARAS, M. *New Experiments upon Vipers*, Paris and London, 1670.

CLARK, G. *Prehistoric England*, London, 1940.

——'The timber monument at Arminghall, and its affinities', in *P.P.S.*, vol. 2, pt. 1, 1936.

CLIFFORD, E. E. 'Excavation of Nympsfield longbarrow, Glos.', in *P.P.S.*, vol. 4, 1938.

COCORAN, J. 'Celtic Mythology', in *New Larousse Encyclopedia of Mythology*, London, 1968.

COOMARASWAMY, A. K. 'The Loathly Bride', in *Speculum*, vol. 20, London and New York, 1945.

COULTON, G. G. *Medieval Panorama*, Cambridge 1938; New York, 1944.

CRAWFORD, O. G. S. *The Eye Goddess*, New York 1956; London, 1957.

CUNNINGTON, M. E. 'The Re-erection of two fallen stones at Avebury', in *W.A.M.*, vol. 38, 1912.

——'The "Sanctuary" on Overton Hill, near Avebury', in *W.A.M.*, vol. 45, 1931.

——*Woodhenge*, London, 1929.

CURWEN, E. C. 'Neolithic Camps', in *Ant.*, vol. 4 1930.

CYRIAX, T. 'Ancient Burial Places', in *A.J.*, vol. 28 1921.

DALTON, G. I. 'The Loathly Lady', in *Folk.*, vol. 82 London, 1971.

DAMES, M. *The Silbury Treasure*, London, 1976.

——*Mythic Ireland*, London and New York, 1992.

DANIEL, G. *Megaliths in History*, London, 1972.

——*A Hundred Years of Archaeology*, London, 1950.

DOUGLAS, M. *Purity and Danger*, London, 1970.

DYER, J. *Southern England, an Archaeological Guide* London, 1973.

DYER, J. AND GRINSELL, L. V. *Wessex*, London, 1971.

ELIADE, M. *Images and Symbols*, London, 1961 New York, 1969.

——*Myths, Dreams and Mysteries*, London, 1960 New York, 1969.

——*Patterns in Comparative Religion*, London and New York, 1958.

——*The Forge and the Crucible*, London and New York, 1962.

——*The Two and the One*, London, 1965; New York, 1969.

EMERSON, W. *Nature*, ed. Bohn, London and New York, 1924.

EMERSON, CHAPMAN D. *Is this your first visit to Avebury?*, London, 1939.

EVANS PRITCHARD, E. E. *Nuer Religion*, London 1955.

——*The Position of Women in Primitive Societies* London, 1965.

FAWCETT, T. *The Symbolic Language of Religion* London, 1970.

FORGE, A. *Primitive Art*, London, 1973.

FRAZER, J. G. *The Golden Bough*, 10 vols, London and New York, 1911–12.

GADON, ELINOR W. *The Once and Future Goddess* San Francisco, 1989.

GIEDION, S. *The Eternal Present*, London and New York, 1962.

GIMBUTAS, M. *The Gods and Goddesses of Old Europe*, London and New York, 1974. Updated as *The Goddesses and Gods of Old Europe*, London and New York 1982.

——*The Language of the Goddess*, London and New York, 1989.

GIRALDUS CAMBRENSIS, *The Historical Works*, ed. T Wright, London, 1863.

GOMBRICH, E. H. *Meditations on a Hobby Horse* London and New York, 1971.

GOVER, J. E. B. *Place Names of Wiltshire*, London, 1939.

GRAY, H. ST. GEORGE 'The Avebury Excavations, 1908–22', in *Arch.*, vol. 84, 1934.

——'Maumbury Rings', in *Proc. Dorset Field Club*, 1913.

GRINSELL, L. V. *The Ancient Burial Mounds of England*, London, 1936.

——*Belas Knap*, H.M.S.O., London, 1966.

——Gazetteer, in *V.C.H.W.*, vol. 1, pt. 1, London, 1954.

GUTCH, M. AND PEACOCK, M. *Folklore of Lincolnshire*, London, 1908.

HALL, T. *Funebria Florae*, London, 1660.

HAWKES, C. 'Unusual finds in New Forest Potteries', in *A.J.*, vol. 18, 1938.

HEDGER WALTERS, R. 'White Cattle in Britain', in *Folk.*, vol. 10, 1899.

HEMP, W. J. 'Bryn Hen Y Bobl', in *Arch.*, vol. 85, 1935.

HOARE, SIR R. COLT *Ancient History of North Wilts.*, 2 vols, London, 1821.

——*Modern Wiltshire*, London, 1826.

HONE, W. *Year-Book of Daily Recreations and Information*, London, 1838.

JACKSON, G. F. *Shropshire Folk-Lore*, ed. C. Burne, London, 1883.

JACKSON KNIGHT, W. F. 'Maze Symbolism', in *Ant.*, vol. 6, 1932.

JAMES, E. O. *From Cave to Cathedral*, London and New York, 1965.

——*Sacrament and Sacrifice*, London and New York, 1962.

——*Seasonal Feasts and Festivals*, London and New York, 1961.

——*The Cult of the Mother Goddess*, London 1959; New York, 1961.

JONES, F. *The Holy Wells of Wales*, Cardiff, 1954.

JUNG, C. G. *The Psychology of the Unconscious*, tr. B. M. Hinkle, London and New York, 1922.

KEILLER, A. 'Avebury', in *Ant.*, vol. 13, 1939.

KEILLER, A. AND PIGGOTT, S. 'The Recent Excavations at Avebury', in *Ant.*, vol. 10, 1936.

KERENYI, I. AND JUNG, C. G. *Introduction to a Science of Mythology*, tr. R. F. Hull, New York and London, 1951.

KIRK, G. S. *Myth*, Berkeley, Calif., 1970; London, 1973.

LEACH, E. R. *Lévi-Strauss*, London and New York, 1970.

——'Primitive Time-Reckoning', in Singer, C. *History of Techonology*, vol. 1, London, 1954.

LÉVI-STRAUSS, C. *The Raw and the Cooked*, tr. J. and D. Weightman, New York, 1969; London, 1970.

——*The Savage Mind*, Chicago and London, 1966.

LEVY, G. R. *The Gate of Horn*, London, 1948.

LIPPARD, LUCY R. *Overlay*, New York, 1983.

LOCKYER, J. N. *The Dawn of Astronomy*, London and New York, 1894.

LOMMEL, A. *Prehistoric and Primitive Man*, London, 1966.

LONG, W. *Abury Illustrated*, Devizes, 1858.

MACKENZIE, D. A. *Scottish Folklore and Folklife*, London and Glasgow, 1935.

MACNEILL, F. M. *The Silver Bough*, 3 vols., Glasgow, 1957.

MACNEILL, M. *The Festival of Lughnasa*, London, 1962.

MALONE, CAROLINE *Avebury*, English Heritage, 1989.

MATTHEWS, W. H. *Mazes and Labyrinths*, London, 1922.

MCGLADE, J. 'Archaeology and the eco-dynamics of human-modified landscapes', in *Ant.*, vol. 69, 1995.

MEREWETHER, J. 'Examination of barrows and earthworks near Silbury', in *P.A.I.*, 1849.

NEUMANN, E. *The Great Mother*, tr. R. Manheim, New York and London, 1955.

NEWHAM, C. A. *The Astronomical Significance of Stonehenge*, London, 1972.

NUTTGENS, P. *The Landscape of Ideas*, London, 1972.

ONIANS, R. B. *The Origins of European Thought*, London, 1951.

OVID, *Metamorphoses*, tr. H. King, London, 1871.

OWEN, T. M. *Welsh Folk Customs*, Cardiff, 1959.

PARINDER, G. *West African Religion*, London, 1961.

PASSMORE, A. D. 'The Avebury Ditch', in *A.J.*, vol. 2, 1922.

——Field Notebook, MS, unpublished, Devizes Museum, *c.* 1919–30.

PEARSALL, D. *Landscapes and Seasons of the Medieval World*, London, 1974.

PEATE, I. C. *Tradition and Folk Life*, London, 1972.

PHILLIPS, C. W. 'Giants' Hills Long Barrow, Lincs.', in *Arch.*, vol. 85, 1935.

PIGGOTT, S. *Excavation of the West Kennet Long Barrow, 1955–6*, London, 1962.

——*Neolithic Cultures of the British Isles*, London, 1954.

——'The First Agricultural Communities', in *V.C.H.W.*, vol. 1, pt. 1, London, 1973.

——'The West Kennet Long Barrow', in *Ant.*, vol. 32, 1958.

——*The West Kennet Long Barrow*, H.M.S.O., London, 1963.

PLATO *Symposium*, tr. W. R. M. Lamb, New York, 1967.

POWELL, T. G. E. *Prehistoric Art*, London, 1966.

RACHEWILTZ, B. DE *Introduction to African Art*, tr. P. Whigham, London, 1966.

RADFORD, E. AND M. A. *Encyclopedia of Superstitions*, London, 1948.

RAWSON, P. *Primitive Erotic Art*, London, 1972.

——*Tantra*, London 1971.

REES, A. AND B. *Celtic Heritage*, London, 1973.

RENFREW, C. *British Prehistory*, London, 1974.

ROBSON, V. E. *The Fixed Stars and Constellations*, London, 1969.

SANDARS, N. K. *Prehistoric Art in Europe*, London, 1968.

SCULLY, V. *The Earth, the Temple and the Gods*, Yale, 1962.

SEWELL, M. F. *The Orphic Voice*, London, 1960.

SIMPSON, D. D. (ed.) *Economy and Settlement in Neolithic Britain*, Leicester, 1971.

SINCLAIR, SIR J. *Statistical Account of Scotland*, Edinburgh, 1794.

SMITH, A. C. 'Excavations at Avebury', in *W.A.M.*, vol. 10, 1865.
——*Guide to the British and Roman Antiquities of the North Wiltshire Downs*, London, 1885.
SMITH, I. F. *Windmill Hill and Avebury, Short Account*, London, 1959.
——*Windmill Hill and Avebury*, London, 1965.
SMITH, M. *The British Amphibians and Reptiles*, London, 1951.
SPEIRS, J. *Medieval English Poetry*, London, 1957; New York, 1958.
SPENCE, L. *Myth and Ritual in Dance, Game and Rhyme*, London, 1947.
——*The Fairy Tradition in Britain*, London, 1948.
STOKES, A. in R. Wolheim (ed.), *The Image in Form*, London, 1972.
STUKELEY, W. *Abury Described*, London, 1743.
——*Gough Maps*, p. 231, MS Bodleian, Oxford.
——*Itinerarium Curiosum*, vol. I, London, 1724.
——*Letters and Diaries*, in Surtees Society, vols. I and 3, London, 1885.
TALBOT, P. A. *Southern Nigeria*, London, 1926.
TATLOCK, J. S. P. 'The Dragons of Wessex', in *Speculum*, vol. 8, 1933.
TAYLOR, T., (trans.) *The Mystical Hymns of Orpheus*, London, 1824.
TEGNER, M. *Roe Deer*, London, 1951.
THOM, A. *Megalithic Lunar Observatories*, London, 1971.
——*Megalithic Sites in Britain*, London, 1967.
THURNAM, J. 'Examination of a chambered long barrow at West Kennet, Wiltshire', in *Arch.*, vol. 38, London, 1860.
——'On Ancient British Barrows', in *Arch.*, vol. 42, London, 1869.

TURNER, V. W. *The Ritual Process*, London and Chicago, 1969.
WAINWRIGHT, G. J. 'A late Neolithic enclosure at Marden, Wilts.', in *A.J.*, vol. 51, pt. 2, 1971.
——'A review of henge monuments in the light of recent research', *P.P.S.*, vol. 35, 1969.
WAINWRIGHT, G. J. AND LONGWORTH, I. H. *Durrington Walls Excavations, 1966–8*, London, 1971.
WEBER, M. *The Protestant Ethic and the Spirit of Capitalism*, tr. Talcott Parsons, London, 1930.
WESTROPP, H. M. AND WAKE, C. STANILAND, *Ancient Symbolic Worship*, London, 1875.
WHITTLE, A. 'A late Neolithic complex at West Kennet, Wiltshire', in *Ant.*, vol. 65, 1991.
——'The Neolithic of the Avebury Area', in the *Oxford Journal of Archaeology*, vol. 12, 1993.
——'West Kennet', in *W.A.M.*, vol. 82, 1988.
WHITTLE, A. AND SMITH, R. 'West Kennet', in *Current Archaeology*, vol. 118, 1990.
WILDE, LADY J. F. *Ancient cures, charms and usages of Ireland*, London, 1890.
WILKINSON, REV. J. 'A report of diggings made in Silbury Hill', in *W.A.M.*, vol. 11, 1869.
WILKINS, E. *The Rose Garden Game*, London, 1969.
The Wiltshire Gazette, Tan Hill Fair Reports, Devizes, 1824–1914.
WOOD-MARTIN, W. G. *Traces of the Elder Faiths in Ireland*, 2 vols., London and New York, 1902.
WRIGHT, A. R. AND LONES, T. E. *British Calendar Customs, England*, 3 vols., London, 1936–40.
ZEVI, B. 'Architecture', in *Encyclop. of World Art*, vol. I, New York, 1968.
ZINZERLING, V. *Women in Greece and Rome*, London, 1973.

Sources of Illustrations

Acknowledgments are due to the following for providing photographs and illustrations:

Aerofilms, pp. 10, 111 (bm); E. Ananti, p. 72 (bm); Ashmolean Museum, Oxford, pp. 2–3, 105; Bath Museum, p. 127 (bm); Bewdley Museum, Worcs., p. 122; Birmingham Reference Library, Stone Collection, pp. 97, 116, 145; Bodleian Library, Oxford, pp. 27, 61, 79, 83, 140, 153 (top), 168, 204; British Museum, pp. 25 (bm), 47 (top), 57, 87 (top), 127 (top); British Tourist Authority, p. 151 (top); Bucharest Archaeo-logical Institute, p. 31; Cambridge University Collection: copyright reserved, p. 91; Cambridge University, Museum of Archaeology, p. 150; Carrasco, Lisbon, p. 44; Harold Chapman, pp. 20–21, 23, 36, 39, 59, 95, 106 (top), 195, 196 (top), 203; Cheltenham Museum, Glos., p. 33; National Museum, Copenhagen, Denmark, pp. 93, 103, 151, (bm), 155; Department of the Environment, pp. 28, 47 (bm), 51, 84, 108–9, 114; Deutsches Archaeologische Institut, Rome,pp. 106 (bm), 141; Devizes Museum, Wilts., pp. 45, 50, 214; Edinburgh National Museum of Antiquities, p. 29; Edinburgh University, Department of Prehistoric Archaeology, p. 43; Frankfurt Stadelschen Kunstinstitus, p. 167; H. St George Gray, pp. 112, 113, 133; Hirmer, p. 169; Horniman Museum, London, p. 132; R. C. Lambeth, p. 25 (top); Tony Linck,

p. 90; Liverpool Museum, p. 143; London Museum, Kensington Palace, p. 153 (bm); J. Mellaart, p. 173; National Gallery, London, p. 211; National Monuments Record, pp. 72 (top), 75 (top), 75 (bm), 174–5, 177; Axel Poignant, p. 88; Reading Museum of English Rural Life, pp. 24, 152; after Hilary Richardson, p. 222 (top); Brian Shuel, p. 18; Edwin Smith, p. 221; Dr I. F. Smith, pp. 129, 180; after S.H. Twohig, p. 222 (bm); National Museum of Wales, pp. 49, 127 (cen.); Christian Zervos, pp. 92, 99, 157, 182.

The maps on pp. 8, 115 and 190 were drawn by Peter Bridgewater. All other plans, diagrams and line illustrations were drawn by the author, with the assistance of Peter Bridgewater except in the case of the last chapter. The author also provided the remaining photographs.

Other sources:
Abury Described (W. Stukeley, 1743), pp. 12, 64–5, 82, 111 (top), 205, 217; *Monumenta Brittanica* (J. Aubrey, 1665–93), p. 202; *Archaeologia* (1860, vol. 38), pp. 34, 160; *A Guide to British and Roman Antiquities* (A. C. Smith, 1885), pp. 198, 209. *Victoria County History, Yorks.* (1907, vol. I), p. 222 (cen.).

2830